D1478445

Yellow Fever, Race, and Ecology

in Nineteenth-Century

NEW ORLEANS

The Natural World of the Gulf South

CRAIG E. COLTEN, Series Editor

YELLOW FEVER
FEVER
RACE
AND ECOLOGY
IN NINETEENTH-CENTURY
NEW ORLEANS

URMI ENGINEER WILLOUGHBY

LOUISIANA STATE UNIVERSITY PRESS

BATON ROUGE

Published with support from the Louisiana Sea Grant College Program,
a part of the National Sea Grant College Program maintained by the
National Oceanic and Atmospheric Administration of the U.S. Department
of Commerce.

Published by Louisiana State University Press
Copyright © 2017 by Louisiana State University Press
All rights reserved
Manufactured in the United States of America
First printing

Designer: Laura Roubique Gleason
Typeface: MillerText
Printer and binder: Sheridan Books

Library of Congress Cataloging-in-Publication Data

Names: Willoughby, Urmi Engineer, 1980– author.
Title: Yellow fever, race, and ecology in nineteenth-century New Orleans /
    Urmi Engineer Willoughby.
Description: Baton Rouge : Louisiana State University Press, [2017] |
    Series: The natural world of the Gulf South | Includes bibliographical
    references and index.
Identifiers: LCCN 2017019253| ISBN 978-0-8071-6774-8 (cloth : alk.
    paper) | ISBN 978-0-8071-6775-5 (pdf) | ISBN 978-0-8071-6776-2
    (epub)
Subjects: LCSH: Yellow fever—Louisiana—New Orleans—19th century. |
    Yellow fever—Louisiana—History—19th century.
Classification: LCC RA644.Y4 W55 2017 | DDC 614.5/410976335—dc23
LC record available at https://lccn.loc.gov/2017019253

The paper in this book meets the guidelines for permanence and durability
of the Committee on Production Guidelines for Book Longevity of the
Council on Library Resources. ∞

For my mother, Madhu

Contents

Acknowledgments

I am grateful for all of the help and support from my mentors, colleagues, friends, and family in the years that it took to complete this book. I am eternally indebted to Terry Burke, who has been a constant source of inspiration, encouragement, and advice throughout my academic career. His guidance and dedication have seen this project through, and I am profoundly thankful for his continued support.

Many people have read chapters or the whole of this manuscript through its numerous iterations over the past ten years. Many thanks to Terry Burke, Lynn Westerkamp, and Ari Kelman, who read the earliest, roughest drafts of my work. Several others have been extremely generous in reading and improving the book. I am lucky to have had some amazing scholars read later versions of my chapters, including Kate Jones, Greg O'Malley, Elizabeth Leonard, and Jenn Tappan. I am deeply indebted to John McNeill, for reading and reviewing the book manuscript, and for bringing mosquitoes the attention they deserve. Jim Webb provided some of the most critical and helpful comments to the manuscript, which I very much needed. Talking through my ideas with Jim, and listening to his thoughtful feedback, has improved the environmental and epidemiological arguments put forth in this book. He and Pat Manning inspired me to think more about the early history of yellow fever in West Africa, an area that I hope will receive more attention from scholars in the future.

Over the years, many great scholars have helped me to answer obscure questions that I could not figure out on my own. Some are dear friends, and others are people who kindly responded to a desperate email from a stranger. Thanks to Jim McCann, Ray Kea, J. N. Hays,

George Dehner, Brooke Crowley, Siobhan Cooke, Bill Horne, Andrew Wegmann, Dave Bright, and John Lienhard for sharing their expertise.

This project was made possible with support from several grants and fellowships from UC Santa Cruz, Colby College, the University of Pittsburgh, and the Tennessee State Library and Archives. I completed the bulk of my research while I was a graduate student at the University of California–Santa Cruz, and I am grateful for all of the opportunities given to me during those years. Without financial support from the Department of History, the Institute for Humanities Research, and Oakes College, I would not have been able to spend time living and working in Louisiana. The archivists and library staff at LSU and Tulane are some of the most helpful people I have met, especially Judy Bolton, Mark Martin, Germain Bienvenu, James Abbott, Nicholas Skaggs, and Sean Benjamin. Thanks also to the wonderful librarians and archivists at the Countway Medical Library, the Southern Historical Collection, the Rudolph Matas Library, and the Tennessee State Library and Archives.

I don't think I could have finished this book without the postdoctoral fellowships I have held after graduate school, at Colby College and the University of Pittsburgh. I am grateful for my time in Waterville, where I did a lot of writing and thinking about what directions to take my research. I am especially grateful to Elizabeth Leonard, my mentor and friend, for her warmth and encouragement. Thanks also to Esther King, who helped me to translate French sources.

I made the most meaningful changes to my work while I was a fellow at the World History Center at the University of Pittsburgh. I am honored to have worked with Patrick Manning, whose brilliant vision gave me countless ideas to improve my research. Thanks to Katie Jones for all of her work in making me feel at home in the Center. The intellectual community at the University shaped my thinking profoundly. Thanks to Diego Holstein, Lara Putnam, and Reid Andrews for their support in helping me to share my work with the talented scholars in Pitt's history department. Thanks also to my close friends and colleagues Mat Savelli, Vincent Leung, Mari Webel, Pernille Røge, David Luesink, Bob Reinhardt, and Molly Warsh.

More recently, I have been lucky to meet some amazing and passionate scholars in the history of disease and medicine, who have served as a source of support and inspiration as I finished my book and presented about it at conferences in the last couple of years. Thanks to Stephen Kenny, Jim Downs, Sharla Fett, Rana Hogarth, Elodie Grossi, Savannah Williamson, Beau Gaitors, Sean Morey Smith, Jessica Wells, and Kathryn Olivarius. I am especially grateful to Elaine LaFay for her enthusiasm that inspired me at a time when I was starting to feel jaded, and most of all for introducing me to the love of my life, Christopher Willoughby.

I am grateful to all of my colleagues at Murray State, who have enabled my work in many ways. Kathy Callahan has been a wonderful and dependable chair, neighbor, and friend, and I am thankful for everything she has done to help me. I am grateful to Staci Stone, Terry Strieter, and Sara Fineman for supporting my research. I am very thankful and humbled by Duane Bolin's enthusiasm for my research, and his advice on all things. Special thanks to Bill Schell, for taking the time to edit this manuscript one last time before I sent it to the reviewers. I am lucky to have such a friendly, collegial department. Thanks to Marjorie Hilton for her spirited energy and friendship, and to my vibrant colleagues who have been incredibly lovely and kind: Christine Lindner, Eleanor Rivera, Selina Gao, David Pizzo, Jim Humphreys, Taufiq Rashid, Ted Belue, Becca Dames, Aaron Irvin, Brian Clardy, Bill Mulligan, and Charlotte Beahan.

I decided to publish this book with LSU Press after discussing my project with Alisa Plant, whose ardent support gave me the confidence to move forward. Everyone I have encountered at LSU has been kind, attentive, and helpful throughout this process. Many thanks to Margaret Lovecraft and Craig Colten, for all of their efforts in critiquing and improving the manuscript. And thanks to Lee Sioles, Kate Barton, Jennifer Keegan, and MaryKatherine Callaway for their work in preparing my manuscript for publication. I am especially grateful to Mary Lee Eggart, who artfully put my data into a visual form that expressed many of my ideas better than my words.

My family and friends have been most helpful over the years, and I cannot thank them enough. Thanks to my oldest friends, Lori Hullings, Meaghan Brewer, Kristin Lorenzo, Emma Jane Browning, for their emotional support and for housing me during my research trips and conferences. I am grateful for all of the great friends I've met in grad school and during my postdocs: Eliza Martin, Marty Renner, Anders Otterness, Chrislaine Pamphile Miller, David Palter, Yajun Mo, Michael Jin, Elsa Fan, Sonja Thomas, Nikky Singh, Meera Sharma, Elspeth Martini, John Stoner, and anupama jain. I am lucky that I met the Willoughbys while finishing up this manuscript. I am grateful to Ruth, Mike, Susanne, Josh, Andrew, and Laura for all of their love and cheer. This book would not be possible if not for the love and support of my mother, Madhu, an amazing woman and feminist role model, who has encouraged and helped me more than I can express. And finally, I am deeply thankful for my amazing partner and best friend, Chris Willoughby, for everything.

Yellow Fever, Race, and Ecology
in Nineteenth-Century
NEW ORLEANS

Introduction

And so, even while we curse, let us also bless the mosquitoes, for
making us move about and root around, instead of dreaming our
lives away.
—LAFCADIO HEARN, 1880

Nineteenth-century depictions of New Orleans tended to emphasize
the city's unusual and exotic qualities, with vivid portrayals of its
distinctive environment, ecology, and culture. Historical representa-
tions of its humid, subtropical climate, precarious geography, and hybrid culture are best understood through a global and ecological lens.
Louisiana historian Joseph Tregle has described the city as "foreign
in its origins, mysterious in its responses and in its customs."[1] By the
nineteenth century, the city's geopolitical status had shifted numerous
times, as Louisiana was claimed by France, Spain, the United States,
and the Confederate States. It captured the imagination of visiting writers and poets, who invoked its colonial past and described its beautiful
and worldly qualities as well its dark side, characterized by death and
disease.

The city fascinated Lafcadio Hearn, who is better known for writing about Japanese culture. His ethnographic style of writing about
the peculiarities of New Orleans preceded his move to Japan, where
he similarly represented local customs and cultures for Western readers.[2] Raised in Greece and Ireland, Hearn lived in and wrote about New
Orleans for ten years between 1877 and 1887. In his vivid portrayal of
the "Creole city," he relished its "quaint houses; its shaded streets; its
suggestions of a hundred years ago; its contrasts of agreeable color;
its streets reëchoing the tongues of many nations; its general look of
somnolent contentment; its verdant antiquity; its venerable memorials
and monuments; its eccentricities of architecture; its tropical gardens;
its picturesque surprises; its warm atmosphere, drowsy perhaps with
the perfume of orange flowers, and thrilled with the fantastic music
of mocking-birds." Hearn, who "grew up keenly aware of his mixed

parentage and the nature of colonial cultural relationships," noted that "all civilized nations have sent wandering children hither," to a city "whose spell is so mystic, so sweet, so universal."[3]

Local writers poetically depicted New Orleans as the "Crescent City," the "City of Dreams," or the "fairest city in the South."[4] The city captivated Abraham Oakey Hall, a self-proclaimed "Manhattaner in New Orleans," who later served as mayor of New York. Hall might have grown up in New Orleans, but his father died of yellow fever when he was five, and his family relocated to New York. He wrote extensively about New Orleans after he moved there to practice law in 1845. Hall described the city as the "Calcutta of America" and often pointed out its similarities to the colonial Caribbean. He wrote that "thwarted enterprise, baffled endeavor, youthful hope, desperate plannings, all emigrate to its precincts to battle with fate, or to court fortune; to amass wealth, and if living after the 'gold hunt is over,' to return home to spend it."[5] Hall, along with other residents and visitors, often referred to yellow fever and the city's high mortality rates. Nineteenth-century writers gave the city creative nicknames such as the "Necropolis of New Orleans" or the "Wet Grave-Yard" or simply described it as a "wet grave." It was feared by newcomers, visitors, and residents alike and was eventually taken as a challenge by the US Board of Public Health.[6]

Historical geographer Peirce F. Lewis has characterized New Orleans as a "world city," comparable to New York, San Francisco, Calcutta, Alexandria, and Shanghai. In the era before air travel, these urban ports linked vast and productive hinterlands to the world.[7] They functioned as outlets that exposed inhabitants to foreign markets, peoples, and diseases. In the nineteenth century, New Orleans, and the sugar country that developed around it, occupied a space that functioned as both metropole and colony within the United States. The story of epidemic yellow fever, a mosquito-borne viral disease that plagued New Orleans for more than one hundred years between 1796 and 1905, reveals the contingent nature of environmental, economic, social, political, and cultural changes that the city underwent during the nineteenth century.

Ecology, Race, and Disease in New Orleans

In the context of colonialism and empire in the eighteenth and nineteenth centuries, medical writers associated diseases found in tropical latitudes with climate, weather, and topography.[8] Contemporaries in New Orleans made similar observations, and they drew connections between the city's ecology and the ubiquitous presence of disease. New Orleans is a lowland subtropical city, located just six degrees north of the Tropic of Cancer. In summer and fall, the city and surrounding environs resemble the tropics, in regard to weather and vegetation. The hot, humid, rainy weather provided conditions for cultivating tropical flora, including sugarcane, bananas, bougainvillea, hibiscus, and passion fruit. The climate and landscape of New Orleans, which expanded into the surrounding swamp country over the nineteenth century, enabled settlers to establish large, lucrative sugar plantations, which turned out to be a major factor in enabling the rise of epidemic yellow fever.

Generations of historians have studied the history of the American South, a region that they have distinguished from the rest of the United States based on particular factors, including its climate, environment, religious fervor, and, of course, its development as a slave society shaped by racial politics. In the nineteenth-century United States, the ways in which people understood race developed in response to African American slavery and its demise. Because American slavery was an institution based on race, proponents of slavery promoted ideas of racial inferiority, and racial difference more generally, to justify the enslavement of Africans and their descendants. Individuals who identified themselves as white saw their whiteness as a characteristic that entitled them to maintain a higher social status than people of African descent. The abolition of slavery led to acute political conflicts and the growth of legally sanctioned racial discrimination, as a way of maintaining social distinctions from the antebellum period. The study of disease, medicine, and public health in the region reveals the intersecting histories of science and the development of ideologies of race in the American South, Latin America, and European colonial spaces throughout the Atlantic world and Asia.

Throughout the nineteenth century, many Americans perceived the warm and humid southern weather as tropical and exotic, comparable to the colonial Caribbean. The social climate in the coastal regions extending from Charleston to the Gulf Coast also resembled that of the Caribbean during the antebellum years. This part of the country was ecologically, socially, and culturally tied to the Greater Caribbean, a geopolitical region that includes the "Atlantic coastal regions of South, Central, and North America, as well as the Caribbean islands themselves, that in the course of the seventeenth and eighteenth centuries became plantation zones."[9] Enslaved Africans and African Americans worked on large plantations, while planters claimed ownership of the land and labor in the region. By the midcentury, a hybrid culture emerged, as the Gulf Coast grew more intimately connected to antebellum plantation cultures that developed across the cotton belt, from east Texas to South Carolina. Many Americans, including those who lived in these regions, perceived illness in the region in relation to the hot climate, the wet vegetation, and the racially mixed population.[10]

After the Louisiana Purchase in 1803, as New Orleans was incorporated into the United States, racial identities in the city challenged conventional perceptions of race in the nation. New Orleans had been home to a diverse and dynamic population of French, Spanish, African, Native American, and Euro- and Afro-Caribbean peoples. In addition to its warm climate and lush vegetation, newcomers from the United States perceived the city as "foreign" because of its mix of European, African, and Caribbean cultural influences.[11] In New Orleans, and in southern Louisiana more generally, racial identities were inconsistent with the binary classificatory system common in the antebellum United States. Conceptions of race varied even within the region, and residents defined and divided themselves along cultural as well as racial lines. The spectrum of racial identities that emerged in eighteenth-century Louisiana was similar to systems of racial classification in the colonial Caribbean. Like many of the islands, lower Louisiana hosted diverse ethnic and linguistic groups throughout the eighteenth century, including French and Spanish colonists, African slaves (primarily from Mali, Senegambia, and the Bights of Benin and Biafra), and several Native American groups including (but not limited to) the Choctaw in the Lower Mississippi Valley, the Attakapa in the bayou country west of the city, and the Houma and Natchez, who lived northeast of the city along the Mississippi.[12] In regard to categories of race, residents distinguished between "negroes," "whites," "Indians," and people of color (*gens de couleur*). In popular and medical sources, people of color were often described in terms of their degree of African ancestry (mulattos, quadroons, octaroons, and so on). However, these classifications were malleable and did not always accurately represent an individual's genealogy.[13] An analysis of the history of racial identification in Louisiana before the Civil War reveals that while race was the most dominant factor in defining one's identity, the construction of racial identities was based on a complex set of factors, including nativity, native language, and perceived ethnic origin, in addition to skin pigmentation and other physiognomic traits. Free people of color, known as *gens de couleur libre* or *affranchis,* also shared an identity that was rooted in their freedom, which elevated their social status. Additionally, many Louisiana natives identified themselves as "Creoles" or were identified as such by newcomers and outsiders.

In this book, the term "Creole" is used synonymously with "native," unless otherwise specified. The term "creole" has been contested and redefined by residents and scholars throughout the nineteenth and twentieth centuries.[14] Etymologically, it is the English equivalent of the French *créole* or the Spanish *criollo,* derived from the Latin *creo* (to create or make), a root that accurately portrays creolism as a new cultural identity that emerged in colonial contexts. Historically, "Creole" appeared in European colonial documents beginning in the seventeenth century, in reference to the descendants of both African slaves and European settlers, who were born in colonial territories, most commonly in the Americas.[15] After the Louisiana Purchase, native Louisianans who traced their ancestry to colonial French, Spanish, African, and Caribbean migrants continued to identify themselves as Creoles, as a way of distinguishing themselves from the growing "American" population, which consisted of free and enslaved migrants from the United States. Though not all native Louisianans identified as Creoles, all individuals in Louisiana who identified as Creoles were native to the Gulf Coast or Caribbean region.[16]

Until the mid-nineteenth century, ideas about racial identity in New Orleans remained similar to systems of racial classification in the French Caribbean. This complex and multitiered understanding of race transformed over the second half of the nineteenth century, as New Orleanians adopted the binary system of racial classification that was common in the rest of the United States. It was during this time that the term "Creole" gained racial connotations. Creoles who identified as white sought to usurp the term, designating Creoles of African descent as "creoles of color." Meanwhile, locals who identified as Americans often portrayed Creoles as a mixed race of French, Spanish, and African ancestry. The work of novelist George Washington Cable, born in

New Orleans in 1844, illustrates the complexity of Creole identity. In response to the question "What is a Creole?," he wrote that "even in Louisiana, the question would be variously answered." He defined the term "Creole" as "a proud appellation," used to designate "the French-speaking, native portion of the ruling class" and explained that over time "the term was adopted by—not conceded to—the natives of mixed blood, and is still used so among themselves." Despite Cable's insistence that the term originally referred only to natives of French and Spanish ancestry, his novels about Creole families depicted them as racially diverse.[17] Changing beliefs about immunity to yellow fever in New Orleans, based on creolism, race, and ethnicity, reveal that conceptions of race were fluid and shaped by interactions between different ethnic and cultural groups.[18]

Throughout the nineteenth century, fevers commonly afflicted residents and visitors, who understood disease as a product of the environment, rather than focusing on microcausal factors that produced and spread disease. In modern medical literature, the term "fever" usually refers to the symptom of high body temperature, which is associated with many illnesses. In the nineteenth century, "fever" referred to what was perceived as an illness, rather than a symptom. Nineteenth-century popular and medical understandings of "fever" resemble current discourses about "cancer," using an umbrella term for numerous ailments with various known and unknown causes and conflating many distinct diseases based on their common symptomatology. Various descriptive terms for fevers included "malarial fever," "bilious fever," "hemorrhagic fever," "broken bone fever," and "fever and ague." In the seventeenth through nineteenth centuries, doctors often identified yellow fever as a pestilential fever, in which the victim exhibited jaundice and internal hemorrhaging and vomited digested blood, which contemporaries described as "black bile." Its early Spanish names, *vómito negro* and *vómito prieto*, derived from this symptom. Early accounts often classified the disease in terms of its symptoms, as hemorrhagic or bilious fever. Observers also classified fevers by their perceived place of origin, for example labeling them as swamp or country fever. They often linked fevers to "miasmas," or foul vapors, which were viewed as part of the atmosphere. They described pestilence in swamps and bayous as a result of miasmas that were distinct from the miasmas and "filth" that were present in urban spaces. These observations reflected the presence of malarial fevers in swamps and prairies, in contrast to the prevalence of yellow fever, cholera, and typhoid in cities.[19]

Currently, yellow fever is classified as an acute viral infection, which is primarily transmitted to humans through the bite of an infected female aedine mosquito. In the nineteenth century, it was most commonly transmitted by *Aëdes aegypti* (*A. aegypti*), a species that has adapted to living in close proximity to humans in built environments, such as cities, maritime vessels, and plantations. Because this book focuses on yellow fever in the nineteenth century, at a time when people did not have a clear understanding of its etiology, contemporary accounts of the disease are interpreted using historical hindsight, relying on medical knowledge produced in the late twentieth and the twenty-first centuries. As a result, this study reveals how early-nineteenth-century witnesses, including scientists and untrained observers, were often accurate in their observations about the relationship between disease and the environment. Despite the absence of advanced microscopic technology, medical researchers who studied yellow fever in the nineteenth century were beginning to understand its patterns of transmission, and they vigorously debated possible causes and treatments.

Over the course of the nineteenth century, local concerns and national politics, as well as intellectual developments in European colonies in the Americas, Asia, and Africa, shaped medical research in New Orleans. In the 1860s and 1870s, medical ideologies shifted across the Americas and Europe; they became less grounded in miasmatic theory and more influenced by the emergent field of bacteriology. This shift inspired medical researchers to search for a yellow fever "germ" and elicited faith in sanitation among public health officials. By the close of the nineteenth century, heightened national political and economic interests in Latin America altered the course of yellow fever research. Geopolitical changes transformed the ways in which contemporaries conceptualized disease, race, and tropical environments. These ideas shaped movements in global health, manifested in the establishment of the field of tropical medicine, which served as the impetus behind yellow fever eradication campaigns in New Orleans. Regional epidemics continued until 1905, when the US Public Health Service intervened and enforced mosquito eradication policies in the city, as part of a series of imperial campaigns that began during the US occupation of Havana after the Spanish-American War. It was not until the 1930s that scientists could finally see the disease-causing agent, as microscopic technology improved and the field of virology developed.

The Argument and Analytical Frame

Ecological changes helped to determine the epidemiological history of New Orleans in the nineteenth century, and these changes in turn affected cultural attitudes about race, health, and the environment. Situating New Orleans and its environs in multiple contexts—as a unique urban space shaped by its geography, a plantation society in the Greater Caribbean, and an entrepôt that linked the Mississippi Valley to the Atlantic World—reveals its distinctiveness in the United States as well as its shared history with cosmopolitan port cities across the hemisphere. The research presented in this book diverges from medical studies that focus on proximate causes of disease; instead, it explores the ecology of disease as a way of understanding the rise and spread of yellow fever. Broadly, global patterns of colonial settlement, cultivation, voluntary and involuntary migrations, landscape alterations, water control projects, and industrial development enabled yellow fever to become a hemispheric pandemic in the seventeenth through nineteenth centuries. Human endeavors served as a catalyst for ecological change, causing unintended and unforeseen consequences that in turn shaped cultural and intellectual perceptions of disease.

By emphasizing the relationship between the local and the global, I present an alternative framework for understanding the city's epidemiological history. Global processes, including the expansion of sugar production in the Americas, the growth of the slave trade in Africa and slavery in the Americas, and the Haitian Revolution, contributed to the prevalence of yellow fever in New Orleans at the turn of the nineteenth century. Demographic and ecological changes, driven by the rise of epidemic yellow fever in West Africa, mid-nineteenth-century conflicts in western Europe, global patterns of migration, industrialization, and revolutions in transportation systems, caused yellow fever to become seasonally endemic in New Orleans during this period. The region's expanding sugar industry and the related effects of urbanization, includ-

8

ing canal construction, swamp drainage, and river clearance, as well as immigration and population growth, created an environment that was hospitable to the virus and its host mosquito, *A. aegypti*. Increasing European immigration in the mid-nineteenth century, prompted partly by famine and revolutionary movements, provided a sizable population of nonimmunes to host the virus. Industrialization fueled the development of steamships, railroads, and water control projects in the Mississippi Valley, allowing yellow fever to spread beyond coastal ports. Approaching the disease from a global perspective highlights connections between the epidemiological and environmental histories of the Atlantic, in relation to political, economic, and social transformations that influenced popular and medical perceptions of yellow fever and shaped public health policy. Unlike most studies of yellow fever in the Americas, this one begins by questioning why the disease appeared at a particular time and place in human history. Yellow fever was absent from the historical record until the mid-seventeenth century, when a series of epidemics occurred in the Caribbean sugar islands. After these epidemics, the disease spread through the Atlantic and regularly appeared in written accounts in the eighteenth and nineteenth centuries. Even though scholars acknowledge its African origin, the history of the growth and spread of yellow fever in West Africa is unknown. Narratives of yellow fever normally emphasize how yellow fever emerged in the Americas as a consequence of the advent of West African slavery and plantation agriculture, which resulted in many more transatlantic voyages between these regions. I present an alternative chronology: historicizing the emergence of endemic yellow fever in coastal West Africa by investigating the growth of epidemics in the late eighteenth and the nineteenth centuries in relation to European colonial expeditions and demographic changes.

A thoughtful consideration of the enigmatic history of the emergence of yellow fever in human history provides a context for understanding the surge in epidemics in antebellum New Orleans. In the first half of the nineteenth century, ecological and demographic transformations related to the rise of sugarcane cultivation led to yellow fever epidemics in the city nearly every other year. The region became increasingly reliant on slave labor upon its admittance to the United States, as large sugar plantations emerged along the banks of the Mississippi and surrounding bayou country. Consequences of the growth of sugar production, including the construction of sugar plantations, the expansion of West African slavery and the slave trade, and the growth of waterfront commerce, immigration, and urban development in the region, directly and indirectly led to the prevalence of yellow fever, by providing numerous breeding places for *A. aegypti* mosquitoes, by frequently exposing the city to the virus, and by providing a renewable host population of non-immune newcomers that enabled the virus to persist.

Tracing the history of yellow fever in the postbellum period exposes the ecological consequences of industrial development. Epidemics subsided during the Civil War and were less frequent and severe during the Reconstruction era, until an outbreak in 1878 initiated a regional epidemic in the Mississippi Valley. Typically, scholars of health and disease in the postwar South emphasize the role of economic decline, poverty, and the lack of public health infrastructure. However, development during the Reconstruction era, including demographic changes and alterations in the region's built environment, unexpectedly allowed yellow fever to reach peoples and places that had never encountered it. Environmental changes tied to industrial development in the postwar South, including the engineering of water management projects, the construction of railroads, and the growth of small outposts along railroad lines, encouraged the habitation of *A. aegypti* mosquitoes and facilitated the spread of the yellow fever virus. Immunological factors related to demographic changes, such as postwar urban migrations and the flight of refugees during epidemics, also fostered the spread of the virus.

The ways in which contemporaries understood (and misunderstood) patterns of yellow fever epidemics and immunity in the nineteenth century reflected local ideas about race, health, and the environment. Individuals who contract yellow fever and survive become immunized; thereafter they can neither host the virus nor experience symptoms. However, concepts of inheritable immunity, based on nativity, ethnicity, and race, developed variously among contemporaries in yellow fever zones across the Atlantic. The new disease environment in New Orleans gradually led to widespread exposure and immunity among native Creole populations, while demographic changes caused ethnic groups who came into contact with yellow fever for the first time to appear to be more susceptible than natives. Across the southern United States, a noticeable change in medical and popular ideologies of immunity occurred between 1817 and 1857. Initially, residents and physicians believed that native populations were immune to yellow fever, but gradually, they began linking immunity and race. This change, combined with the amplification of local racial tensions before the Civil War, led to an increasingly racialized view of bodies among medical professionals. Local ideas reflected a global pattern in the development of racial thought that developed in European colonial spaces throughout the Caribbean, Asia, and Africa. Racial anxieties, intensified by the gradual abolition of slavery around the world, influenced medical ideas about tropical bodies and tropical environments, hardening beliefs about innate biological differences expressed in terms of race. Ideologies of racial immunity solidified after the Civil War, in tandem with the escalation of racist ideologies and racial violence toward African Americans. After the epidemic of 1878, scientists, public health authorities, and untrained observers abandoned their ideas of Creole immunity and increasingly connected disease immunity with race. Proponents of theories that emphasized innate racial types used the notion of racial immunity as proof of biological difference.

Nineteenth-century views of racial immunity have shaped historical interpretations of yellow fever, and historians continue to raise the question of whether West African and African American populations enjoy some degree of genetic protection against the disease.[20] My critique of claims of racial immunity is directed toward scholars who uncritically accept that individuals of African descent inherited immunity and/or were more resistant to yellow fever than whites, and use this premise to make arguments about political, socioeconomic, and cultural developments. My theoretical approach is informed by critical scholarship in the fields of science studies and the social construction of race, which are often grounded in Michel Foucault's work. While many researchers argue that immunity to yellow fever can be acquired only by contracting and surviving the disease, other scholars, including Kenneth F. Kiple, who has served as editor of the *Cambridge World History of Human Disease,* argue that blacks enjoyed some degree of genetic resistance that made them more likely than whites to survive if they became infected. Scholars of southern history often cite Kiple's pioneering studies of Afro-Caribbean health and disease. World historians of disease, including Philip D. Curtin and Sheldon Watts, maintain that yellow fever immunity depends upon surviving the disease.[21] My analysis applies this world historical framework to the American South, raising questions about studies that have erroneously depicted African Americans as immune or resistant to yellow fever.[22]

Contextualizing the history of disease, medicine, and public health in New Orleans in global terms explains seemingly unique qualities of the city's epidemiological history. In particular, the development of public health institutions in the South was part of a larger pattern of the growth of the field of tropical medicine at the turn of the twentieth century. Studies of tropical diseases (including yellow fever, malaria, dengue, and others) normally focus on colonial territories in Asia, Africa, the Caribbean, and South America but evade the southern United States as an area of study.[23] However, late-nineteenth-century social and economic conditions in New Orleans were comparable to those in colonial regions, similar in terms of widespread poverty, economic stagnation, racial segregation, and violence. Further, local businesses were integral to supporting public health research and mosquito eradication programs in Latin America. The development of medical authority and public health institutions, directed toward the prevention of yellow fever and other tropical diseases, occurred simultaneously in the American South and the colonial world.

Ecological conditions produced by colonialism and imperial expansion resulted in the escalation of epidemic yellow fever (and other diseases) across the Atlantic, and imperial military interventions were necessary to control their spread. However, the underlying theme of unintended outcomes applies to disease eradication efforts as well as to environmental engineering and demographic change. In the nineteenth century, epidemic yellow fever emerged in the Americas and Africa as an unforeseen consequence of colonial expansion and maritime trade, and the disease became prevalent with the rise of plantation slavery, sugar production, and urban growth in swamps and prairies. Similarly, twentieth-century public health programs aimed at controlling yellow fever, including the sporadic use of pesticides and vaccines, have had consequences that are becoming increasingly apparent, such as the evolution and immunity of disease-causing agents and the growing toxicity of water systems.

1

A Disease Sui Generis

YELLOW FEVER IN WORLD HISTORY

Yellow fever had no discernible impact on human history until the mid-seventeenth century, when a series of epidemics took place in the Caribbean sugar islands.[1] Although the disease had been absent from the historical record prior to these epidemics, it quickly spread throughout the Americas and regularly appeared in written records during the eighteenth and nineteenth centuries. The yellow fever virus and its host mosquito originated in tropical Africa, but epidemics were not documented on that continent until the late eighteenth century. The rise of epidemic yellow fever, and the subsequent emergence of endemic yellow fever zones in the tropical Atlantic, is intricately tied to global developments in the sixteenth through nineteenth centuries, including the maritime revolution, the growth of plantation agriculture (particularly sugarcane), the slave trade, urban growth, migrations, and the ecological changes that these processes engendered.[2]

Landscapes of Fever in the Atlantic World

Since the 1970s, scholars including Alfred Crosby, William McNeill, and Philip Curtin have studied the role of diseases in shaping historical developments in the Atlantic. Crosby has shown the profound effect of the transport of pathogens in the Columbian Exchange on the history of colonization and settlement in the Americas, since native populations' lack of exposure to "old world" pathogens made them vulnerable to diseases such as smallpox, measles, diphtheria, whooping cough, and chicken pox. The "Great Dying" killed the majority of native populations throughout the Caribbean and the continental Americas and, in turn, allowed Europeans to establish colonies more easily. Philip Curtin has emphasized the role of African diseases, particularly malaria and yellow fever, in shaping histories of colonization, slavery, and colonialism in the Americas and Africa. More recently, J. R. McNeill has explicated the role of differential immunity to yellow fever and malaria in affecting outcomes of colonial and imperial wars in the Greater Caribbean.[3]

Between the late seventeenth and the mid-nineteenth centuries, the tropical and subtropical Atlantic developed as an endemic fever zone, owing to a conjuncture of transatlantic ecological exchange and landscape transformations, which facilitated the spread of both malaria and yellow fever. Despite the presence of *falciparum* malaria in southern Europe and other temperate zones, historians often group these diseases together as the two primary "diseases of warm climates" or "tropical diseases" that caused widespread illness in the Atlantic and were more threatening to Europeans and people of European descent than to "blacks" and people born in endemic zones.[4] The two diseases share some common traits, including their African origin, some similar symptoms, and their dependence on primates and mosquitoes for survival. Their reliance on mosquitoes ultimately caused them to spread in similar climates and seasons, in conditions that were warm and wet enough to sustain insect populations.

However, because they are carried by different mosquitoes, with distinct habits, yellow fever and malaria have vital differences in their epidemiology. As a result of mosquito preferences and human endeavors, malaria flourished in swamps, irrigated fields, and other aquatic habitats, while yellow fever thrived in cities and onboard ships. Because of the distinctive features of the yellow fever virus compared to the parasitic *plasmodium* that causes malaria, yellow fever often caused epidemics on ships and at urban ports, while malaria became endemic in less populated wetlands and rural environments. Although both pathogens are African in origin, the relationship between *Plasmodia* and humans has a much longer known history. James L. A. Webb has shown how West African communities that settled in tropical riverbanks dealt with the burden of malaria prior to the Neolithic revolutions, and how indigenous "encounters with falciparum malaria . . . intensified with the shift from paracultivation to cultivation" in "cleared woodlands or in rainforest openings" when humans created these microenvironments before the eleventh millennium BCE.[5] Further, from about 1500 BCE through the seventh century BCE, descriptions of malaria appeared in historical accounts across Eurasia, from Greece to the Indus and Yangtze River Valleys.[6] However, accounts of yellow fever do not occur until the modern period, and reports of outbreaks prior to the seventeenth century are rare and uncertain.

Yellow Fever Epidemiology and Ecology

Yellow fever is an acute viral infection, caused by an arbovirus (a virus carried by arthropods) that is transmitted to humans through the bite of an infected female aedine mosquito, most commonly of the species *A. aegypti*.[7] These mosquitoes are also able to transmit dengue fever, chikungunya, and the Zika virus. Dengue and yellow fever share similar symptoms and epidemic patterns; they are caused by viruses that belong to the genus *Flavivirus,* which also includes the Zika and West Nile viruses and Japanese encephalitis.[8] In the late eighteenth and the nineteenth centuries, dengue fever was reported in tropical and subtropical regions across the globe. In the nineteenth century it appeared most frequently in Asia, in regions where yellow fever failed to cause epidemics. While yellow fever and dengue are caused by a virus, malaria is caused by a protozoan parasite. There are at least five known malarial parasites of the genus *Plasmodium* that can infect humans (*P. malariae, P. vivax, P. falciparum, P. ovale,* and *P. knowlesi*) through the bite of an infected *Anopheles* mosquito (primarily *A. gambiae* in West Africa, *A. albimanus* in the Caribbean, and *A. quadrimaculatus* in North America).[9] The two species that have the greatest global impact are *P. vivax,* which transmits a form of malaria that epidemiologists describe as comparatively mild, and *P. falciparum,* which transmits one that has severe symptoms and results in higher mortality rates.[10] While malaria and dengue spread throughout the world, yellow fever remained confined to the Atlantic.[11]

Researchers have identified three transmission cycles of yellow fever: sylvan (or jungle), intermediate (or savannah), and epidemic (or urban), in which the virus follows different epidemiological patterns. Sylvan yellow fever is maintained primarily by tree-dwelling monkeys and transmitted by wild mosquitoes (primarily *A. africanus* in Africa and various species of *Haemagogus* mosquitoes in South America) that live in the forest canopy. The intermediate cycle marks the transfer of the virus from nonhuman to human primates by a variety of "semidomestic" species of *Aedes* mosquitoes that feed on monkeys and humans.[12] This cycle typically occurs when humans enter sylvan regions (often to hunt or fell trees), with the potential of causing major epidemics among humans engaged in clearing and cultivating forested areas. Urban yellow fever, by contrast, infects only humans and is transmitted by *A. aegypti,* an "urban species" that has "proved to be remarkably adaptable to living close to humans, thriving in their cities by changing its preferred breeding sites to artificial containers and by changing its preferred blood meal to human blood."[13] Like all mosquitoes, *A. aegypti* females lay their eggs in water. However, they seem to have a unique preference for man-made containers, especially those made of wood, cement, or clay. Included are large reservoirs and cisterns, in addition to flower pots, "gutters, water barrels, cans, jars, or those many little niches found in such places as junk yards."[14] Essentially, *A. aegypti* can breed in any crevice that can hold a small amount of rainwater, causing them to prefer urban environments, as opposed to malaria-carrying *Anopheles* mosquitoes, which flourish in undeveloped and rural environments. The species of anophelines that thrived in the Americas during the sixteenth through nineteenth centuries, *A. albimanus* and *A. quadrimaculatus,* bred in freshwater and brackish swamps, ditches, and canals, in addition to agricultural ponds and irrigated fields.[15] As humans entered wetlands and wooded areas and cleared them for cultivation and urban development, these regions functioned as ecological borderlands, where malaria and yellow fever coexisted.

SYMPTOMS

Perhaps the most distinctive features of the yellow fever virus are its rapid passing through the body and its macabre symptoms. The *A. aegypti* bites humans in the daytime and evening, and symptoms of yellow fever begin to appear after three to six days. Symptoms range from mild to severe and occur in two distinct phases. In the first phase, an infected person will experience mild symptoms, which usually last for three to four days; the victim initially has chills, followed by high fever, slow pulse, headache, intense muscle and back pains, loss of appetite, nausea, and vomiting. Most infected individuals will improve within three to four days, but about 15 percent will enter the second (toxic) phase. In the eighteenth and nineteenth centuries, individuals who experienced mild symptoms would be unlikely to know that they had been infected with yellow fever. Victims who progressed to the toxic stage experienced a relapse of fever, combined with severe symptoms including liver failure, jaundice, abdominal pain, internal hemorrhaging, and decreased kidney function, which could cause albuminuria (protein in urine) or kidney failure. During the final stages of the disease, the victim vomits coagulated blood known as "black vomit," "black bile," or *vómito negro,* which many late-eighteenth- and nineteenth-century observers described as being of the consistency of coffee grounds. This unique symptom is the only way to identify the presence of yellow fever in historical records with any certainty. Black vomit indicates that death is imminent, and most yellow fever victims who show that symptom die within ten to fourteen days. Preceding death, they often hallucinate, have fits of convulsions, and/or fall into a coma.[16]

Despite the distinctive symptoms of yellow fever, it is impossible to retrospectively diagnose its presence with certainty. Even today, doctors would have difficulty diagnosing yellow fever based on its mild symptoms, which resemble mild symptoms of malaria, dengue fever, chikungunya, typhoid, and various other febrile diseases. In the eighteenth- and nineteenth-century Atlantic, physicians often conflated yellow fever, dengue, malaria, and other diseases that exhibited similar symptoms. Though yellow fever victims notably exhibited jaundice, both dengue and yellow fever could cause joint or muscle pain and internal hemorrhaging. Thus, early cases of yellow fever could not be positively diagnosed, and it is likely that contemporaries recorded only severe cases that resulted in death, overlooking mild cases. Additionally, cases that doctors identified as bilious or hemorrhagic fevers may have actually been yellow fever, described as such because victims exhibited symptoms of vomiting and internal or external hemorrhaging.

IMMUNITY AND THE EMERGENCE OF
ENDEMIC YELLOW FEVER ZONES

Humans can acquire immunity to yellow fever by contracting and surviving the disease. Healthy children who contracted yellow fever often exhibited only mild symptoms and survived, thus gaining lifelong immunity to the disease. Adults were more likely to experience severe symptoms and die within two weeks of contracting the virus.[17] In the Atlantic Americas, reported mortality rates during epidemics commonly reached 40 to 50 percent in adult populations.[18] Since physicians and families did not recognize cases of yellow fever among children unless they were severe, and generally children who reached the severe stages of the disease did not survive, it is probable that childhood cases of yellow fever were often misdiagnosed or unrecorded. Because immunity prevents a victim from hosting the virus again, only nonimmune individuals infected with the disease, including humans and other primates, can spread yellow fever. They are in fact necessary for it to appear in epidemic or endemic form.[19] The establishment of endemicity can thus be identified on the basis of records of severe epidemics prior to records of the disease's constant or seasonal presence.

As a result of acquired immunity in regions that underwent numerous epidemics, yellow fever could become endemic if the population size and density was high enough to sustain the virus. Natives to endemic zones would be likely to contract the disease during childhood and acquire immunity. As relative "newcomers to their society," usually children were the only group susceptible to the disease; since most adults would have likely contracted the virus and acquired immunity as children, they could not be reinfected.[20] Thus it is probable that epidemics, and the growth of regional endemic zones, may have occurred as a result of migrations and trade in the region.

The history of yellow fever in tropical Africa before the nineteenth century remains a severely understudied topic, and historians have yet to find evidence of yellow fever in early African sources. The lack of records of early epidemics in tropical West Africa has caused many researchers to assume its endemicity in West Africa as a constant feature of the region's environment. Because of this immunological pattern, combined with notions of tropicality and febrile diseases, until the twentieth century nearly all naturalists, physicians, and untrained observers noticed that peoples who were native to regions where the disease was endemic seemed to be immune.[21]

While there is no compelling evidence of genetic resistance to yellow fever, genetic mutations among some tropical African populations have provided effective resistance to certain malaria parasites. Across West and West Central Africa, the Duffy Red Blood Cell antigen negativity

(Duffy negativity) has offered generations of indigenous peoples protection against *P. vivax*, while the sickle cell trait has given them a smaller degree of protection from *P. falciparum*.[22] Whereas the yellow fever virus passes through the body rapidly, within two weeks, malaria can cause chronic illness, in which victims are reinfected. Malarial symptoms can last for years or a lifetime, causing intermittent symptoms. Further, since *P. vivax* can remain dormant for years, even when mosquitoes are hibernating, malaria can remain endemic for long periods of time, even without the introduction of new human populations. *P. falciparum*, however, can remain dormant only for a few months before disappearing.[23]

ORIGIN AND EARLY EPIDEMICS

Although both the yellow fever virus and *Aedes* mosquitoes originated in Africa, epidemics were not recorded until the late eighteenth century, more than one hundred years after the earliest reports of epidemics in the Americas. Until the twentieth century, most contemporary medical researchers believed that yellow fever originated in the Americas because of the lack of evidence of the disease in Africa in the pre-Columbian period. Further, since yellow fever appeared for the first time in Europe in the eighteenth century, more than seventy-five years before the earliest recorded epidemics in West Africa, its African origin was not apparent. Additionally, nineteenth-century proponents of this theory pointed to evidence from Native American sources, as described in early European colonial accounts of travels and encounters in the Americas. Although current scholars hold that the diseases described in pre-Columbian sources could not have been yellow fever, throughout the nineteenth and early-twentieth centuries several notable medical researchers, including Carlos Finlay, W. C. Gorgas, and Rubert Boyce, believed that it was present in the Americas when Europeans arrived in the fifteenth century.

Carlos Finlay, known for his pioneering research on the role of mosquitoes in the transmission of yellow fever, "noted in his early studies of that disease that the vicinity of Veracruz, as well as parts of the Yucatán peninsula in Mexico, has been repeatedly depopulated by epidemics of what the Aztecs called *cocolitzle*. According to Finlay, the clinical description of and epidemiology of *cocolitzle* corresponded to that of yellow fever."[24] Physician and surgeon William Crawford Gorgas of Mobile, known for his successful mosquito eradication campaigns in Havana and Panama during the construction of the Panama Canal, thought that early English settlers in Jamestown and Plymouth might have died from yellow fever. He and Finlay both believed that *cocolitzle* eventually became known as *vómito negro* and was endemic in Veracruz in pre-Columbian times, citing Spanish historian Father Lapey's account of yellow fever in Yucatán in 1648, in which he refers to the disease as *cocolitzle*.[25] Several nineteenth-century writers maintained that Hernán Cortés found yellow fever prevailing in Mexico, where it was known as *matzlazahuatl*.[26] Professor Rubert Boyce of Liverpool, who wrote extensively about mosquito-borne diseases, maintained this view in a textbook on yellow fever that he published in 1911. He claimed that it was endemic in the West Indies when Spanish colonists arrived, based on records of an epidemic at Isabella on Santo Domingo in 1493, after the first Columbian voyage. According to Boyce, subsequent epidemics occurred in Puerto Rico (1508), Cuba (1620), and Guadeloupe (1635).[27]

Over the twentieth century, medical researchers and scholars debated about the precise origin of yellow fever. Since the 1980s most specialists have agreed that both the virus and the *A. aegypti* mosquito are native to tropical Africa. The consensus in the literature regarding the West African origin of yellow fever stems from late-twentieth-century genomic research, while previous researchers who believed that yellow fever originated in the Americas based their conclusions on empirical evidence of yellow fever epidemics mentioned in historical accounts. Late-twentieth-century medical research on the West African origin of yellow fever is compelling because it incorporates the findings of recent studies in the fields of genetics, epidemiology, entomology, and evolutionary biology. These fields can inform historical arguments by exposing inconsistencies between historical records and laboratory research.

In the case of yellow fever, its West African origin raises questions regarding its apparent emergence in the Caribbean and the lack of recorded outbreaks in West Africa until the eighteenth century. Assessing the causes of this discrepancy elucidates the role of human activity in shaping epidemic patterns. The first recorded epidemics that can be clearly identified as yellow fever took place in the 1640s, in colonial settlements and plantations in the Caribbean and Gulf Coast regions of

North America; there were large-scale outbreaks in Barbados (1647), Guadeloupe (1648), St. Kitts (1648), Yucatán (1648), and Cuba (1649).[28] Within fifty years, it appeared in temperate colonial port cities in North America, first in Boston, Philadelphia, and Charleston in 1693, and then in New York (1702), Halifax (1710), and Norfolk, Virginia (1737). The first documented epidemics in Europe occurred simultaneously, not surprisingly in temperate port cities along the Iberian coast: Cádiz (1700), Lisbon (1723), and Málaga (1741).[29]

For more than a century, European medical reports described yellow fever epidemics in the Caribbean, North America, and Europe, but not in Africa. Descriptions of disease in Africa included various other fevers, including malaria. Fifteenth- and sixteenth-century Portuguese and Dutch sources documented various diseases with symptoms that were similar to the milder symptoms of yellow fever, such as muscular pain, fever, jaundice, and inflammation of the liver.[30] However, these accounts did not describe the black vomit that is unique to yellow fever.

The earliest medical account that suggests black vomit comes from West Central Africa, indicating that yellow fever may have been present in late-sixteenth-century Angola.[31] In 1520 Portuguese traders had begun to occupy the coast, and in the 1570s the port city of Luanda was actively involved in the transatlantic slave trade. From 1575 through the turn of the century, the majority of slaves that the Portuguese brought to Brazil came through Angola.[32] In a report of observations of disease in Angola and Brazil between 1594 and 1606, Portuguese army surgeon Aleixo de Abreu documented a disease natives and colonizers called "the worm's disease" (*enfermedad del gusano*), with a symptom that he described as *regueldo caliente*.[33] This symptom could be interpreted as hot or bloody vomit, indicating yellow fever, or it could suggest a soil-transmitted parasitic tapeworm that caused nausea and vomiting. This rare description raises the possibility that yellow fever may have traveled from Angola to Brazil, where epidemic yellow fever was reported in Bahia and Pernambuco in 1685–92.[34]

The Rise of Endemic Yellow Fever in Coastal West Africa

As yellow fever appeared more frequently in the Caribbean, North America, and Europe in the mid-eighteenth century, a few sources indicated outbreaks in West Africa. Some of the earliest descriptions that suggest the presence of yellow fever are in reports from medical officers on British expeditions in the Senegal and Gambia Rivers. The area between the shores of these rivers was one of the first parts of sub-Saharan West Africa to come into maritime contact with Europe. The region was heavily involved in the slave trade prior to 1600; possibly more than one-third of the slaves exported from Africa in the sixteenth century came from this area.[35] Portuguese, Dutch, French, and British traders purchased slaves from coastal ports, located at the mouths of both rivers. By 1600 an Afro-Portuguese community dominated trade in the Gambia region, and by the 1690s French merchants occupied a fortified post in the north, at Makhana. Meanwhile, British traders resided at an unfortified port at Albreda and traded with Afro-Portuguese and African merchants near the Gambia.[36] Despite this rich history of trade and cross-cultural exchange, there is no compelling evidence that indicates the presence of yellow fever in this coastal region before the mid-eighteenth century.

In 1758, during the Seven Years' War, British forces took control of French settlements in Saint-Louis, sent a detachment up the Senegal River, and occupied the French factory fort at Galam (Gajaaga). Galam, located about seven hundred miles inland, marked the "outer limits of the Atlantic trade networks under direct European control."[37] The British made the fatal mistake of traveling upriver during the rainy season. A medical officer who accompanied the troops described the fort's surroundings as a heavily forested environment, with numerous tigers, serpents, crocodiles, elephants, ostriches, baboons, sand flies, and mosquitoes, which he referred to as their "most distressing enemies."[38] Within six weeks, more than one-third of the troops died of unidentified fevers.[39] In less than a year, during the next rainy season, "the mortality was so great among the soldiers sent from Senegal to relieve them, that not above three or four reached the fort alive."[40]

Physician James Lind described the epidemic fever that Europeans encountered in Senegal as a "low malignant fever," which occurred during the rainy season. According to his report, the dry season lasted for about eight months, and the rainy season, which he described as the "season of sickness," lasted about four months. He wrote that during the dry season, the "country was as healthy and pleasant as any in the world," but when the rainy season commenced, "a low malignant fever constantly spread itself among the Europeans." He described how the fever "seemed to proceed from a poison, as it were, which had got into the stomach, beginning with severe retchings, and often the vomiting of bile." Lind also noted that "in some, the fever was very malignant, and the patient died soon after its attack, the corpse appearing of a yellow color and the skin stained with livid spots or blotches."[41] Despite these symptoms, Lind classified the disease as distinct from yellow fever, which he characterized as a disease of the West Indies. However he also noted that, "having now considered this disease with attention, I am now of the opinion, that the remarkable dissolution of the blood, the violent haemorrhages, the black vomit, and the other symptoms which characterize yellow fever, are only accidental appearances in the common fever of the West Indies."[42]

Although Lind's account of the epidemic lacks a detailed description of black vomit, the circumstances suggest that it might have been an early and unusual account of the intermediate cycle of yellow fever transmission, in which the disease transferred from monkeys to humans. Yellow fever may have been endemic among monkey populations in the forests of the lower Senegal River valley. The medical officer on the British voyage to Galam reported that "the baboons were so numerous, that [the troops] made them their principal amusement; they clothed them with the regimentals of the soldiers who died, they made them walk erect . . . and in some respects even made them serve them in their houses."[43] This type of close contact with baboons, who may have carried yellow fever, could explain how British troops came into contact with the disease. Another factor suggesting that British troops came into contact with yellow fever, rather than malaria, is that they took quinine bark and it had no effect.[44] While quinine served as effective antimalarial medicine, it did not affect one's susceptibility to the yellow fever virus. By the 1830s, British expeditions in West Africa used quinine to abate the threat of fevers and significantly decreased their mortality rates.[45] Since quinine had effectively reduced the risk of fevers on commercial expeditions in the Niger River in the 1830s, it is probable that yellow fever was not present in the regions they explored.

While it remains unclear whether the disease mentioned in Lind's account was actually yellow fever, about a decade later, in 1768 and 1769, two accounts of shipboard epidemics also suggest the possible presence of yellow fever. In the summer of 1768, the British sloop *Merlin* entered the Gambia River with a crew of about ninety healthy men. After six days, several men left the ship, to engage in "wooding and watering." It is not evident how many were assigned this task, or exactly where they went, but a few days after they got back on the ship, they became sick with fever. They died within six or seven days, and soon afterward their shipmates contracted the same disease.[46] Although there is no clinical description of the symptoms, two factors indicate that this might have been yellow fever. First, since the men who were logging initially became sick and the men who remained on the ship did not, the loggers probably came into contact with the virus while they were in the woods. Second, the incubation time and the timing of the deaths correspond with the known incubation period of yellow fever and the period after which death occurs.[47] However, since many different lethal pathogens could cause death in a short period of time, these descriptions cannot be definitively regarded as yellow fever.

Another account that suggests the appearance of yellow fever in the Senegambia region comes from Robert Robertson, a naval surgeon on board the *Weasel*, a British warship that set sail on the Gambia River during the rainy season in 1769. He wrote a lengthy description that included many symptoms of yellow fever, including back pain, irregular pulse, jaundice, and violent vomiting.[48] However, he failed to mention the fever's characteristic bloody vomit as he had in earlier accounts.[49] While these accounts imply the possible presence of yellow fever, they fail to provide definitive evidence, since they describe symptoms and epidemic patterns that could be dengue, malaria, or possibly chickungunya.

The first epidemic that historians decisively recognize as yellow fever in West Africa occurred in 1778, at the end of a period of colonial warfare between French and British forces. J. P. Schotte, surgeon-in-chief of the British garrison at Saint-Louis, documented the disease in detail.[50] He arrived in Senegal in 1775 and in 1782 published a report that he had presented to the Royal Society in 1780, describing an epidemic in Saint-Louis. In the summer of 1778, the rains began earlier than usual and were especially frequent and heavy.[51] The British garrison and inhabitants of Saint-Louis had been "remarkably healthy" until early August, when a "sudden and most dreadful disease broke out." The epidemic "raged" from this time until the middle of September.[52] Of the 92 whites living in Saint-Louis, 59 died. On the island of Gorée, out of a total European population of about 150, 43 died. In addition to killing more than 40 percent of the European population, the epidemic killed an unidentified "great number of the native mulattoes and blacks."[53] In his report, Schotte described the telltale symptoms of yellow fever: a constant and unrelenting high body temperature, convulsions, aches and back pain, and finally, "throwing up . . . great quantities of a black matter, which resembled the grounds of coffee," followed by delirium and death. He described the vomit in great detail, noting that "the bile, which was before thrown up of a yellow colour, and in a liquid state, was now changed both in colour and substance. It became green, brown, and at last black, and was coagulated in small lumps." He identified the disease as "*synochus atrabiliosa*" and distinguished it from yellow fever and other bilious fevers by noting the severity of its symptoms, particularly the black vomit and hemorrhaging.[54] Although he didn't classify the disease as yellow fever, his descriptions of the symptoms were identical to contemporary descriptions of yellow fever in the Caribbean. Other sources describing the 1778 epidemic, and a second epidemic in 1779, confirm this as well.[55] After this outbreak, no reports of yellow fever appeared in Senegal for more than thirty-five years, between 1779 and 1815.[56]

Shortly after the epidemics in Senegal, there is some evidence of yellow fever among British newcomers on the island of Bolama, off the coast of Sierra Leone, on the passenger ship *Calypso* in 1792. The *Calypso* was one of three ships that sailed toward Bolama in 1792 on an "antislavery expedition" to colonize and settle the island, with the goal of eventually establishing sugar, cotton, and indigo plantations. Like the British naval officers in Galam, the passengers on the Bolama expedition came into close contact with monkeys as they moved inland and explored the island's mangrove swamps. Colonists described seeing "thousands of monkeys," which they killed and ate as they simultaneously felled trees for timber. As they continued to survey the island's low-lying forests, they frequently found dead monkeys, signifying the possible presence of a sylvan yellow fever epidemic.[57] As Billy G. Smith has argued, "by repeatedly disrupting the African forest habitat, the

European settlers unwittingly exposed themselves to a radically new epidemiological environment."[58] These British newcomers transformed the island's ecology in several ways. By cutting down trees and altering the physical environment, they provided new breeding spaces for *A. aegypti* mosquitoes and destroyed the habitats of birds that preyed on insects. Further, by inserting themselves into the sylvan habitat, they provided a large number of new human hosts for the virus. This incident marks another striking example that indicates the intermediate cycle of yellow fever, in which the virus was transmitted from monkeys to humans. The reaction of the colonists to the outbreak demonstrates its unusual occurrence among Europeans in Africa in the late eighteenth century. They described the disease as "mysterious" and labeled it "Bolama fever," signifying its unique association with Bolama island.[59] In 1793 the fever spread from Bolama to several British vessels in the Cape Verde Islands, and then to various ports in the Caribbean (on the islands of Grenada, Jamaica, Barbados, Hispaniola, Dominica, and Antigua), and eventually to Philadelphia. Contemporaries described it as a distinct illness, which they called Bulam fever or *fièvre de Boullam*. Some doctors believed it was a more virulent form of yellow fever. Dr. William Carpenter of New Orleans argued that "in 1792, a new era occurred in the history of yellow fever on our continent, and it assumed a type more malignant than ever."[60]

In tropical West Africa, yellow fever spread from sparsely populated, forested regions to more densely populated coastal ports after 1815, and by the 1820s it caused frequent epidemics in port cities in Sierra Leone, Ghana (Gold Coast), Benin, and several islands off the coast, including Bioko (Fernando Po) and the Canary and Cape Verde Islands.[61] After its reappearance in Senegal in 1815, epidemics escalated between 1840 and 1872.[62]

By the 1850s, as French colonizers took control of inland regions in the Senegal River Valley, Saint-Louis developed as a thriving Atlantic entrepôt. During this period, epidemics were so frequent along the West African coast that most late-nineteenth-century medical experts concluded that yellow fever had become endemic in this region, even if they believed that it originated in the Americas.[63] By the late nineteenth century, colonial medical officials viewed epidemics "as a simple transformation from endemic to epidemic disease under the pressure of climatic conditions and the natural and social environment."[64]

Colonial medical authorities consistently emphasized the vulnerability of white populations and the relative lack of vulnerability of native populations. They often reasoned that records of high mortality rates among Europeans compared to Africans implied that yellow fever must have been endemic in some parts of Africa. However, several descriptions of high mortality rates among native populations during early epidemics demonstrate that the disease might not have been widespread in the mid to late nineteenth century. For example, Lind, in his description of the "fluxes and fevers" that were particularly fatal to Europeans, noted that "the natives themselves are not exempted from those diseases."[65] Epidemics in Gorée and Saint-Louis in 1830 "carried off a large number of blacks—nearly as many as whites."[66] Records from the epidemic in 1867 in Saint-Louis account for the deaths of about three hundred Europeans and "hundreds of Africans."[67] Official records attempted to account for all European deaths, while neglecting to count deaths of native populations. For example, reports from a major epidemic in Saint-Louis in 1879 show that 652 (of a population of 1,300) Europeans died, along with "an undetermined number of middle class residents and *indigènes*."[68] This data suggests that many indigenous Africans in the coastal Senegambia region had not been previously exposed to yellow fever. However, within a few generations, it is probable that their descendants could have acquired immunity. Rather than providing medical care for *indigènes,* colonial medical officials viewed them as a threat to the health of Europeans and enacted public health policies that resulted in their segregation and economic marginalization.[69] Further, in 1868 French medical authorities in Senegal claimed that yellow fever was not endemic there, but that it was imported from Gambia or Sierra Leone. Dr. J. P. F. Thévenot observed that outbreaks in Senegal did "not spare the indigenous population," and he reasoned that because it came from the South, it did not "have the same predilection for Europeans as has been seen in the Antilles; which seems to prove that the disease is a result of an accident in the climate."[70] As late as the turn of the twentieth century, there is some evidence to suggest that yellow fever might not have been endemic along the West African coast, but that it appeared sporadically. In 1901 Dr. Ronald Ross, a pioneer in the field of tropical medicine, noted that "malaria and elephantiasis prevail all down the coast; and many medical men of repute consider that yellow fever also has existed there from time to time."[71]

Yet, in the early decades of the twentieth century, many medical authorities in the United States claimed that yellow fever was endemic along the West African coast and determined that it had originated in West Africa. They came to this conclusion not only because of the rise of yellow fever in the area, but because of their belief in African immunity. For example, a posthumous volume published by Henry Rose Carter of the US Public Health Service and his associates in 1931 argued that African immunity was "biological evidence" that indicated the African origin of yellow fever. He reasoned that observing differential mortality rates could serve as a way of identifying disease outbreaks, noting that "an epidemic . . . with a higher mortality among negroes is little apt to be yellow fever," while "an epidemic with a decidedly *higher* mortality among blacks than whites is apt to be smallpox, influenza, pneumonia, [or] plague."[72] Many historians share this view, and some argue that resistance can be an inherited trait.[73]

However, it is more likely that many West Africans across the Atlantic, and their descendants, acquired immunity to yellow fever in the late seventeenth through the early nineteenth centuries, as did most groups who spent long periods of time in places where the disease became endemic, including pirates, laborers, and natives in port cities that yellow fever frequently visited. As in the Americas, environmental modifications associated with colonization and the slave trade contributed to the expansion of endemic yellow fever zones in West Africa. Despite a lack of evidence of inheritable immunity or resistance to yellow fever, some scholars have pointed to differential immunity among people of African descent to explain the growth of African slavery in the tropical and subtropical Americas (as opposed to European indentured servitude or the enslavement of Native American populations) and the continued enslavement of their descendants.[74] While differential immunity to malaria might have affected the demography of plantation labor systems, there is little evidence that yellow fever immunity had a similar effect.

Ironically, the intensification of enslavement practices likely resulted in increased exposure to port-dwelling *A. aegypti* mosquitoes and viral pathogens among captives. The holding of slaves in coastal West Africa, and especially in the Caribbean, increased the probability that they would encounter yellow fever. Combined with the subsequent growth of sugarcane production and shipping and of urban development, which led to the emergence of endemic yellow fever in Atlantic port cities that were actively involved in trading sugar and slaves, the material circumstances of the slave trade caused enslaved Africans to be exposed to yellow fever and acquire immunities. European observers connected their observations of immunity to their ideas of racial difference, which hardened over the course of the nineteenth century.

The Long Nineteenth Century of Fever

As yellow fever became endemic along the West African coast in the late eighteenth century, it appeared more frequently in the Caribbean, North America, and Europe, and by the mid-nineteenth century, it reemerged in Brazil. The rise of yellow fever across the Atlantic in the late eighteenth and early nineteenth centuries was tied to ecological and demographic impacts of several global processes, including the expansion of large-scale sugar plantation zones, the peak of the West African slave trade to the Americas, the extension of eighteenth-century transatlantic trade networks, and the subsequent growth and development of urban ports in coastal West Africa, the Caribbean, and the Gulf of Mexico.[75]

Between 1775 and the early twentieth century, yellow fever thrived across the Atlantic. It had become endemic in several Caribbean port cities (including Havana and Port-au-Prince) after a series of regional epidemics. In North America, yellow fever epidemics appeared frequently in port cities across the eastern seaboard between 1793 and 1820, including Charleston, Norfolk, Baltimore, Philadelphia, New York, and Boston and reaching as far north as Portsmouth, New Hampshire, and Quebec City. The first recorded yellow fever epidemic in New Orleans occurred in 1796.[76] After 1811 the frequency of epidemics escalated in New Orleans and other Gulf Coast cities, including Mobile and Galveston. Simultaneously, the frequency of epidemics decreased in the north, and by the 1820s yellow fever no longer appeared in northeastern cities. In Europe, yellow fever was most active between 1800 and 1880. In 1800 it broke out in Seville and Cádiz and spread across the peninsula, instigating epidemics in Córdoba, Grenada, Valencia, Catalonia, and Gibraltar by 1804. In 1819 it appeared again in Cádiz, apparently brought by a vessel bearing "public treasure" from Havana, and then spread to Seville, San Fernando, Port St. Maria, Rota, Sanlúcar de Barrameda, and Jerez de la Frontera. Other major epidemics took place in Barcelona and Palma, Majorca, in 1821, Gibraltar in 1828, and Lisbon in 1857. Smaller epidemics occurred in western France and in Britain, in the cities of Brest (1802 and 1856), Southampton (1852), Saint-Nazaire (1861), and Swansea (1865).[77]

The growth of the Atlantic slave trade had unforeseen ecological impacts, especially at its peak in the late eighteenth century. As demand for slaves increased in the Americas, slave traders acquired human captives from diverse environments, including remote regions in the Senegal River Valley, Sierra Leone, Guinea, Congo, and Angola, where yellow fever may have been endemic among nonhuman primates or among African populations. Growing demand for slaves led to an increase in slave prices after 1770, but the price of slaves exported from Angola remained considerably lower than for slaves sold from Senegal or the Gold Coast. As a result, between 1770 and 1790, the number of slaves taken to the Americas from West Central Africa doubled (from roughly 225,000 to 450,000).[78] By the late eighteenth century, many enslaved Africans who wound up working on American plantations were native to regions of West and West Central Africa, where sylvan yellow fever might have been present.

By the close of the eighteenth century, owing to increasing demand for slave labor on American plantations, contact between inland and coastal regions in West Africa increased, facilitating the spread of yellow fever. Common trade practices further exacerbated the threat of epidemics. For example, historian James Searing explains, "The majority of slaves exported from Senegal were purchased from three hundred miles or more upriver . . . [and] could only be shipped downriver during the three months of high river coinciding with the rainy season. When they arrived on the Atlantic coast, they had to be held for several months, because of the wind and weather patterns that regulated the patterns of the transatlantic shipping in the eighteenth century."[79] Africans who traveled by river from inland villages to coastal ports during the rainy season might have encountered yellow fever along the way. Holding enslaved Africans at slave castles further increased their likelihood of exposure to yellow fever prior to traveling to the Americas. In addition to demographic changes produced by the expansion of the slave trade, the growth of urban port cities transformed the ecology of Central Africa and the West African coast.

Numerous factors made urban ports an ideal space for yellow fever to thrive. Port cities offered the vital conditions for both the yellow fever virus and the *A. aegypti* mosquito because of demographic and environmental changes associated with the growth of trade and urban development. The virus could sustain itself most effectively if it was regularly introduced to nonimmune populations, so cities that were most often stricken by yellow fever had a regular flow of migrants, including African slaves and European immigrants. In addition, the *A. aegypti* population flourished in tropical and subtropical port cities because their warm climates and built environments provided ideal living and breeding conditions, which suited the preferences of the mosquitoes. While yellow fever thrived in cities, it was also frequently present onboard maritime vessels in the Atlantic. Ships offered the necessary conditions to sustain yellow fever by providing breeding receptacles and nourishment for *A. aegypti*.[80] As they traveled from port to port, they encountered infected mosquitoes and humans. Contemporaries commonly noted the occurrence of fevers in port cities and on ships and drew connections between the two. While some reports observed that ships spread yellow fever from infected ports, others considered the possibility of the fever arising because of poor sanitary conditions on the vessels. By the mid-nineteenth century, contemporaries associated yellow fever with ships and with particular cities where yellow fever appeared to be endemic, including Havana, Veracruz, and New Orleans.[81]

At the center of the growth of slavery, shipping, and development in the Atlantic was the rise of sugar production and the sugar plantation complex, which fostered a series of ecological changes that contributed to the rise of yellow fever. Curtin has argued that the sugar revolution in the eastern Caribbean produced a "new version of the plantation complex" that was "more specialized, more dependent on networks of maritime, intercontinental communication."[82] The intensification of sugar production and consumption transformed landscapes and ecologies across the Atlantic, causing yellow fever to become endemic in large-scale sugar-producing regions, beginning in the eastern Caribbean and then spreading to Saint-Domingue, Jamaica, Cuba, Brazil, and Louisiana.

The process of sugar production and the establishment of large-scale sugar plantations facilitated the propagation of yellow fever in several ways. First, the construction of the sugar plantations involved heavy deforestation, as planters cleared land for cultivation and used wood to fuel sugar mills. The clearing of forests resulted in the eradication or near eradication of numerous animal species, particularly those that lived in the forest canopy, including large mammals, rodents, bats, and birds. Bird and bat communities that resided highest in the canopy typically fed on insects, and their extermination opened a viable niche for mosquitoes.[83] Second, sugar plantations contributed to the spread of yellow fever through their involvement in transatlantic trade and shipping. Plantations were built in close proximity to river ports or canals and were in frequent contact with urban port cities via riverboats. The infrastructure used to move sugar from the plantations to port cities also transported infected mosquitoes. Third, the plantations created a sustainable breeding environment for *A. aegypti*. Plantations usually had an abundance of cisterns, water barrels, and clay pots, which offered ample breeding spaces for the mosquitoes. Even small plantations needed hundreds of clay pots, used to clarify crystallized sugar.[84] Larger plantations could have more than ten thousand pots in use over the course of one year. Even pots that were broken or discarded could still hold a small amount of rainwater, enough to provide breeding spaces for *A. aegypti*.[85] Fourth, in addition to supplying ample breeding spaces for mosquitoes, sugar plantations provided nourishment. Entomologists have shown that *A. aegypti* "do not live by blood alone" and "are especially attracted to sweet fluids," including "fruits, honey, flowers and sugar."[86] Though female mosquitoes need human blood in order to lay eggs, they also feed on sucrose. Researchers have found that mosquitoes are likely to lay more eggs when they feast on human blood, but adding sucrose to their diet can increase the lifespan of the *A. aegypti*.[87] Sucrose was available throughout the year on Caribbean sugar plantations in various places and forms: on used sugarcane that was discarded after it had been pressed (*bagasse*), in cooling vats that held boiling cane juice, and in the runoff from the clay pots that held the crystallized sugar.[88]

Mosquitoes could also find sucrose on docks, harbors, and ships, in wooden sugar-barrels used to store sugar for export.

The apparent connection between sugar production and yellow fever provides a compelling explanation of why the first yellow fever outbreaks appeared in the Caribbean, rather than in Africa. Europeans began colonizing Barbados in the 1620s, and they established sugar plantations over the next two decades. Initially, colonists did not grow sugar; they grew tobacco and cotton, using indentured servants for agricultural labor. During this period, the population of Barbados experienced many health problems; generally these were familiar maladies that had been present in Afro-Eurasia, such as malaria, tuberculosis, hookworm, yaws, guinea worm, leprosy, elephantiasis, and venereal diseases.[89] Sugar planting on the island expanded rapidly between 1640 and 1643, when Dutch traders supplied English sugar planters with slaves and techniques for processing the cane.[90] In 1647, the first appearance of yellow fever on the island was unusual; residents were not familiar with the disease, and it was exceptionally overwhelming because it reached epidemic proportions, killing roughly 15 percent of the population.[91] The epidemic proved to be so devastating that British newcomer Richard Ligon "thought it as bad as the plague in England."[92]

The sugar revolution in the Caribbean catalyzed the acceleration of the Atlantic slave trade, which in turn enabled the proliferation of sugar production in the Americas. As Curtin has argued, the sugar revolution in the eastern Caribbean was "an important step into the North Atlantic, and it was, incidentally, the stepping-stone that brought the African slave trade and a peripheral version of the plantation complex to the United States."[93] Yellow fever emerged in Saint-Domingue, Cuba, and Louisiana as these regions began to engage in large-scale sugar production and exportation. It reemerged in Brazil in the mid-nineteenth century as the sugar industry underwent a period of revitalization and rapid expansion after the Haitian Revolution.[94]

Throughout the Atlantic World, doctors and untrained observers did not recognize yellow fever as a disease sui generis until the mid-seventeenth century. Since the mid-nineteenth century it has been known in English as yellow fever, in French as *fièvre jaune*, in Portuguese as *febre amarela*, and in Spanish as *fiebre amarilla*, although earlier Spanish records refer to it as *vómito negro*, emphasizing the unusual symptom of

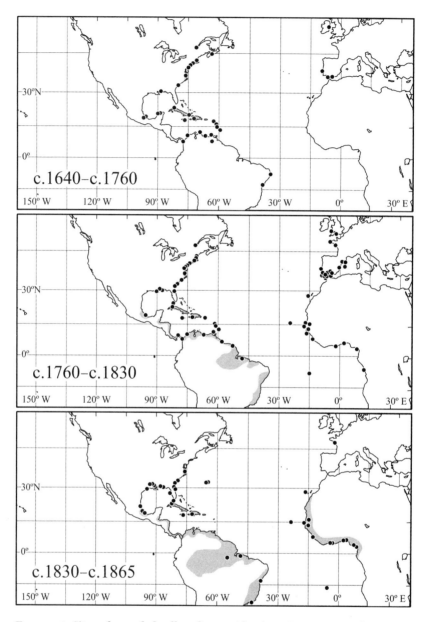

FIGURE 1. Sites of recorded yellow fever epidemics, 1640–1865. Epidemics increased and endemic fever zones grew in the tropical Americas and West Africa between 1760 and 1860. (Compiled from numerous sources, including Augustin; Boyce, "History of Yellow Fever"; Viesca-Treviño; and McNeill, *Mosquito Empires.* Cartography by Mary Lee Eggart.)

black vomit. When yellow fever appeared for the first time in Spain in the eighteenth century, it was known as *vómito prieto,* another reference to dark-colored vomit. Seventeenth-century French historian Raymond Breton wrote that yellow fever was known to the Caribs of Guadeloupe as *iepoulicáatina,* the equivalent of the French *coup de barre,* "expressive of the muscular pains of the fever, as if produced by blows from a stick."[95] These symptoms resembled dengue fever, which was also called "break bone fever."[96] After its emergence in Guadeloupe, *coup de barre* was widely understood to mean yellow fever among French-speaking Creoles throughout the Caribbean in the nineteenth century, and even in the southern United States.[97]

When yellow fever first appeared in the Americas, colonists named the new disease according to its perceived geographic origin. For instance, after repeated epidemics in Barbados during the seventeenth century, it was known in the Atlantic colonies as "Barbados distemper."[98] An epidemic that began on Martinique in 1690 and spread throughout the Caribbean was widely known as *mal de Siam* because it had arrived on the French war vessel *Oriflamme,* which had reportedly come from Bangkok.[99] For many years after the epidemics that contemporaries believed originated in Bolama, medical writers described epidemics in the Caribbean and Iberia as Bulam fever. Some believed that Bulam fever was in fact yellow fever, while others argued that it was a distinct disease.[100] In the late eighteenth and the nineteenth centuries, it was often called "yellow jack" because of its prevalence on ships, which were required to display a yellow quarantine flag (or jack) when carrying infected passengers.

From about 1780 onward, as yellow fever ravaged coastal cities and maritime vessels in temperate zones across the Atlantic, it gained a fearful reputation among medical professionals in the Americas and Europe. Scottish physician Gilbert Blane remarked that yellow fever seemed "the hurricane of the human frame, equally uncertain in its recurrence, equally dark and inscrutable in its cause, equally and deplorably certain as to the reality of its existence."[101] By the mid-nineteenth century, it aroused tremendous panic, fear, and anxiety in the American South. Popular references to yellow fever often invoked gruesome images of its symptoms, indicating a sense of terror and horror that increasingly became associated with yellow fever in the antebellum era. In this period, doctors described the disease as the "scourge of the South" and the "scourge of the tropics" and increasingly associated it with warm climates and tropical geographies.[102]

In New Orleans, the confluence of related processes, including the growth of slavery, sugar production, and maritime commerce, contributed to the rise of yellow fever in the nineteenth century.[103] Chapter 2 explores the development of these processes, in addition to other factors, such as the influx of newcomers (including migrants from the eastern United States and European immigrants) and the proliferation of water-related construction projects (including the construction of levees, artificial waterways, and swamp drainage) that shaped the city's ecological and epidemiological history.

The diverse demographic composition of New Orleans provides a unique case study of the development of ideologies of immunity based on factors such as nativity, ethnicity, and race. Louisiana historian Paul F. LaChance argued that "antebellum New Orleans struck contemporaries and continues to strike historians as *sui generis* in the ethnic composition of its population."[104] In a travel account published after his visit to the Atlantic Americas in 1833, British captain James Edward Alexander remarked, "Let no one judge of America from New Orleans, for it is altogether *sui generis*." Like many visitors to the city during this time, he commented on the prevalence of disease during the "sickly season," warning readers, "Above all let no future traveler visit it in autumn, unless he wishes to 'shake off this mortal coil,' and save the coroner some trouble."[105]

2

Sugar Fever

THE RISE OF CANE SUGAR AND YELLOW FEVER
IN LOWER LOUISIANA, 1796–1850

The growth of large-scale sugarcane production in southern Louisiana in the early nineteenth century altered the landscape and ecology of the Lower Mississippi Delta, creating a built environment that contributed to the emergence and prevalence of epidemic yellow fever in New Orleans. Both the virus and its host mosquitoes presumably came to New Orleans from West Africa via the Caribbean, on maritime vessels that transported enslaved Africans and sugar in the Atlantic. Sugar cultivation increased rapidly in lower Louisiana in the early nineteenth century, after the Haitian Revolution. The growth of global sugar markets precipitated economic growth and fostered the physical expansion of the city, creating an urban landscape that attracted *A. aegypti* mosquitoes during the summer, resulting in seasonal epidemics. Urban port cities, with abundant ships, harbors, and migrant populations, provided the ideal conditions for epidemic yellow fever.

In Louisiana, ecological changes caused by the growth of sugar plantations included land clearance, deforestation, and numerous water management projects, which primarily consisted of digging canals, draining swamps, and constructing levees. These activities, combined with heightened maritime activity, urbanization, and demographic changes instigated by the productive sugar industry, transformed the city and its surroundings into an environment that was extremely hospitable to mosquitoes and mosquito-borne diseases, especially yellow fever and malaria. Between 1830 and 1860, the burgeoning sugar industry led to rapid economic growth and attracted European immigrants, who served as the primary host population for the yellow fever virus in the 1840s and 1850s. The growing population escalated urban development and suburban expansion in the cypress swamps and wetlands surrounding the city, which created a greater niche for *A. aegypti*.[1]

Environmental Conditions in Colonial Louisiana

The unique environmental conditions at the site of New Orleans generated many challenges for early settlers, owing to the surrounding swamps and the constant threat of flooding. Craig Colten has argued that "New Orleans's physical geography is interlaced with its local history" and that "keeping the city dry . . . has been the perpetual battle for New Orleans."[2] When French colonial expeditions into the Mississippi Delta region began early in the eighteenth century, various Native American and European communities inhabited the historical geopolitical area that became known as the Louisiana territory (La Louisiane), which extended from Canada to the Gulf of Mexico and was bordered by the Appalachian and the Rocky Mountains.[3] Before the settlement of New Orleans, Jean-Baptiste Le Moyne de Bienville, traveling south from Canada with his brother Pierre Le Moyne d'Iberville, established small colonies near present-day Mobile (Fort Louis de La Louisiane) and Biloxi (Fort Maurepas). In 1718 Bienville positioned the French capital of La Louisiane on a crescent-shaped section of rare high ground along the natural levee of the Mississippi, formed by alluvial soil deposited by the river that a "local Native American guide had pointed out . . . approximately two decades earlier."[4] Bienville named the city L'Isle de la Nouvelle Orléans because it appeared to be surrounded by water, bounded in the south by the Mississippi River and in the north by cypress swamps that extended to Lakes Pontchartrain and Borgne.[5] Ari Kelman has described the surrounding swampland as "a place of seemingly interconnected marshes, swamps, and bayous, with little solid land anywhere in sight." He added, "Cattails, irises, mangroves, and a wide variety of grasses thrive in the Delta's soggy environment. Muskrats, otters, minks, raccoons, and of course alligators all inhabit this watery world, while crawfish, or 'mudbugs,' as locals call them, burrow in a constantly replenished supply of muck."[6] In a 1958 report to the US Army Corps of Engineers, geographers Charles Kolb and Jack Van Lopik called this environment "a land between earth and sea—belonging to neither and alternately claimed by both."[7]

As French colonists slowly established settlements in the Louisiana territory in the early eighteenth century, they depended on the region's natural resources for trade goods, particularly furs and timber.

However, French migrations "failed to provide Louisiana with a large, stable, agrarian population essential for the colony's continued growth and economic development." Between 1712 and 1731, Louisiana failed to attract French immigrants because of its image as an "inhospitable land." French sources depicted the Mississippi Valley as "an enormous, fertile wilderness populated by wild beasts and cruel, heathen savages who capitalized on every opportunity to waylay, murder, or torture Europeans."[8] Despite this image, roughly two thousand French settlers and soldiers, along with about thirty-eight hundred slaves, occupied the territory in 1732. For more than a century, the population of enslaved and free people of color outnumbered white settlers. Gwendolyn Midlo Hall's research shows that "a free population of African descent emerged quite early in New Orleans," and that group grew after 1722 as a result of intermarriage and slave manumissions.[9] The Native American population of the Louisiana territory at that time, though in decline from disease (primarily smallpox) and warfare, has been estimated at thirty thousand. By the 1720s, French settlers had established trade relations with neighboring Native American nations, including the Choctaw and the Caddo. French colonials conformed to Native American trade practices by participating in "such formal ceremonies as gift giving and smoking the calumet." While they established alliances with some Native American groups in the Mississippi Delta region, they came into conflict with northeastern nations (north of Baton Rouge) including the Chickasaw and the Lower Creeks, who allied with British colonials, and the Natchez, who allied with Spanish settlers and African slaves. In 1729 the French defeated the Natchez and claimed a portion of the land that they inhabited, located on the Mississippi about 170 miles north of New Orleans.[10]

Throughout the eighteenth century, French colonial sources described the general presence of disease and vaguely described fevers in Louisiana, noting that *la maladie* was most prevalent during the summer. While some evidence indicates the brief appearance of yellow fever at nearby ports, including Biloxi (1702) and Mobile (1705) upon their settlement, mid-eighteenth-century French sugar prospectors believed that La Louisiane was more healthful than the Caribbean colonies, speculating that "if the crop of the Louisiana planter produces less than that of Saint-Domingue, the farmer has the advantage of having to put out only a fourth of the costs that occur elsewhere and can count on keeping his working force intact during the entire year, without fear of the sicknesses and deaths that are only too frequent in the islands."[11]

Sugarcane cultivation in Louisiana did not advance in the eighteenth century because of a combination of environmental and political obstacles. The landscape and the subtropical climate in southern Louisiana was not propitious for growing cane, especially when compared to the tropical Caribbean. The variety of cane grown in the islands, known as "Creole cane," grew swiftly in the tropical Caribbean climate (roughly 10 to 24 degrees north latitude). It required a long, frost-free growing season of 14 to 24 months, with year-round sunshine and temperatures averaging about 75 degrees, well-distributed annual rainfall of about sixty inches, and fertile, drainable soil.[12] The subtropical climate of the southern regions of Louisiana (28 to 31 degrees latitude), along the geological Mississippi Delta, offered arable conditions for roughly 8 months. However the area was prone to cold weather and frost in the winter, and the soil was difficult to drain. Until the development of frost-resistant cane in the twentieth century, frost damage was the greatest threat to the region's cane crop. Commonly "frost damage was followed swiftly by a warming front, which triggered oxidation; as a result, the freshly extracted cane juice became so excessively thick and viscous that it failed to crystallize upon evaporation." As a result, planters cut the growing season in half to 9 months, producing cane with 7 to 8 percent sucrose by volume, compared to Caribbean cane, which matured for 18 to 20 months and produced 14 to 15 percent sucrose by volume.[13] Thus, while Louisiana planters were able to annually harvest a viable product, Caribbean planters utilized their land to constantly produce sugar. In addition to the region's climate, the landscape presented challenges to early planters. Swamps covered most of the interior, and even levee lands were at risk of flooding.

Despite the difficulty of growing cane in Louisiana, settlers had attempted to cultivate sugar since the mid-eighteenth century. Their efforts met with little success. In 1751 Jesuit planters sent knowledgeable slaves and Creole cane from Port-au-Prince to New Orleans and began experimenting with sugarcane cultivation. The Jesuits acquired Bienville's plantation, which extended fifteen arpents (about half a mile) from the riverfront, adjacent to the Vieux Carré, in 1726.[14] Jesuit planters did not produce large quantities of granulated sugar; instead, they made a small amount of liquid sugar or syrup that was not sold commercially. Several other planters also experimented with sugarcane in the 1750s and 1760s, including Joseph Villars Dubreuil, a French militia captain who established a sugar plantation on the estate of Chevalier de Mazan, across the river from the city. He exported cane to France, where refiners processed it into sugar.[15]

For nearly fifty years, prospective sugar planters tried but failed to grow and manufacture a granulated product that could compete with the sugar produced in the islands. Local growers produced small amounts of sugar, and they sold cane products in town markets in the form of cane syrup, raw cane for "chewing purposes," and tafia, a cheap liquor distilled from molasses.[16] During this time the region's agricultural exports included tobacco and indigo, and its primary exports were furs and cypress, in the form of lumber and wooden boxes that Caribbean planters used to transport sugar.[17] During this initial period of swamp clearance, drainage, deforestation, and cultivation in cleared lands, it is likely that malaria became endemic in the wetlands surrounding the city.

Political conflicts between France, Britain, and Spain also interfered with the establishment of sugar plantations in Louisiana. The Seven Years' War, the cession of Louisiana to Spain in 1762, and the rebellion in 1768 disrupted plantations that were established during the French period. While warfare and political tensions disrupted trade and commerce, immigration to the colony increased after France lost its colonial possessions. Between about 1765 and 1790, thousands of Francophone Acadian (later known as Cajun) refugees settled along the Mississippi (about seventy miles upriver from New Orleans) and Bayou Teche, at Attakapas and Opelousas, after their expulsion by the British.[18] Between 1778 and 1780, as the Spanish Crown declared war against the British, more than two thousand Canary Islanders (*Isleños* or *Islingues*) settled along the Mississippi, about ten miles downriver from New Orleans along Bayous Terre-aux-Boeufs and LaFourche.[19]

After 1763, settlers who had established plantations on the outskirts of the Vieux Carré sold their properties, providing space for residential development. These small suburban *faubourgs* eventually became incorporated into the city as both residential and commercial zones.

After the Spanish Cabildo expelled the Jesuits from their plantation, the French administration divided the land into smaller plots and sold them. In 1785 Madame Marie Josephe Deslondes Pradel and her second husband, Bertrand Gravier, acquired a large section of the former Jesuit plantation, including the riverfront. By the 1790s Gravier further subdivided and sold the lands, naming the *faubourg* after his wife. This suburban region, called Faubourg St. Mary (Faubourg Sainte-Marie), was eventually incorporated into the city after the Louisiana Purchase, as the Second District or the "American Quarter."[20] The creation of *faubourgs* surrounding the Vieux Carré resulted in significant alterations to the land, as a result of residential development and, eventually, the construction of rail lines.

By the 1780s Louisiana sugar planters grew a small amount of cane, but the colony continued to import rum and syrup from Cuba.[21] The Cuban sugar industry rapidly expanded between 1763 and 1792, and by the late eighteenth century, Cuban sugar planters had depleted the island's forests. Early-nineteenth-century Cuban sugar technician José Ignacio Echegoyen observed that "the sugarmill's need for firewood is alarming—and where are the forests that can meet it?"[22] Cuban sugar producers needed wood for sugar crates as well as for fuel. A 1772 royal decree that banned the use of cedar for making sugar crates prompted mill owners to search for alternatives. They began buying cypress from Louisiana; it was shipped from New Orleans to Havana. By the early nineteenth century, Cuban sugar plantations depended on timber imports from the United States, particularly pine and cypress from the Lower Mississippi Valley.[23] After the Haitian Revolution, Cuba replaced Saint-Domingue as the world's top sugar-producing colony.

The Haitian Revolution and the
Emergence of Louisiana Sugar Country

Documented outbreaks of yellow fever appeared in New Orleans after the Haitian Revolution and the subsequent "rise of the plantation complex" in lower Louisiana, following a similar pattern to its emergence and prevalence in the Caribbean sugar islands in the mid-seventeenth century. Philip Curtin has shown that as a result of the change from "settlement to plantation" that occurred in French and English sugar colonies after planters began using African slave labor and mass-producing sugar in the seventeenth century, Europeans and Native Americans were exposed to African diseases, most significantly, yellow fever and malaria (both *falciparum* and *vivax*).[24] Additionally, as shown in chapter 1, this transformation resulted in African populations' exposure to yellow fever when it became endemic along the West African coast in the nineteenth century, as slave traders increasingly acquired slaves from further inland and relocated them to West African port cities before sending them to the Americas.

By 1791 Saint-Domingue produced more sugar than any other colony, providing sugar for roughly one-half of the world's markets.[25] Immediately after the slave revolt and revolution, sugar production came to a halt in the former French colony, opening a market for prospective sugar planters in Louisiana. The Haitian Revolution also instigated a series of migrations to Louisiana, and a large proportion of those refugees had worked in the Saint-Domingue sugar industry. The influx of Saint-Domingian refugees helped to establish Louisiana's sugar industry by bringing technical knowledge and labor from planters and slaves who had been successfully growing cane for generations.

During the revolution, yellow fever killed the majority of French and British troops who tried to reestablish control in Saint-Domingue.[26] European military records did not account for slave deaths, and this lack of official record-keeping makes it impossible to determine the degree to which yellow fever affected former slaves in the wake of the revolution. However, demographic records reveal that the enslaved population of roughly 500,000 in 1790 shrank to 342,000 adult Haitians by the time French troops withdrew from the island in 1804. In 1790 residents of the colony also included roughly 70,000 free people, described by historian J. R. McNeill as "forty thousand French and thirty thousand free people 'of color.'" Presumably the category "French" included French Creoles as well as French immigrants. Similarly, the figure of half a million slaves included both Creole slaves and West African newcomers, who made up the majority of the enslaved population.[27]

Tens of thousands of refugees, primarily French and Creole planters (including whites and people of color), fled Haiti in the aftermath of the revolution. Some returned to France, but thousands fled for refuge to American port cities, including New York, Philadelphia, and New Orleans. In fact, the famous yellow fever epidemics of 1793 in Philadelphia and New York were "introduced by vessels from the West Indies, many of which brought refugees who fled from St. Domingo to escape a general massacre."[28]

The first documented outbreak of yellow fever in New Orleans occurred a few years after the epidemics in Philadelphia and New York, in the summer of 1796. The same year, Etienne de Boré, who has been called the "father of Louisiana sugar" and "savior of Louisiana," famously grew and granulated sugar.[29] He produced a large crop of one hundred thousand pounds, initiating an era of large-scale sugar production in the region.[30] A native of the Illinois district of French Louisiana, de Boré had studied in France before settling in New Orleans in 1771. He inherited his plantation, adjacent to the present site of Audubon Park and six miles upriver from the Vieux Carré, through his wife's father, Jean Baptiste D'Estréhan des Tours, who had served as royal treasurer under the French colonial administration.[31] For more than twenty years prior to 1796, de Boré had experimented unsuccessfully with indigo, which proved to be an unstable crop in Louisiana.

De Boré successfully produced a large crop of sugarcane in 1796 because of his association with Antonio Méndez, a Cuban emigrant who had recently purchased a sugar plantation at Terre-aux-Boeufs, and Antoine Morin, an experienced Saint-Domingian sugar maker who had fled the island after the Haitian Revolution.[32] In 1794 and 1795, the local indigo crop failed because of heavy fog and worms. Afterward, in a letter to the Spanish governor Esteban Miró, local distillery owner Joseph Delfau de Pontalba wrote, "Our planters are founding all their hopes on sugar cane, with which they flatter themselves they will at least make syrup and tafia. Mr. Boré has a superb stand of cane which is very promising, and he counts on making syrup and tafia this year. He has brought in a good refiner and distiller, and is getting prepared to distill."[33]

Other local planters had engaged in cane farming before de Boré's famous successful crop. Joseph Solís, a native of Cuba, emigrated to Louisiana in the 1780s with his father, along with the large group of Canary Islanders that settled at Terre-aux-Boeufs between 1778 and 1780. From Havana, he brought fresh cane and "a 'wooden mill' to grind cane for the purpose of making syrup or rum."[34] He hired Saint-Domingian refugee sugar-maker Antoine Morin and successfully produced cane in 1793, but he sold it to planters rather than making sugar.[35] In 1794 Méndez bought Solís's entire operation (including land, equipment, livestock, cane, and five slaves) and produced "a few small barrels of sugar" but was not successful in growing large quantities.[36] One year later, in 1795, De Boré purchased cane from Méndez and hired Antoine Morin, who was likely the "good refiner and distiller" that Pontalba had mentioned in his letter.

After de Boré successfully produced a large quantity of granulated sugar, prospective planters became increasingly interested in the viability of sugarcane cultivation in Louisiana. In 1797 Saint-Domingian newcomers brought Otaheite (also called Otaheiti, Tahiti, or Bourbon) cane to Louisiana. Compared to the common Creole variety, Otaheite cane was longer, thicker, and slightly more resistant to cold temperatures, but extremely susceptible to wind damage.[37] Nonetheless, the Otaheite cane proved to be more suited to Louisiana's climate than the Creole cane that the region's pioneer sugar planters had cultivated.

The rise of Louisiana's sugar industry coincided with early land and water management projects that facilitated the spread of yellow fever, particularly swamp drainage and canal construction. Epidemics in 1796 through 1797 coincided with a major canal-building project, aimed to connect the Vieux Carré to Lake Pontchartrain and Bayou St. John. In June of 1795, while Etienne de Boré was experimenting with sugarcane, the governor, Baron Frances Louis Hector de Carondelet, began construction of a 1.6-mile canal. Observers noted that "fevers during the period of digging this canal were awful in its neighborhood" and that "all of the laborers engaged in the work were carried off by yellow fever, and a violent epidemic ensued."[38] Succeeding epidemics in 1811, 1817, 1819, and 1822 coincided with canal repair work and were particularly severe when the canal was cleaned and deepened.[39]

During these years, several waves of Caribbean migrants arrived in the city. Nathalie Dessens's study of migration from Saint-Domingue to New Orleans after the Haitian Revolution reveals that by the turn of the century, Louisiana had become the primary destination of refugees. "Between 1791 and 1815, fifteen thousand (and possibly close to twenty thousand) refugees from Saint-Domingue settled in the Lower

Mississippi region, 80 to 90 percent in New Orleans and vicinity."[40] More than ten thousand Saint-Domingian refugees settled in the city after the war, including a company of French comedians and actors who fled Cap-Français (now Cap-Haïtien) and established one of New Orleans's first theaters.[41] Large waves of migrations occurred from 1803 to 1809, during the final French evacuation of the island.[42] After Napoleon's invasion of Spain in 1808, nearly nine thousand exiles arrived in New Orleans from Cuba. This migration included many experienced sugar planters who had fled from Saint-Domingue to Cuba during the Haitian Revolution, who once again had to vacate the plantations they had built roughly fifteen years earlier. Early planters depended on Saint-Domingian "free refugees of color and white refugees who became managers, overseers, or technical assistants," in addition to Caribbean "slaves, who provided semi-skilled labor and who were thus in high demand among Louisiana planters."[43] Caribbean migrants established sugar plantations on the natural levees along the banks of the Lower Mississippi and the surrounding bayou country southwest of the city, along Bayous Lafourche and Teche, former tributaries of the Mississippi.[44]

Sugar production evolved in the context of colonial Louisiana, but it was transformed in the early decades of the nineteenth century after the United States purchased the territory and created the state of Louisiana in 1812, with its capital at New Orleans. Louisiana was made up of the former Territory of Orleans and the Florida parishes on the eastern bank, which the United States acquired in 1810. In addition to Caribbean migrants, tens of thousands of Anglo-American migrants settled in this region after the Louisiana Purchase. These newcomers included planters and slaves who had previously grown cotton, tobacco, indigo, and rice in the southern United States. Upon arriving in Louisiana, they built sugar plantations north of New Orleans along the Mississippi's natural levees. Presumably, refugee planters and slaves, particularly those native to Hispaniola and Cuba, had encountered yellow fever before they arrived in southern Louisiana and were more likely to have acquired immunity than newcomers from the eastern United States who began migrating to the region after the Louisiana Purchase. Plantations expanded and sugar production grew after 1812, facilitated by the steam revolution and funded by investments from migrants from the eastern United States.

The Expansion of Louisiana Sugar Country
and Epidemic Yellow Fever, Post-1817

Until 1817, yellow fever epidemics occurred sporadically in New Orleans and generally were confined to the city.[45] After a severe outbreak in 1817, yellow fever appeared in New Orleans nearly every summer and occasionally spread to smaller ports and towns along the Mississippi. The rise of yellow fever in New Orleans can be attributed to ecological changes produced by the developing sugar industry, including the expansion of Louisiana "sugar country" in the Delta region, the growth of New Orleans as an Atlantic entrepôt, urban and suburban expansion, and immigration from Europe and the eastern United States.

Sugar production in southern Louisiana increased dramatically after 1817 as a result of technical improvements, including the introduction of cold-resistant ribbon cane, the steam revolution and the subsequent use of steam-powered sugar mills, and other technological implements such as the vacuum pan and the centrifuge.[46] These innovations enabled Louisiana planters to produce large quantities of sugar and compete with Caribbean producers, causing New Orleans, which connected the interior of the United States to Atlantic markets, to emerge as an active commercial center in the Atlantic world. Its growing economic and political importance attracted thousands of prospective planters and urban migrants, leading to significant demographic growth and metropolitan expansion during this period. Between 1803 and 1830, the city's population grew from roughly eight thousand to fifty thousand.[47]

Sugar historian J. Carlyle Sitterson has argued, "It would be impossible to overemphasize the importance of ribbon cane to southern sugar development." Ribbon cane, also known as Batavian Striped or Black Java, "grew rapidly and ripened earlier than the Creole and Otaheite, and its thicker bark . . . increased its resistance to cold. With this new cold resistant variety, sugar planters could move northward, considerably enlarging the sugar area."[48] Until 1817 Louisiana planters planted two varieties of cane: Creole and Otaheite. Neither variety grew easily in the region's climate, because of seasonal cold weather. Dutch sugar planters on St. Eustatius had been cultivating ribbon cane since the mid-eighteenth century, but this variety was not cultivated in North America until the nineteenth century. After successfully growing a small crop in Savannah in 1814, Georgia planter John J. Coiron moved to Louisiana with his cane and in 1817 established a plantation at Terre-aux-Boeufs. During the 1820s, Coiron supplied neighboring planters with cane, and "soon ribbon cane was being planted by scores of planters, and its superior adaptability to the South enabled it to displace the older varieties rapidly."[49]

The steam revolution in the United States shaped the sugar industry in New Orleans by bringing steam-powered vessels to the Lower Mississippi and introducing steam-powered sugar mills. The era of steam in the Lower Mississippi began in 1811 when an entrepreneurial trio of Americans known as the Fulton group, consisting of Robert Fulton, Robert Livingston (US minister to France, who helped to negotiate the Louisiana Purchase), and Nicolas Roosevelt (Theodore's great uncle, of the New York Roosevelts), gained exclusive access to the use of steamboats in the Territory of Orleans.[50] However, after a series of disputes, the group lost its monopoly in 1817, and the city's waterfront, known as the levée, became a "public space," where all persons and commercial vessels had free access to the port. Not surprisingly, river traffic in New Orleans increased dramatically after the space became open to the public. In 1817 the wharf register recorded the arrival of just seven steamboats. But within ten years more than one hundred steamboats passed through New Orleans.[51] The growth of the levée as a public space allowed unrestricted access to the city for vessels arriving from the Caribbean, Brazil, West Africa, and western Europe.

Additional technical changes that planters implemented in the first half of the nineteenth century included the use of the steam-powered sugar mill, the vacuum pan, and the centrifuge. The steam-powered grinding mill allowed faster and more efficient processing of cane than previous mills that were powered by animals, wind, or water. The vacuum pan and the centrifuge enhanced the amount and quality of granulated sugar that was evaporated from cane juice. These innovations "transformed sugar manufacture from an artisanal process depending upon the particular knowledge of the refiner to a scientific process resting upon standardization, measurement, and systematic application of chemistry and physics."[52] Between 1820 and 1825, Louisiana plantations produced about twenty-five thousand to thirty thousand hogsheads of sugar per year, and by 1830 the average grew to more than seventy thousand.[53]

As Louisiana's sugar industry grew during the first half of the nineteenth century, patterns of consumption changed in the United States. Sidney Mintz, in his influential analysis of the growth of sugar production and consumption in world history, has shown how sugar went from being a luxury item to a primary source of calories in the English diet over the course of the eighteenth century. By the nineteenth century, sugar became commonplace in both American and European diets, used as a sweetener and a preservative and for decorative purposes.[54] After 1820 sugar became more common in the United States, and it became popularized in forms such as chocolates, ice cream, hard penny candies, and soda fountains.[55]

THE ECOLOGY OF CANE SUGAR PRODUCTION

As outlined in chapter 1, ecological changes resulting from the establishment of large-scale sugar plantations facilitated the expansion of *A. aegypti* populations. Sugar plantations were particularly inviting to *A. aegypti* because they created new breeding spaces and contained an abundance of sucrose. In addition, sources of processed sugar could regularly be found at the port of New Orleans, where the "fermenting drainage of sugar and molasses hogsheads on the Levée" provided nourishment for mosquitoes.[56]

The proximity of early sugar plantations to the waterfront, combined with the presence of sugar in both agricultural and urban spaces, fostered the development of an attractive niche for *A. aegypti* mosquitoes. In lower Louisiana, the growth of plantations severely altered the landscape surrounding New Orleans as a result of land clearance, drainage, and other construction projects. Large-scale cane cultivation required systems of water control, including irrigation, canal-building, river clearance, and swamp drainage. The water management infrastructure on plantations, in surrounding areas, and in cities also encouraged the habitation of mosquitoes. Drainage ditches and artificial waterways created habitats for *Anopheles* mosquitoes, while plantations and cities created niches for *A. aegypti*. During the construction of these projects, a hybrid environment that attracted both species emerged. Deforestation,

FIGURE 2. Sugar barrels at the New Orleans waterfront. The original caption read "The sweetest spot on earth: sugar levee beside the Mississippi, New Orleans, Louisiana." (New York Public Library.)

combined with ecological shifts that resulted from the intensification of water management projects, created a distinct environment that was particularly hospitable to West African diseases, especially yellow fever and malaria.

Sugar planters relied on drainage canals and ditches to keep their sugar crops from flooding. Early planters established plantations along natural levees, because these elevated regions provided the only well-drained soil in the region that was relatively safe from floods. Plantations occupied land tracts at a ninety-degree angle to the rivers and bayous, so each had access to riparian space and could build drainage canals to the backswamp. Because levee land was required for a viable plantation, demand for levee property increased as more prospective sugar planters moved to the region in the early decades of the nineteenth century,

and "since the better drained land lay nearest the river, earliest settlement faced the river while latecomers settled farther back."[57] By 1820,
newcomers from the eastern United States had established plantations
along levees of the Mississippi as well as along Bayous Lafourche and
Teche.[58] However, even levee sites were susceptible to flood damage,
particularly on plantations located along the Mississippi. Historical geographer Sam B. Hilliard notes that "periodic high water topped the levees damaging crops and buildings and in severe cases, literally wiping
out entire plantations."[59] Planters responded by ordering slaves and hir-
ing laborers to dig ditches and drainage canals and to reinforce natural
levee lands by building artificial levees. Despite these early engineering
projects, high water would often cause levees to crack. A breach (or *cre-
vasse*) in a levee could result in devastating floods that lasted for weeks,
causing severe crop damage. In his manual on sugarcane cultivation,
Benjamin Silliman advised planters:

> The draining of the land, notwithstanding the importance attached to
> it in Louisiana, still merits sugar planters generally, a higher degree
> of attention than it has received. It is only when the drains are suffi-
> ciently frequent and deep, and carried far back into the swamps, that
> the land can be delivered, with the requisite rapidity, of the water from
> the rains, and the filtration which takes place through the banks of the
> river during the spring, when its level is above that of the land. Unless
> the land is capable of rapid drainage, it is impossible to deprive it of its
> coldness and clamminess; both of which are hostile to the early bud-
> ding of cane plants.[60]

While most planters relied on African American slaves for agricultural labor, they often hired Irish and German immigrants to perform
construction-related labor on plantations, including the arduous tasks
of repairing levees, digging ditches and drainage canals, and clearing
swamps, rivers, and bayous. Some Irish immigrants worked for "local
contractors, who hired out teams of immigrants to conduct laborious
and hazardous plantation maintenance knee-deep in disease-infested
waters." According to one overseer, planters chose to hire workers for
these tasks because "it was much cheaper to have Irish do it, who cost
nothing to the planter, if they died, than to use up good field hands in
such severe employment."[61] Malaria-carrying *Anopheles* mosquitoes
often resided in undeveloped swamps, bogs, and marshes. The process

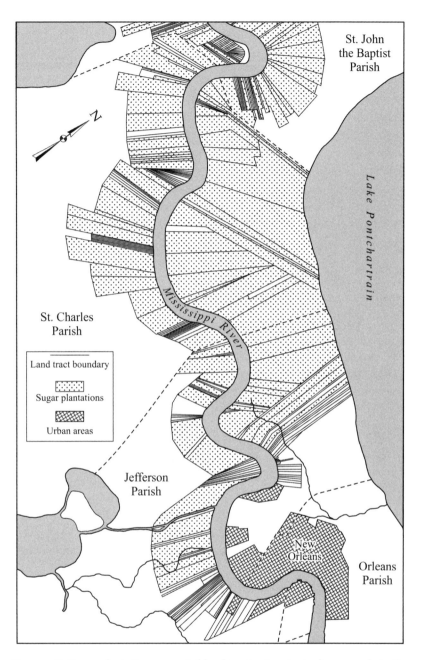

FIGURE 3. Sugar plantations occupied land tracts at a ninety-degree angle to the rivers and bayous, so each had access to the waterfront and could build canals that drained excess water into the backswamp. (From Colton, Norton, and Persac. Cartography by Mary Lee Eggart.)

of clearing and developing swamps for settlement and cultivation created a niche for *A. aegypti,* alongside *Anopheles* mosquitoes. As a result, immigrants who worked as ditchers and delvers encountered both types of mosquitoes and were exposed to both malaria and yellow fever. Since most European newcomers had not had contact with these fevers prior to their immigration to Louisiana, they were particularly susceptible, and large numbers of them died during yellow fever epidemics. Thus, during the 1830s and 1840s, residents of New Orleans and visitors perceived yellow fever as a "stranger's disease" and believed that natives (described as Creoles) were generally immune.[62]

URBAN DEVELOPMENT AND IMMIGRATION, 1830–1853

The growth and expansion of Louisiana's cane industry in the 1830s and 1840s not only altered landscapes through the construction of plantations; it also transformed New Orleans into an active urban center, owing to increased port traffic, suburban development, and demographic growth, largely enabled by industrialization. Alongside the construction of artificial levees and canals, development was characterized by the expansion of urban zones and increased immigration. In this period, yellow fever occasionally spread to regions connected to the port of New Orleans by rivers, canals, and railroads.

In the 1830s and 1840s, the links between canal construction and yellow fever were becoming apparent. The growth of canal-building projects in the city coincided with epidemics, and local medical authorities connected epidemics with ecological changes resulting from their construction. For example, local physician E. H. Barton argued that the New Basin Canal, which paralleled Bayou St. John, coincided with major epidemics in 1832 and 1833. He drew further connections between canal work during the epidemics of 1837 and 1850, claiming that "digging . . . extensive trenches and canals" caused severe epidemics of yellow fever and cholera. He believed that yellow fever resulted from "the excessive disturbance of the original soil of the country," which included "large excavations on miles of streets . . . for laying down gas and water pipes and making relaying pavements."[63]

In the 1850s the impacts of the growth of steam traffic intensified along New Orleans's waterfront, or levée. In 1849, New Orleans physician E. D. Fenner noted that "the levée, to the extent of three or four miles, is lined the greater part of the year with every variety of water craft, from the most magnificent ships and steamboats down to small schooners, oyster boats and flatboats."[64] By 1860, more than 250 steam-boats passed through New Orleans, in addition to countless small boats, barges, and sailing ships. Observers described the view from the riv-erfront as "a forest of masts" and remarked that "steamboats were the waterfront's signal feature." The scene on the New Orleans levée "pre-sented an awesome spectacle, with a confluence of technologies, goods, and people that was amazing in an age when successful challenges to the boundaries of space and time were just becoming commonplace."[65] In 1851, A. Oakey Hall spoke of a "panorama of trade" at the waterfront in the morning, with the levée surrounded by "a wilderness of ships and steamboats," as "thousands of hogsheads, bales, and bags and packages crowd and jostle and hedge each other in."[66] The development of New Orleans's riverfront as an urban public space, combined with increased port traffic, provided a large supply of human blood and desirable breed-ing spaces for *A. aegypti* and further increased the likelihood of people's exposure to the yellow fever virus. S. R. Christophers, in his study of the species, has argued that "at the dock side and water front of teeming harbours in moist and rainy tropical climates, with miscellaneous col-lections of water in machinery, country boats and even in the old days in ships, whereby it is spread to other ports and harbours, the species obtains conditions optimal for its proliferation."[67] *A. aegypti* thrived at New Orleans's waterfront because of the growth of port traffic, which was mostly due to the thriving sugar trade, and the expansion of its hab-itat as a result of urban construction.

The city's water management challenges exacerbated the environ-mental impacts of urban development. The physical expansion of the city prompted severe ecological changes, notably continued clearance and drainage of cypress swamps behind the city. Swamp drainage en-abled urban development in lowland regions, which extended from be-hind the Vieux Carré and the American Quarter along the natural levee of the Mississippi north to Lake Pontchartrain.[68] After the land was drained, however, it remained marshy and prone to flooding. Follow-ing heavy rains and floods each summer, puddles of water collected in low-lying regions, providing additional breeding spaces for *A. aegypti*. In J. D. Gillett's study of the species, he argued that "female mosquitoes can detect the whereabouts of even the smallest traces of water" and said the fact "that patches of darkness rather than the presence of water itself is the first thing to attract the gravid female makes it easier for us to understand how certain species of *Aedes* deposit their eggs in dry places liable to flooding."[69]

In addition to prompting the growth of commercial development,

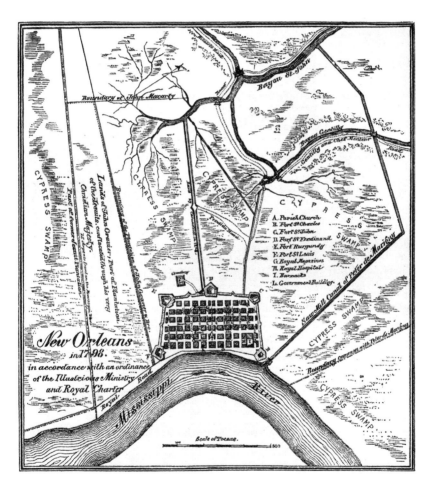

FIGURE 4. By 1798, canals and roads extended across the cypress swamps surrounding the city, connecting the Vieux Carré to large bayous. Construction and repairs coincided with epidemics. (Courtesy University of Texas Libraries, the University of Texas at Austin.)

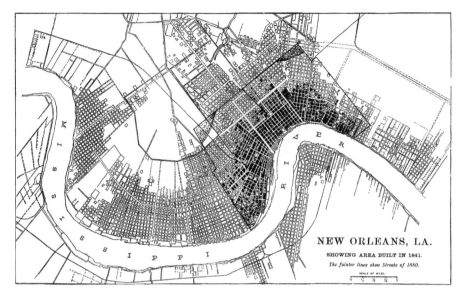

NEW ORLEANS, LA.

SHOWING AREA BUILT IN 1841.

The fainter lines show Streets of 1880.

SCALE OF MILES.

FIGURE 5. By the 1840s, urban and suburban development in New Orleans expanded into the lowlands surrounding the Vieux Carré. (Courtesy University of Texas Libraries, the University of Texas at Austin.)

suburban growth in New Orleans led to an increase in the construction of residential neighborhoods and of cemeteries, which contributed to the creation of built environment that allowed the prolific breeding of *A. aegypti*. Christophers argues that *A. aegypti* "does not find conditions so suitable where communities are well housed with a permanent water supply and good drainage system and tidier house habits. . . . Here, with the domestic water pot, the cistern . . . the flower vase and the shaded rooms with cupboards and hanging equipment and with man to feed upon, *Aedes aegypti* . . . finds a very suitable *locus*."[70] Residential areas attracted *A. aegypti* mosquitoes by offering an abundance of breeding spaces, in a variety of urban water containers including cisterns, architectural ornamentation, and various other small crevices that collected water during the summer.

Despite being virtually surrounded by water, New Orleans lacked a source of clean groundwater. Because of the city's high water table, residents could not dig wells and instead depended on cisterns to collect and store rainwater for drinking and bathing. Open-water cisterns proved to be a highly favored breeding space for *A. aegypti*. Early-twentieth-century medical authorities referred to it as the "cistern mosquito."[71] As the city's population grew, so did the number of cisterns. Because the region's wet season, from roughly May through September, was also the warmest time of the year, mosquitoes thrived during this period, which became known as the "sickly season."

By the 1830s, the physical expansion of the city prompted the construction of short rail lines. More extensive railroad construction projects began in the 1840s and 1850s, but many of these lines were destroyed during the Civil War. Louisiana's first line, the Pontchartrain Railroad, went through the Third District, connecting the Mississippi River to Lake Pontchartrain. In 1835 the city's second line, the New Orleans and Carrollton Railroad, extended six miles from the Vieux Carré to the Carrollton suburbs, through Faubourg St. Mary. Construction of the city's third line, the Mexican Gulf Railroad, began in 1839. That line aimed to connect the city to the Gulf of Mexico via Lake Borgne, but financial difficulties prevented its completion, so the line stopped at the entrance of Bayou Terre-aux-Boeufs in St. Bernard Parish.[72] In the 1840s new railroads began construction, including the Clinton and Port Hudson Railroad, the West Feliciana Railroad, and the Red River Railroad. In the 1850s several long-distance lines were constructed, including the New Orleans, Opelousas, and Great Western Railroad, the New Orleans, Jackson, and Great Northern Railroad, and the Vicksburg, Shreveport, and Texas Railroad.[73] The development of antebellum rail lines connected sugar plantations to the city and facilitated the growth of New Orleans as a major interstate slave port.

Ecological changes resulting from railroad construction facilitated yellow fever epidemics, and completed lines enabled the virus to spread from the city to nearby plantations and towns. Like the laborers who built canals, immigrants who worked in railroad construction suffered in great proportions during epidemics.[74] By the 1850s, contemporaries noticed connections between railroad construction and yellow fever, particularly the high death rates among workers. In 1853 Barton, who served as president of the Louisiana State Medical Association at the time, noted that "during the last season, extensive embankments of earth and excavations were made for the Opelousas Railroad, [and] the fever broke out and devastated that village; of 350 hands employed on the road, three hundred fell victims to it." On the Jackson Street Railroad, in the Fourth District, fifty of eighty construction workers died.[75] Similarly, a large proportion of workers died during construction of the Great Northern Railroad, which extended more than two hundred miles from Carrollton to Jackson, Mississippi, and cut through several sugar plantations. In addition to deaths among workers, Barton observed an "unprecedented amount of fevers on plantations, near and in the rear of which these embankments were made." In suburban Carrollton the fever appeared for the first time, and mortality was "very great." Barton wrote that 1853 was "probably the first time yellow fever was in any of these rural districts on either side of the river."[76]

New Orleans grew rapidly between 1830 and 1861, demographically as well as physically. Within thirty years, the documented urban population increased from about 50,000 to nearly 175,000. Between 1837 and the start of the Civil War, more immigrants entered the United States through New Orleans than through any other city, with the exception of New York.[77] The demographic consequences of European immigration to New Orleans, particularly after 1848, contributed to the prevalence of yellow fever by providing a population of nonimmunes to host the virus every year. Changing conditions in Europe during the nineteenth century, including unprecedented demographic growth, crop failures, and political conflicts during the 1840s, caused European immigration to the United States to increase during this time. In 1848, national struggles in France, Hungary, Germany, and Ireland led to the flight of millions of refugees. In Ireland and Belgium, potato blight and poor grain harvests caused widespread famine and resulted in large-scale migrations from both regions after 1845.[78] The majority of immigrants to New Orleans arrived from Ireland, Prussia and other German states, France, Great Britain, Spain, and Italy; significantly fewer came from Austria, Switzerland, Denmark, Sweden, Russia, Holland, and Belgium.[79] These newcomers, who had not been previously exposed to yellow fever, provided a large population to host the virus when it was reintroduced to the city from Caribbean vessels during the summer.

The city's ethnic geography also contributed to the increased exposure of immigrants to yellow fever, particularly those who worked in canal and railroad construction. Affluent families occupied elevated sections of the city, while middle- and working-class families lived in the backswamp, away from the riverfront. Immigrants who arrived in New Orleans during the 1820s through the 1850s settled in these lowland areas. Geographer Richard Campanella has shown that "areas farthest from the river were lowest in elevation and closest to the mosquito infested, flood-prone swamp" and that this "so-called back-of-town suffered environmental risks and primitive infrastructure, cost little, and inspired the humblest housing stock." Thus, immigrants who lived and worked in these regions, where they found "both affordable housing and low-skill employment at flatboat wharves, warehouses, slaughterhouses, tanneries, and in public-works projects for canals, drainage, and railroads," were likely to come into contact with infected mosquitoes.[80]

CITY OF THE DEAD

Yellow fever victims quickly filled the city's graveyards. Since its settlement, the city's environmental attributes had shaped the funerary practices of its residents. The high water table made interment difficult, and by the 1830s many residents opted for above-ground vaults. In 1819 architect Benjamin Henry Latrobe observed that eight or nine inches below the surface, tombs "filled with water and were not three feet deep," and "thus all persons here who are interred in earth are buried in the water."[81]

Beginning with the establishment of the city's first cemetery in 1725, local observers associated swampy cemeteries with pestilence, including cholera, malaria, and yellow fever. Many eighteenth-century residents buried their dead along the riverbank or in the St. Peter Street Cemetery, located on a "low and swampy site" behind the Vieux Carré, surrounded by ditches used to raise the land. After a devastating flood, fire, and epidemic in 1788, the Spanish administration, "realizing that the cemetery was filled and being warned by local physicians that the proximity of the cemetery to the city could cause another outbreak of pestilence . . . ordered a new cemetery to be established farther from the center of population." In 1789 the new cemetery, known as St. Louis Cemetery I, occupied a space "at the edge of the city," forty yards from the Charity Hospital Garden.[82] Following the severe yellow fever epidemics of 1817–20, the city council ordered the construction of a new cemetery even farther from the riverfront. The St. Louis Cemetery II, established in 1823, was located about eighteen hundred feet behind

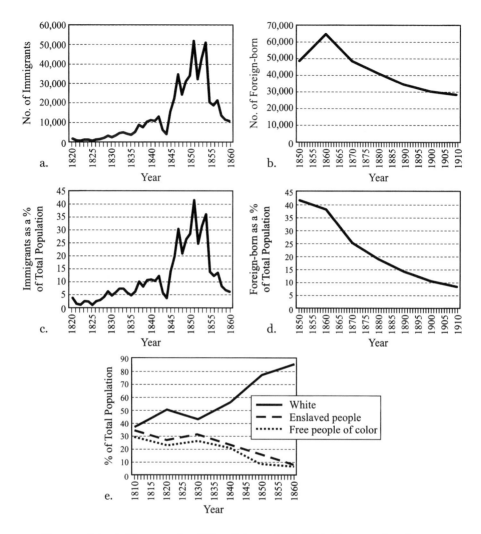

FIGURE 6 (a–e). Demography of New Orleans, 1810–1910. European immigrants made up the majority of yellow fever victims in the 1850s. (Based on data from the US Census Bureau, Population Division; and Spletstoser. See also Campanella, *Geographies of New Orleans*. Graphs by Mary Lee Eggart.)

a. Number of immigrants arriving in New Orleans, 1820–1860.

b. Immigrants arriving in New Orleans as a percentage of the population, 1820–60.

c. Foreign-born population of New Orleans, 1850–1910.

d. Foreign-born population as a percentage of the population, 1850–1910.

e. Racial identification of New Orleans, 1810–60. The white population grew from an influx of Anglo-American migrants after 1810 and with increasing European immigration after 1830.

Rampart Street.[83] Urban development in the 1830s and 1840s enclosed the cemetery, which was located "on semiswampland [that] frequently flooded after heavy rains."[84]

In addition to the St. Louis Cemetery II, seven new cemeteries were established between 1820 and 1848. The Girod Street Cemetery, located behind the Second District (the American Quarter), was constructed in 1822, and the St. Vincent de Paul Cemetery, on Piety Street in the Third District (between the American Quarter and Vieux Carré), was built in 1844. Additional cemeteries were established on a section of rare high ground known as Metairie Ridge, including the Hebrew Rest (1828), Cypress Grove (1840), St. Patrick's (1841), Odd Fellows' Rest (1847), and Charity Hospital (1847) cemeteries.[85]

Irish immigration notably increased during the 1830s, and St. Patrick's expanded rapidly as Irish immigrants quickly succumbed to yellow fever. Following the disastrous epidemic of 1853, more than eleven hundred Irish immigrants were buried during the month of August. The cemetery did not have the facilities to bury such a large number of people in such a short time, and many individuals "had to be buried in hastily dug graves which were at times mere ditches or trenches."[86]

Nineteenth-century cemeteries, often called "cities of the dead," presented an inviting locale for A. aegypti to live and breed. New Orleans's cemeteries contained a variety of monuments, including marble vases, statuary, and architectural embellishments that filled with water when it rained. Cemeteries became a distinctive feature in New Orleans's urban landscape as the city expanded, despite early attempts to locate them away from the city. Christophers described the proliferation of mosquitoes in developed areas, explaining that A. aegypti "breeding may occur in "flower pots, . . . upturned bottles used for decorative purposes, . . . [and] stagnant ornamental fountains."[87] During the 1830s and 1840s, "modest tombs began to give way . . . to more elegant and expensive monuments as family prestige, status, and fashion influenced funerary design."[88] Many graves in the Metairie cemeteries contained underground tombs, but cemeteries located in lowland spaces contained exclusively above-ground vaults, decorated with various embellishments that could collect rainwater. Cemeteries built in the nineteenth century, which provided ample breeding spaces for A. aegypti, were increasingly situated near new residential developments. In 1849 Fenner reported that cemeteries "are encroached on by progressive improvements, and, before many years, the dead will have to give place to the living. The Protestant cemetery, near the new basin, is already surrounded by houses."[89]

The encroachment of urban dwellings in the swamp and bayou country of lower Louisiana, combined with the growth and expansion of sugar plantations, continued until the Civil War. Economic growth, tied to the booming sugar industry, created jobs and wealth in New Orleans and was integral to urban expansion during the antebellum period. By 1848 a substantial population of *A. aegypti* mosquitoes had effectively settled in the city and the surrounding sugar country. This environment became home to a species that was capable of causing yellow fever epidemics whenever the city was exposed to the virus, which thrived especially with the yearly introduction of nonimmune newcomers. As the incidence of yellow fever increased during the 1840s and 1850s, visitors and residents grew accustomed to its seasonal presence and considered the disease as a factor that distinguished the region from temperate parts of the United States.

3

Imagined Immunities

IDEOLOGIES OF RACE, ECOLOGY, AND
DISEASE RESISTANCE, 1840–1861

The regular appearance of yellow fever in antebellum New Orleans shaped the culture of the city, which gained a fearful reputation in the United States. Physicians who studied the causes and prevention of yellow fever often focused on the role of environmental features. They developed notions of immunity and resistance based on factors including city creolism (nativity) and race; categories of class, age, and gender; and social behaviors. Cultural attitudes about the environment, race, and the relationship between climate and race affected medical professionals' and untrained observers' perceptions of yellow fever immunity and resistance.

The development of local ideologies of immunity were linked to seemingly unconnected global processes, including the simultaneous rise of endemic yellow fever in coastal West Africa and the upsurge in immigration to the United States that resulted from mid-nineteenth-century political and social revolutions in Europe. The frequency of yellow fever epidemics in New Orleans led to widespread exposure and immunity among native populations, while global demographic changes brought more susceptible newcomers into contact with yellow fever for the first time. Examining the changing views about yellow fever immunity in the mid-nineteenth century reveals how political and social tensions influenced popular and medical ideologies. After the Louisiana Purchase, popular views of immunity based on creolism and nativity reflected tensions between American newcomers and Creoles. In the 1830s and 1840s, a binary (black and white) system of racial classification began to supplant the multitiered system by which Louisianans had been identifying themselves, and medical authorities increasingly advocated theories of racial immunity and resistance. Among medical professionals, notions of race-based resistance were grounded in observational data, combined with ideological preoccupations that caused them to focus on racial differences. Ideas about race among doctors in New Orleans came about simultaneously and in connection with theories of scientific racism developed by researchers and medical authorities in the northern United States, Europe, and colonial spaces throughout the Caribbean, Latin America, and South Asia. By the 1860s, conflicts over slavery and colonialism caused ideas about race and biological difference to solidify.

A Culture of Fever: Ecological Perspectives

The ubiquitous presence of yellow fever shaped the culture of antebellum New Orleans. In the 1850s it appeared to become more severe, causing higher mortality and frequently spreading outside of the city, to towns and cities that had not previously experienced epidemics. Responses to the persistent threat of severe yellow fever outbreaks in New Orleans ranged from blithe acceptance to grave concern among residents and visitors. Newcomers reacted with fear and panic and fled the city during the summer if they were able. Local physicians wrote extensively about the disease, trying to figure out its causes, treatment, and prevention. Core concerns among local elites included the economic and social consequences of both epidemics and preventive measures.

Responses to epidemics in the 1850s reveal the complex ways in which people understood the relationship between health and the environment. Nancy Stepan has argued that before the advent of bacteriology in the 1860s, the dominant framework for understanding disease could be described as "environmentalist." Rather than searching for microscopic causes of disease, doctors understood illness as caused by complex and interrelated environmental variables including climate, latitude, topography, soil conditions, temperature, rainfall, changes in seasons, and other meteorological events. This view was common among European colonial doctors who practiced in tropical regions, as well as physicians who practiced in the Gulf South. They drew connections between environments and diseases that they associated with warm climates, particularly fevers. New Orleans physicians often linked illness with atmospheric conditions, theorizing that diseases had to do with local "foul airs" or "miasmas," which they believed emanated from swamps and decomposing matter.[1] In the urban environment of New Orleans, doctors were especially concerned with "filth," an ambiguous term that they often used to refer to organic waste that accumulated in cities.

Throughout the antebellum period, many medical professionals conflated malaria and yellow fever, though gradually physicians determined that yellow fever was a distinct disease. Some physicians considered yellow fever to be an extreme form of intermittent or malarial fever. As late as 1861, Glasgow physician Andrew Anderson argued that the "well-known pestilential yellow fever . . . is hardly to be distinguished symptomatically from the more severe continued forms of malarious fever."[2] Since at this time they lacked knowledge of specific disease pathogens, physicians labeled fevers variously and inconsistently. Many doctors described fevers based on their additional symptoms, using terms such as bilious fever, hemorrhagic fever, and broken bone fever. Fevers were often accompanied by chills and described as "chills and fever" or "fever and ague." In the Gulf South, fevers described as remittent and intermittent fevers, continued fever, and malarial fever most likely were malaria, while fevers described as bilious fever, hemorrhagic fever, and bilio-gastric fever might have been yellow fever. Southern doctors often conceived of fever in terms of its ecological attributes, alluding to specific environments, geographies, and climatic patterns, using terms such as swamp fever, country fever, summer fever, and autumnal fever.[3]

By the 1850s, most physicians practicing in the Gulf Coast and Caribbean region identified yellow fever as a distinct disease, though they had diverse and often conflicting views about its causes and prevention. However, most considered the role of environmental conditions and ecological transformations in their assessment of its cause and connected the appearance of disease to factors including the presence of stagnant water, mosquitoes, and urban development. While many residents commented on the growth of local mosquito populations, they did not presume that mosquitoes carried the disease. However, a few witnesses made explicit connections between stagnant water, mosquitoes, and epidemics. These observations, though often quite accurate, did not influence local government officials to pass any sort of public health legislation.

STAGNANT WATER AND FILTH

In New Orleans, several doctors associated the presence of stagnant water with fevers. Some observed the common occurrence of mosquitoes and other insects in these environments, but they usually did not consider the role of mosquitoes in spreading fevers. Many physicians associated stagnant water with general unhealthfulness, linking the presence of fevers with the environmental attributes of swamps and marshes.[4] In 1849 New Orleans physician E. D. Fenner drew a connection between mosquitoes, stagnant water, and sickness in the city, arguing, "There is still a considerable number of vacant lots in the city, many of which are lower than the level of the streets, and, during wet weather, contain stagnant water, which breeds myriads of musquitoes and evolves deletrious [*sic*] effluvia. Stagnant water is also to be found under many houses."[5]

Doctors often associated stagnant water with filth, which was tied to cultural attitudes about cleanliness and purity that went along with social behaviors, notably temperance. Discourses on temperance commonly highlighted the dangers of intemperance in warm climates. In 1850 E. H. Barton, while serving as president of the Louisiana State Board of Health, argued that disease in New Orleans was caused by stagnant water in addition to "bad air, bad habits, and bad milk." He claimed that "the greatest sources of *impurity of air* [arose] from privies, the offal from kitchens, stables, stores, markets, streets, manufactories, etc.," that stagnant water was contaminated with filth, and that "the effects of intemperance, especially in a warm climate," were the greatest cause in "undermining the constitution" and "increasing the liability to disease."[6] Barton's views illustrate the ways in which doctors drew connections between social and environmental conditions, which they linked to the pervasiveness of disease. In his assessment of the causes of the yellow fever epidemic of 1853, Barton emphasized meteorological conditions and changes to the landscape, which he identified as "terrene conditions." He said yellow fever was caused by changes to environment, including urban construction and land clearance projects, particularly the digging of ditches and canals, in addition to unusually early high temperatures and increased rainfall. The stagnant water that accumulated in low-lying lots and streets throughout the city as a source of filth, he ultimately argued, was the primary cause of the epidemic. Barton used the metric of filth to explain why yellow fever was more severe in certain locales than others, noting that yellow fever in its most "malignant and revolting aspect" ravaged a portion of the city that he described as "disgusting and revolting beyond all expression. . . . Filth of every character crowded the streets, gutters, pavements, and even the houses."[7]

Physicians' preoccupation with filth often caused them to ignore the impacts of clean sources of stagnant water. However, urban architecture, including gardens, cisterns, and cemeteries, contributed to the propagation of *A. aegypti*, since the mosquitoes preferred to breed in clean water receptacles. Barton did notice that cisterns served as mosquito breeding spaces and suggested methods to prevent the growth of mosquito larvae. He wrote that water "should be filtered as it comes from the roof through the gutters into the cistern, by passing through a bed of charcoal, and its power of absorbing atmospheric impurities and a nidus for musquitoes checked by having a float of wood on the surface of the water in the cisterns." He further advised residents that "if, notwithstanding all these precautions, animalculae should be found in it, . . . the liability of being a breeding place for musquetoes, as all stagnant waters are, may be obviated by placing small fish in the cistern."[8] Barton's concerns about animaculae and mosquitoes were rooted in his views about the dangers of filth, particularly in water used for drinking and cooking.

URBAN DEVELOPMENT

Although most physicians agreed that stagnant water was unhealthful, they commonly viewed urban development and drainage as improvements that would better the overall health of the city. In 1849 Fenner optimistically reported:

> This vast swamp has undergone a wonderful amelioration in the last twenty-five or thirty years. The part within two miles of the city has been pretty thoroughly drained, by which means a large extent of valu-

able land has been reclaimed, and in a few years will be covered with buildings and gardens. The surface is gradually becoming more elevated, the streets are annually extended in that direction, and thus the spot, which, a few years ago, was a *pestiferous fen,* will probably soon become the abode of a dense and active population.[9]

It is probable that swamp-dwelling *Anopheles* mosquitoes lived in the backswamp before it was drained and urbanized. While development may have slightly diminished the ecological niche occupied by malaria-carrying anophelenes, city-dwelling *A. aegypti* mosquitoes thrived in the urban metropolis.

A few physicians, including Josiah Clark Nott, who practiced in Mobile and New Orleans, directly linked yellow fever with urban development. His observations documented the process of ecological transformations that led to the prevalence of malaria in the early stages of land clearance and construction, followed by yellow fever during periods of rapid urban growth. Nott explained that "when the forest is first leveled and a town commenced, intermittents and remittents spring up. . . . As the population increases, the town spreads, and draining and paving are introduced, yellow fever, the mighty monarch of the South, who scorns the rude field and forest, plants his scepter in the centre, and drives all other fevers to the outskirts."[10] A few doctors outside of the region made similar observations. In 1861 Andrew Anderson also noted the uniqueness of yellow fever as a disease that prevailed in cities, particularly those that were situated near the sea.[11]

MOSQUITOES

Visitors and residents in antebellum New Orleans commonly remarked on the presence of mosquitoes, but they often viewed them as a nuisance rather than a cause of disease. Living in New Orleans from 1846 to 1848, A. Oakey Hall described the "cunning and sagacity" of local mosquitoes and concluded simply that the "mosquito is a sad drawback to the sunny days and pleasant nights of a New Orleans exile. The mosquito! whose bark is perhaps more disagreeable than his bite."[12]

Numerous local physicians remarked on the unusual abundance of mosquitoes in 1853. Dr. Fred R. Harvey, of East Feliciana Parish, noted that in July "musquetoes [were] uncommonly numerous, both night and day." A doctor in Centreville, located along Bayou Teche, wrote,

"There appeared to be more musquetoes, the past summer, than I ever noticed in any previous year." He also commented that there had been some clearing and "considerable opening of ditches . . . late in the summer."[13] Nathaniel Houghton, a doctor who had practiced in New Orleans since 1845, wrote, "I noticed no particular change in the health or condition of animals, except, perhaps, I may mention that the musquetoes were more numerous than was ever known before."[14]

In addition, locals who were not medical professionals noticed the growth of mosquito populations in the early 1850s. Judge Lewis Selby described the first appearance of yellow fever in Lake Providence in 1853, located about 250 miles upriver from New Orleans. He was especially perceptive in noticing not only a greater preponderance of mosquitoes, but also that a new species had become abundant in the region. He observed that "musquetoes seemed multiplied a hundred-fold, commonly here they are a dirty yellow, but these had gray rings around their bodies, bit quicker and stung much harder than heretofore."[15] Selby's description of these new mosquitoes provides a remarkably accurate depiction of *A. aegypti*, later described by entomologist L. O. Howard as "strikingly marked," with "silvery white" bands on its thorax and abdomen. This physical characteristic is common among *Aedes* mosquitoes and distinguishes them from *Anopheles* mosquitoes, which entomologists have described as "pale" and "yellow."[16] Selby also drew a connection between the decline of bird populations during the epidemic, noting that "during the sickness, and for some time before, and since, nor yet do I recollect of having seen a blue-bird or wood-pecker within the bounds of the disease—the martins were very scarce, and the few that were here left early—while at the same time, in ordinary seasons there have been, perhaps, a hundred mocking birds, this season, during the sickness, I only saw two; and for weeks only heard one sing."[17] Selby's description of declining bird populations and growing mosquito populations provides compelling anecdotal evidence of ecological changes that would have contributed to the likelihood of yellow fever, since several bird species, including martins, bluebirds, and woodpeckers, feed on insects and their larvae.

Although observers frequently commented on the abundance of mosquitoes, they rarely made a direct connection between insects and yellow fever. However, a few local doctors, including E. H. Barton and

Josiah Nott, considered the potential role of insects. Barton, mentioned earlier, drew connections between mosquitoes, filth, and disease and advocated methods of killing mosquito larvae in cisterns. In 1848 Nott argued that yellow fever was a disease sui generis, distinct from malarial and bilious fevers. He rejected miasmatic theories of yellow fever transmission, arguing that "the morbidic cause of Yellow Fever is not amenable to any of the laws of gases, vapors, emanations, &c., but has an inherent power of propagation, independent of the motions of the atmosphere, and which accords in many respects with the peculiar habits and instincts of insects." He concluded that the "specific cause" of yellow fever must "exist in some form of Insect life."[18] Nott drew his theory from his observations in Mobile and New Orleans. However, he did not attempt to test his ideas or identify a species that carried yellow fever. Nott erroneously hypothesized that insects also spread cholera. British surgeon-general Daniel Blair made a similar observation about yellow fever in British Guiana, noting that epidemic patterns resembled "to the imagination the attributes of insect life."[19]

The most accurate description of the causes of yellow fever prior to Carlos Finlay's pioneering research on the mosquito vector comes from Louis Daniel Beauperthuy, a Creole physician born in Guadeloupe and trained in Paris. He believed that mosquitoes caused yellow fever by obtaining infectious material from "soil or decomposed matter." In an essay published in 1853, based on his observations of yellow fever in Cumaná, Venezuela, he claimed that "the affection known as yellow fever, or black vomit, is due to the same cause as that producing intermittent fever. . . . The mosquito plunges its proboscis into the skin . . . and introduces a poison which has properties akin to snake venom." He argued against miasmatic theory, stating that "marshes do not communicate to the atmosphere anything more than humidity, and the small amount of hydrogen they give off does not cause in man the slightest indisposition in equatorial and intertropical regions renowned for their unhealthiness. Nor is it the putrescence of water that makes it unhealthy, but the presence of mosquitoes." He might even have identified *A. aegypti,* in his claim that the most dangerous mosquito was the *zancudo bobo.* His description of the *zancudo bobo* as a "house-haunting" mosquito, with white stripes on its legs, is a remarkably precise representation of the domestic preferences and physical attributes of *A. aegypti.*[20]

THE EPIDEMIC OF 1853

Late in the summer of 1853, New Orleans experienced its most devastating epidemic yet, in terms of its morbidity, mortality, and spread outside of the city. Fenner described it as "more malignant and more unmanageable than ever seen here before."[21] The epidemic reached cities connected to New Orleans by river, causing outbreaks in Baton Rouge; Natchez; Vicksburg; Greenville, Mississippi; and Memphis, and by rail, spreading to Opelousas, New Iberia, Shreveport, and Jackson. Beyond these cities, yellow fever appeared sporadically in nearby towns and plantations.[22] By 1853 New Orleans's population had grown to more than 120,000, with immigrants accounting for more than 40 percent. The city suffered extremely high morbidity and mortality rates, as the fever killed roughly 10 to 15 percent of the population.[23]

Responses to the epidemic reveal numerous insights about the way doctors and other observers understood the relationship between environmental characteristics and ecological changes, including land and

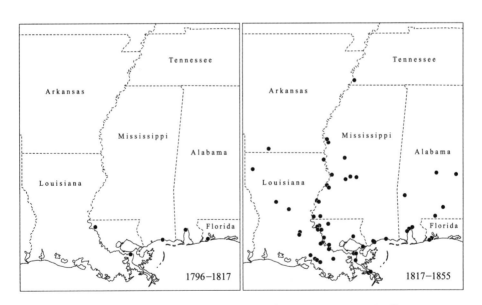

FIGURE 7. Map of the spread of yellow fever in the Lower Mississippi Valley, 1795–1855. (Compiled from articles published in the *New Orleans Medical and Surgical Journal* and the *New Orleans Medical News and Hospital Gazette;* and Augustin. Cartography by Mary Lee Eggart.)

water control projects.[24] After the epidemic, the New Orleans Sanitary Commission solicited reports from doctors and other residents. In addition to collecting morbidity and mortality statistics and descriptions of cases, the commission compiled detailed, narrative descriptions of environmental conditions to assess the "sanitary condition" of the city. Locals were asked to record detailed information about local environmental features alongside each locality's demographic data and "social condition."[25] Local medical authorities were particularly interested in transformations to the landscape, water sources, soil quality, local flora and fauna, and weather patterns. The commission's questionnaire solicited information about recent "extensive clearing of lands in the vicinity, or disturbance of the soil from the digging of wells or canals, making levees, improving roads, draining or paving of streets, or any upturning of the soil." Further, informants were questioned about the position of their locale in regard to "rivers, bayous, swamps, marshes, [and] stagnant lakes or pools of water," and they were asked to specify whether the area was prone to collecting stagnant water. The questionnaire asked, "Does the water run off freely or does it accumulate, and if so, how near your place?" Reporters were also to include a description of local drinking water sources, specifying whether they were well, cistern, or spring water. The commission was very specific in regard to questions about climate and weather patterns. They asked respondents to state "the condition of the weather as to dampness or dryness, the temperature whether hot or cold, whether very hot in the sun, or cool in the shade, the prevalence of rains and fogs . . . and the prevalence and direction of winds during the existence of the fever, and for a month or two previous." In addition to these categories, the commission asked observers to record "anything remarkable in the Animal or Vegetable Kingdoms, prior to, or during the epidemic." This category specified whether they had noticed changes "such as . . . the inordinate presence of flies, mosquitoes, &c."[26]

As a result of this line of questioning, which encouraged witnesses to consider links between ecological and health conditions, locals produced numerous detailed accounts of environmental changes. The accounts illustrate the intimate knowledge that locals had of their surroundings and reveal how changes to the built environment contributed to the severity of the epidemic. Reporters from across the Lower Mississippi Valley and the Gulf Coast outlined local conditions, focusing on soil quality, drainage, changes in the land use, and descriptions of nearby water sources, including swamps, lakes, marshes, and other stagnant pools of water. They also recorded rainfall patterns and temperature and wrote detailed descriptions of local vegetation and animals.[27] Based on these characteristics, medical authorities believed that certain environments were prone to malarial fevers but safe from yellow fever.

Perceptions and Patterns of Immunity and Resistance

In addition to drawing connections between the environment and disease, antebellum medical authorities linked environmental conditions, particularly climate, with ideas about race and yellow fever resistance. Broadly, the idea that some individuals are born with genetic characteristics that cause them to be more or less susceptible to a particular disease has been advocated and contested by scholars, including medical researchers and historians of disease and medicine. They have pointed to numerous other factors that can influence a person's susceptibility to disease, such as diet, locality, and labor conditions. Issues related to socioeconomic status have a direct impact on these factors. However, most experts agree that any individual can acquire lifelong immunity to various diseases (including smallpox and yellow fever) if the person contracts the disease and survives.[28]

In histories of the early modern and modern Atlantic, the question of genetically determined immunity, resistance, and susceptibility to yellow fever continues to elicit varied responses from current scholars, especially concerning the perception that people of African descent are less likely to contract the disease and more likely to recover if they do.[29] This notion gained widespread acceptance in the mid-nineteenth century among both medical authorities and other witnesses, including European colonials who traveled to the tropical Americas, Africa, and Asia, as well as physicians who practiced in the antebellum United States. Ideologies of racial difference informed contemporary medical research and methods in the American South and the Greater Caribbean, in large part owing to the legal structure of racial inequality that served to legitimate the prevailing social and economic system of plantation slavery.

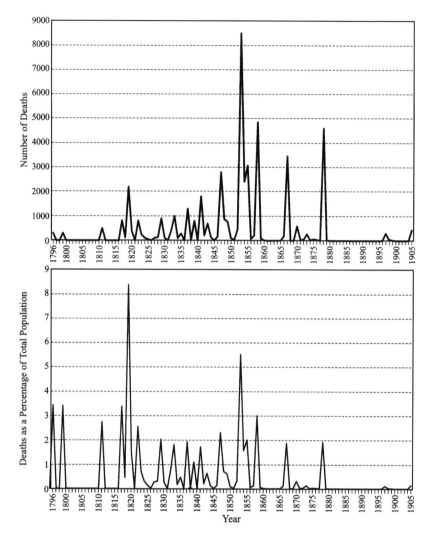

FIGURE 8. Graphs of reported yellow fever mortality in New Orleans, 1796–1905, based on official records, which did not include many nonwhite victims. Unofficial anecdotal accounts by witnesses are the only evidence of most nonwhite victims' deaths. Estimated mortality rates vary significantly in some years, notably 1841. (Compiled from articles in the *New Orleans Medical and Surgical Journal* and the *New Orleans Medical News and Hospital Gazette*. See also Augustin; Aiken; Carpenter; Dromgoole; Touatre; Patterson; Humphreys, *Yellow Fever*; Bloom. Graphs by Mary Lee Eggart.)

ANECDOTAL EVIDENCE OF AFRICAN SUSCEPTIBILITY

Anecdotal evidence from the eighteenth- and nineteenth-century Caribbean reveals several instances of African susceptibility to yellow fever, the details of which were not reported in contemporary medical accounts. By the late eighteenth century, as yellow fever appeared more frequently in West African and Caribbean port cities, enslaved Africans were more likely to encounter the virus before their arrival in New Orleans. They risked exposure to yellow fever while gathered in West African coastal ports, onboard maritime vessels in the Atlantic, and upon their arrival in Caribbean cities and plantations.[30] Chapter 1 demonstrates that during the first recorded yellow fever epidemics in Gorée and Saint-Louis, anecdotal sources suggested high mortality rates among African populations, and French colonial medical authorities failed to account for these deaths. Additionally, a critical analysis of evidence from slave ships raises questions about the cause of death among slaves during their jouney to the Americas. Further, accounts from the Caribbean and Brazil demonstrate the vulnerability of African populations. As late as the mid-nineteenth century, there is compelling evidence that African newcomers in the Caribbean suffered from yellow fever and that their deaths were unrecorded.

The lack of quantitative medical records of slave deaths obscures studies of disease and mortality among African captives on Atlantic vessels. There is very little data before the late eighteenth century, when yellow fever began to appear more frequently in coastal West Africa. Philip Curtin has shown that mortality from disease in the eighteenth century often ranged from 10 to 25 percent of slaves, with a higher percentage of deaths among crew members.[31] Between 1700 and 1789, planters in Saint-Domingue imported 900,000 slaves; yet by 1789 fewer than 450,000 slaves resided in the colony. Historians have estimated that in Barbados, the "entire slave population . . . had to be renewed every sixteen years."[32] Prior to the late 1770s, slaves were less likely to have been exposed to yellow fever before arriving in the Americas. While colonial records often accounted for the deaths of European newcomers, they did not record details of deaths among Africans. Since the majority of demographic data comes from late-eighteenth- and early-nineteenth-century voyages, it is difficult to discern the endemicity of yellow fever prior to this period. Owing to the absence of substantive medical records or descriptions of slave deaths when compared to mortality records kept on European passenger ships, scholarship that relies exclusively on statistical analyses are prone to conclude that blacks were less susceptible to yellow fever than whites.[33]

Sources from early Caribbean epidemics also reveal possible high death rates among Africans. Richard Dunn, in his study on sugar and slavery in Barbados, argues that slaves suffered from both yellow fever and malaria in the 1640s and 1690s.[34] Since sugar planters did not keep detailed records of the births, deaths, and marriages of slaves during this time, vital records fail to provide an accurate or complete list of yellow fever victims.[35] The absence of slave deaths in most accounts can be attributed to the lack of medical care for slaves during yellow fever epidemics, as physicians and coroners could not even manage to care for the white population. In Bridgetown, yellow fever claimed so many victims that bodies were thrown into the swamp near the town.[36] Although mortality records of slaves are incomplete, observers noticed the presence of yellow fever among slaves. John Oldmixon, in his account of the yellow fever epidemic of 1691 in Barbados, wrote that the outbreak killed large numbers of "inhabitants, masters, servants, and slaves."[37]

Seventeenth-century Portuguese accounts also suggest that African newcomers in Brazil were susceptible to yellow fever. Stuart Schwartz has argued that during the first recorded epidemics, between 1686 and 1692 in Bahia and Pernambuco, yellow fever "decimated the slave population."[38] Further, Curtin has shown that in seventeenth-century Brazil, "newly arrived Europeans and Africans both died in greater numbers than old residents," although records of European death rates were higher than African death rates.[39] Early-nineteenth-century sources also reveal high death rates among African newcomers to the Caribbean. In an essay containing practical advice on disease and slave management in the West Indies, a Scottish doctor who resided in St. Kitts wrote that it took at least one year for slaves arriving from Africa to be "seasoned."[40]

Records of high mortality among British-led "negro regiments" in Jamaica illustrate the process of acquired immunity. William Walker, who led a filibuster war to expand plantation slavery into Nicaragua between

1855 and 1857, acknowledged that in Jamaica, "the average mortality is greater among the negro than among European regiments," which led Josiah Nott to consider the possibility that "tropical America is not suited to the African." However, Walker argued that "negro blood seems to assert its superiority over the indigenous Indian of Nicaragua," based on his observation that "the blacks who have gone thither [Nicaragua] from Jamaica are healthy, strong, and capable of labor."[41] Nott's analysis suggests that soldiers who came to the Caribbean from Africa may have been more susceptible to endemic fevers than Afro-Caribbeans, while Walker's observations reveal that Africans and people of African descent probably acquired immunity in Jamaica.

The most compelling evidence of yellow fever among Africans in the Caribbean comes from one of the few existing accounts from a Cuban native who was raised as a slave on the Flor de Sagua sugar plantation during the 1860s. Esteban Montejo lived on the plantation until he escaped in 1868. He remained in hiding in the forests of central Cuba until the end of the Ten Years' War. In his autobiography, he described his experiences with disease in the barracoons, or slave quarters, noting that "the worst sicknesses, which made a skeleton of everyone, were smallpox and black sickness." The disease that Montejo described as the "black sickness" resembled yellow fever in terms of its symptoms as well as in its name, which was similar to the Spanish term *vómito negro*. Montejo recalled, "The black sickness took [Negroes] by surprise; it struck suddenly and in between one bout of vomiting and the next you ended up a corpse."[42] His description of the symptoms of "black fever" was strikingly similar to Scottish physician Andrew Anderson's fanciful description of yellow fever in 1861, in which "a man walking along in health feels as if struck across the back with an iron bar." Anderson described the final stages of yellow fever, in which the patient became jaundiced and exhibited "bilio-gastric symptoms; intense epigastric pain, purging, vomiting, the matter vomited being characteristically 'black,'—altered, decomposed blood."[43]

Montejo's account shows the degree to which enslaved Africans underwent disease outbreaks that were not witnessed by Europeans. Such accounts call into question the notion that Africans had any genetic protection from yellow fever and demonstrate the greater likelihood that they acquired immunities in the late eighteenth and nineteenth centuries as a result of increased exposure to yellow fever. Contemporary medical authorities observed this pattern among Africans and Caribbean natives that they identified as Creoles.

Race and City Creolism in Antebellum New Orleans

Prior to the Louisiana Purchase, the system of racial classification adopted by New Orleanians was similar to the one found in other Caribbean colonies and coastal ports in Mississippi, Alabama, and Florida that had been French or Spanish colonies in the eighteenth century. Residents of the city had multiple identities. Native New Orleanians often identified as "Creoles" and understood race as a malleable category that included "negroes," "mulattoes," "quadroons," "octaroons," and so on. By 1803, most Louisiana natives and Caribbean newcomers emphasized their Creole identity, which functioned as a cultural identity that remained distinct from their racial identity.[44]

Along with the political status of Louisiana, regional conceptions of creolism and race transformed between the colonial period and the mid-nineteenth century. In the mid-eighteenth century, the colonial governments of France and Spain disputed the political and legal status of Louisiana, and for a brief period between 1762 and 1768, after the Seven Years' War, when the French ceded the territory to Spain, it was unclear to which empire it belonged. During the following period of Spanish rule, immigration increased and the population grew rapidly. The sparsely populated Louisiana territory served as a refuge during the Seven Years' War and again during the Haitian Revolution. Despite the official presence of the Spanish Crown in the late eighteenth century, the Francophone population grew during these years. After 1765 thousands of French-speaking Acadians (Cajuns) fled Canada and settled in the bayou country north of New Orleans. Between 1778 and 1780, thousands of Spanish-speaking Isleños migrated from the Canary Islands to southern Louisiana, where they settled in the bayou country downriver from New Orleans.[45] In the wake of the 1791 slave revolt and revolution in Saint-Domingue, more than fifteen thousand refugees came to the southern United States, between 1791 and 1815. Nearly 90 percent of these individuals settled in New Orleans and its vicinity—a migration that more than doubled the city's free population of color.[46] The social composition of the region, and particularly the city of New Orleans, underwent considerable change during those years. By the close of the eighteenth century, the territory was composed of multiple generations of Creoles of French, Spanish, and African descent. In 1804 the city's population exceeded 17,000, with a majority consisting of nearly 6,000 slaves and about 5,000 free people of color, and a minority of roughly 6,300 whites.[47] The city had an unusually high percentage of free and enslaved people of color who were native to the Caribbean, where yellow fever was endemic.

After the Louisiana Purchase in 1803 and the admission of the state of Louisiana to the Union in 1812, thousands of English-speaking American migrants, including planters and slaves, settled in the city and surrounding sugar parishes. Newcomers from the eastern United States challenged and redefined local customs of racial identification. During the years immediately following the acquisition of the Louisiana territory, tensions between Anglo-Americans and Creoles became more pronounced. Public controversies contributed to the increasing anti-Anglo-American sentiment among the French- and Spanish-speaking residents, who united as *l'ancienne population* and identified as Creoles.[48] The city's free population of color, known as the *gens de couleur libre*, also maintained a Creole identity. They sought to distinguish themselves from African American slaves, who arrived in large numbers with Anglo-American planters and served as a substantial portion of the region's labor force. In the 1820s and 1830s, New Orleans emerged as a critical entrepôt in the domestic slave trade. Hundreds of thousands of slaves passed through the city on their way from the eastern United States to plantations in Louisiana, Mississippi, and Alabama.[49]

In the 1840s, newcomers to the region included not only Anglophone planters and slaves from the eastern United States. Several groups of foreign migrants arrived in New Orleans, including a growing number of German, Italian, and Irish immigrants who settled in the city, thousands of undocumented African captives who arrived via Galveston and moved to work on plantations, and a smaller number of indentured laborers from China and South Asia, known as coolies. By this time, communities in New Orleans and the surrounding prairies, marshes, swamps, and bayou country, including plantations in the Mississippi

Delta, had developed a distinctive complex system of cultural and racial identification.

Between 1820 and the Civil War, nearly all residents and visitors to New Orleans described the presence of yellow fever during the "sickly season," which usually fell between July and October. As yellow fever epidemics broke out in New Orleans almost every year between 1817 and 1857, residents grew accustomed to the presence of the disease in the city each summer and "came to regard it as an inevitable fact of life, and they accepted its almost yearly ravages with fatalistic complacency."[50] Residents of New Orleans came to view yellow fever as a "strangers' disease," because the majority of its victims were newcomers, particularly European immigrants and migrants from the eastern United States, who attributed their vulnerability to yellow fever to their status as "strangers." During the late antebellum years, most travelers avoided visiting New Orleans during the summer because of the threat of yellow fever. Further, many affluent New Orleans residents who did not identify as Creoles left the city during the summer to avoid epidemics. In 1850 A. Oakey Hall described the emptiness of the city during the summer: "Juleps and iced ale are in demand until the sunny hours of August, when Yellow Jack comes into town, and the room echoes to the tread of some score or so, whom death nor disease can frighten from the worship of the appetite; or who, secure by acclimation, over their clinking glasses or ice ringing goblets laugh at the passing terrors of the 'grim conqueror.'"[51]

Individuals who had acquired immunity to yellow fever lived in locales where it was prevalent, notably southern port cities in the antebellum United States, including New Orleans, Mobile, Savannah, Charleston, and Galveston. Individuals who remained in these southern port cities during the summer would likely be exposed to the virus, and thus would be more likely to acquire immunity. As shown in chapter 2, by the 1850s the fever spread from cities to hinterland towns and plantations more frequently along with the construction of canals, railroads, and towns in the Lower Mississippi Valley.

Until the mid-1850s, most residents and visitors to antebellum New Orleans believed that Creoles were immune to yellow fever, regardless of their racial or ethnic identity. Most physicians agreed that Creoles and long-term residents of New Orleans seemed to enjoy some degree of immunity, especially compared to newcomers from both Europe and the eastern United States. Many local medical authorities believed that individuals also gained immunity by undergoing a process of "acclimation," "acclimatization," or "seasoning," which current researchers describe as "acquired immunity." Though most antebellum observers maintained that nativity was a factor in yellow fever resistance, many also considered theories of yellow fever immunity based on familiarity with the disease. Since they did not identify most cases of yellow fever among children, many nineteenth-century physicians concluded that acclimation could be attained by long-term residence in the city. This notion resembled perceptions of immunity in the Caribbean colonies and remained unrelated to conceptions of race. Physician P. H. Lewis of Mobile wrote, "Natives, and those who have long resided in Mobile or New Orleans, are equally exempt with those similarly situated in the West Indies."[52]

Local medical authorities debated about whether immunity could be acquired by long-term residence. While some physicians viewed long-term residence as a process of acclimation or seasoning, which led to immunity, others insisted that immunity could be acquired only by surviving the disease. In 1850 Bennet Dowler, who worked as a medical researcher and served as editor of the *New Orleans Medical and Surgical Journal*, argued, "Long urban residence is, in a sanitary sense, an equivalent to nativity, among the people of the city. It is a kind of naturalization, or rather creolization."[53] E. H. Barton believed that although yellow fever was known as "the great acclimating fever," the term "acclimation" was imprecise, and immunity was not a certain result of long-term residence in the city but rather an effect of surviving the disease. He explained, "The term acclimation is very indefinite, so as to apply to records in civil life that can be of any use to the statistician. If it is confined to *yellow fever*, there is no record of it unless the subject falls victim to it, and the cemetery records show the fact that people sometimes die of yellow fever after having been here five, ten, or more years."[54] E. D. Fenner was more ambivalent. He thought "acclimation may be attained without sickness; but that, most generally, it requires the endurance of one or more spells of customary endemic fevers." However, he also noted that "creoles, or natives of New Orleans, may have yellow fever—though generally, they have it in a very mild form."[55]

CHILDHOOD EXPOSURE AND IMMUNITY

Perceptions of Creole immunity and resistance can be explained by considering the number of undocumented cases of yellow fever survivors, including many children. Many adult immigrants died from yellow fever, leaving their surviving children as orphans. In New Orleans, several women established orphanages in response to the increased demand for orphan care during the yellow fever epidemic of 1853.[56] Because epidemics occurred nearly every year during the 1840s and 1850s, most children who resided in the city encountered yellow fever. Thus, most children who remained in New Orleans during an epidemic either died or acquired immunity, while children who left the city during epidemics were less likely to contract the virus. Although most local physicians did not focus on the category of race in their studies of immunity, they often remarked that "creoles" and "negroes" were less susceptible than foreigners.[57]

The issue of varied rates of childhood exposure between different social and economic classes exposes patterns of acquired immunity, which explain the perceived resistance that observers attributed to creolism and race. For example, many affluent residents of New Orleans left the city during the summer if yellow fever appeared or if it was rumored to be present; as a result of their absence during epidemics, their children would have had fewer encounters with the virus. British traveler Alexander Mackay, during his visit to the United States from 1846 to 1847, observed that during epidemics, residents who usually left New Orleans included a large proportion of Anglo-Americans, while "creoles," "negroes," and people of "mixed races," remained in the city:

> The inhabitants of New Orleans may be . . . divided into its resident and its peripatetic population. The former include the creoles—few of whom, being natives to the town, ever leave it; and the negroes, and the mixed races, who have no option but to remain. The latter, the transitory population, are chiefly composed of Anglo-Americans; a small proportion of whom are natives to the city, and the bulk of them abandoning it on the approach of the sickly season. A little more than one-fifth of the whole population thus annually migrate from the town, the

runaways returning as soon as the dangerous period for such as are unacclimated is past.[58]

Mackay's observations explain perceptions of immunity based on city creolism and race, by revealing that Creoles and people of African descent whom he categorized as "negroes" and "mixed races" had a higher chance of being infected with yellow fever and acquiring immunity than white residents. Because children who survived were likely to exhibit only mild symptoms, doctors did not record these cases. Since a large proportion of children who remained in the city during epidemics were nonwhite and native, contemporaries often perceived these groups as being immune to yellow fever.

Residents commonly observed that many children appeared to be immune or exempt from severe symptoms during epidemics. Doctors reported that cases of yellow fever among children were usually mild and that most native children survived and acquired a lifelong immunity to the disease. James Jones, a professor of medicine at the University of Louisiana, argued that immunity could be acquired only by undergoing infection. In 1858 he claimed, "The symptoms in all young children, during our ordinary epidemics, are by no means grave, and among the native are frequently so light and transient as to escape the observation their scientific important demands."[59] Because they did not typically exhibit severe symptoms, physicians failed to recognize these cases as yellow fever and they remained absent from medical records. Also, since yellow fever prevailed in urban New Orleans (owing to the breeding habits of *A. aegypti*), children who lived in remote, rural regions generally did not have as many opportunities to contract the disease until the growth of railroads in the 1850s. When epidemics spread to these areas for the first time, doctors often recorded an "unusual" high number of child victims.[60]

LABOR CONDITIONS AND CLASS DISPARITIES

By the 1830s, Irish and German immigrants comprised the majority of newcomers in New Orleans. More immigrants than Anglo-American migrants settled in the city during th 1840s and 50s. Many worked as servants and laborers, effectively replacing the population of urban slaves. This demographic shift led to a decline in the number of black

New Orleanians after 1840; the black population went from a numerical majority to a minority within a decade.[61] The high percentage of yellow fever victims among the European immigrant population of New Orleans can be attributed to three factors: their status as nonimmunes, their economic condition, and their proximity to mosquitoes. First, since most immigrants came from Europe and had probably never encountered the virus during childhood, they had not had the opportunity to acquire immunity. Second, since most immigrant laborers resided in the city during epidemics, they were more likely to be exposed to yellow fever than residents who left during the summer. Finally, the living and working conditions of immigrants may have contributed to their exposure to infected mosquitoes. Richard Campanella's mapping of New Orleans's ethnic geography shows that many immigrant families lived in recently cleared wetlands that were prone to flooding and attracted mosquitoes. Further, immigrants frequently performed construction-related labor, building and repairing canals and railroads. They often labored in shallow, stagnant water, in close proximity to mosquitoes and maritime vessels that may have been carrying the virus.[62] Additionally, dock workers and others who labored near the waterfront would have been exposed to incoming river traffic, including ships carrying yellow fever.

In fact, several local observers noticed apparent differences in rates of infection based on socioeconomic and labor conditions. While many native New Orleanians believed that the disease was confined to foreigners, elite foreigners believed the disease was confined to immigrant laborers. When Alexis de Tocqueville visited New Orleans in 1832, he asked the French immigrant Etienne Mazureau, who had settled in New Orleans in 1804, "Is it true that yellow fever is as much of a scourge here as supposed?" Mazureau replied, "I think they exaggerate the evil. My experience has taught me that of ten foreigners who live wisely and allow themselves no excesses of any sort, but two die. I am speaking of people who do not have to work with their hands in order to live. Of the same number belonging to the working classes and passing the day in the open air, perhaps seven or eight succumb."[63] Mazureau's perspective demonstrates how popular notions of disease susceptibility echoed medical views that associated yellow fever epidemics with ecological transformations, and susceptibility with temperance. Perceptions of differential rates of infection and immunity resulted from material conditions caused by socioeconomic conditions. Laboring classes had fewer opportunities to leave the city during the summer and were more likely to work in outdoor environments close to stagnant water, especially when employed in land clearing, water management, and railroad construction projects.

In addition, some observers perceived different rates of infection based on gender and saw differential mortality between men and women. Many claimed that women were less vulnerable to yellow fever than men, some attributing the relative lack of female victims to their temperance.[64] Observations of fewer women victims may have been a result of the greater proportion of men who worked in construction. Dr. M. Amic of Martinique believed that "creoles are almost never attacked [by yellow fever]. . . [and] the negroes are never attacked," while "women and children appear to enjoy the greatest immunity." However he witnessed "numerous exceptions . . . to this rule" in 1853. Doctors often expressed surprise when they observed high morbidity and mortality rates among women, just as they did regarding "creoles," "negroes," and children.[65] Massachusetts doctor Elisha Barlett maintained, "It is quite certain that yellow fever destroys very many more males than females," and he reasoned that this was a result of their increased likelihood of being exposed to the disease.[66] Doctors who speculated about differential immunity in regard to gender or sex usually did not emphasize biological differences. Moreover, most contemporaries did not focus on these categories, instead concentrating on creolism, nativity, and, by the mid-nineteenth century, race.

Ideologies of Racial Immunity and Black Resistance

During the 1850s, many medical professionals in New Orleans abandoned previous notions of Creole immunity or acclimation and emphasized race as a factor in determining yellow fever resistance. The widespread acceptance of race-based ideologies of immunity was grounded in the misinterpretation of observational data, resulting from the pervasiveness of racial thought among scientists in the antebellum United States. This perception can be understood by considering the impacts of local, regional, and global processes on patterns of acquired immunity, such as immunological changes caused by the growth of endemic yellow fever in coastal West Africa, the Caribbean, and the Gulf of Mexico and demographic changes resulting from increased immigration from Europe to North America. These processes contributed to the pervasive notion that, compared to people of European descent, people of African descent had some sort of innate resistance to yellow fever. This idea became increasingly common during the 1850s, owing to escalating racial tensions in the American South and in European colonial territories. In New Orleans, racial tensions were rooted in political conflicts surrounding slavery and its expansion. Racialized views of immunity gained widespread acceptance after the devastating epidemic of 1853. Despite evidence of African and African American victims, doctors consistently noted that yellow fever was less severe among people of African descent.[67]

The simultaneous processes of the rise of endemic yellow fever in coastal West Africa and the growth of western European immigration to the United States led contemporary naturalists and trained medical practitioners to notice that individuals whom they identified as "colored" suffered lower morbidity and mortality rates than those whom they classified as "white." By the mid-nineteenth century, yellow fever had become seasonally endemic in New Orleans and endemic in major port cities in the Caribbean and West Africa. As explained in chapter 1, yellow fever epidemics escalated in West Africa after 1820 and by the mid-nineteenth century had become common along much of the West and West Central African coast. By the 1850s there were frequent epidemics in cities in the Ascension and the Cape Verde Islands, and by the 1860s epidemics were frequently reported in Senegal, Gambia, Guinea, Sierra Leone, the Gold and Ivory Coasts, Benin, and Angola.[68] By this time nearly all Africans who came to the Americas, and all people of African descent native to the Caribbean and the Gulf Coast, would likely have been exposed to yellow fever as a result of spending time in endemic zones, often as youths. In tandem with this process, changing conditions in Europe in the mid-nineteenth century led to an unprecedented increase in immigration to North America during the 1840s and 1850s. Population growth, combined with famine because of crop failures and the Irish potato blight, along with revolutionary political movements of 1848, resulted in the immigration of hundreds of thousands of Europeans to New Orleans. The majority of immigrants came from Ireland and Germany, and they made up the vast majority of yellow fever victims.[69] As a result of these dual processes, by 1853 yellow fever seemed to attack whites more than people of color.

The epidemic of 1853 presents an expository case for examining shifting views of immunity in connection to the growth of racial tensions, as physicians emphasized race over factors such as creolism, nativity, and residence. Because of the regularity of yellow fever epidemics in New Orleans during the first half of the nineteenth century, presumably most residents had been exposed to the disease, except for European immigrants and residents who vacated the city during the summers. The city's population doubled between 1830 and 1840. In the following decade, the proportion of foreign-born whites in the population rose to 40 percent. The population of New Orleans in 1850 has been estimated at between 119,000 and 130,000. In 1851 alone, more than 52,000 immigrants arrived in New Orleans; between 1850 and 1854, more than 160,000 immigrants arrived, primarily from Ireland and Germany.[70] European immigrants formed slightly less than half of the city's population in 1853, yet they accounted for 90 percent of the recorded yellow fever deaths. Irish and German immigrants constituted the majority of yellow fever victims during the epidemic, accounting for nearly six thousand out of more than eight thousand reported deaths.[71] Though fewer in number, immigrants from Holland, Belgium, Austria, and Switzerland died in a greater proportion than any other migrant group.[72] In statistical analyses, authorities consistently classified these groups as white.

Scholars including Ari Kelman and Jo Ann Carrigan have examined the connection between racial tensions (manifested in whites' anxiety and fear of slave revolts) and ideologies of race-based yellow fever immunity, particularly during the epidemic of 1853. Kelman's research reveals a link between the epidemic and the rumored slave insurrection that prompted city officials to send out local militia to patrol the streets and "demand that free and enslaved people of color not be allowed to walk the streets after dark, that businesses ('Negro groggeries') serving alcohol to *gens de couleur libres* be shuttered immediately, and that all slaves with reputations for violence or even insolence be locked up."[73] Kelman questions the existence of genetic resistance among African Americans and considers the visual symptoms of the disease in relation to the construction of racial identities. He argues that "in a city like New Orleans, whose complicated racial categories had more in common with parts of Latin America—where subtle shades of color mattered far more than in the typically biracial United States—jaundice thus not only trumpeted a person's grave illness, but also raised questions about the malleability of a victim's race."[74]

In contrast to Kelman's position, Carrigan accepts the notion of race-based immunity and argues that blacks were less susceptible to yellow fever than whites, though not necessarily "immune." Citing Kenneth Kiple, she contends that, "as the widespread epidemics of the 1850s clearly demonstrated, blacks were not immune to yellow fever, but they usually presented mild symptoms, and relatively few died of the disease."[75] In her analysis, she shows how various groups interpreted black yellow fever resistance, arguing that some northern abolitionists viewed black resistance as a "penalty or punishment" to southern slaveholders, who in turn "contended that the relative immunity of blacks from the ravages of the fever provided a strong argument in favor of slavery."[76] Carrigan further speculates that "blacks must also have observed their apparent resistance to the disease," since "blacks were sometimes employed as nurses and gravediggers during epidemics because of their presumed immunity."[77] While her analysis reveals the implications of contemporary perceptions of race-based immunity, it fails to include a critical assessment of the professional acceptance of a racialized view of resistance.

Carrigan is critical of the existence of Creole immunity, yet she accepts the notion that blacks were less susceptible to yellow fever. Under the subheading "The Myth of Creole Immunity," she considers the role of childhood exposure as an explanation for local beliefs in Creole immunity. However in her analysis of race-based immunity, she uncritically states that "yellow fever in children, as well as in blacks, was usually mild and rarely fatal" and concludes that "persons of African ancestry, in striking contrast to whites, historically have exhibited some innate resistance to the lethal effects of yellow fever—not absolute immunity but some defensive mechanism than enhances survival."[78] Carrigan's stance is representative of many studies of the antebellum South. Since historians agree that Creoles clearly constituted a socially and culturally constructed category, they commonly question the legitimacy of the contemporary belief in Creole immunity. However, many scholars fail to challenge contemporary ideas about racial immunity. Even those who question the notion of race-based immunity are open to the possibility that people of African descent may have experienced milder symptoms than whites and were more likely to survive.[79]

After the epidemic of 1853, many physicians in New Orleans noticed an apparent increase in Creole and nonwhite victims, and some began to question previously held notions of acclimation and immunity. However, they maintained a racialized view of resistance, dependent on an individual's degree of African ancestry. Fenner, in his report on the epidemic of 1853, observed that the epidemic attacked a large number of "creoles or natives" and "negroes" and noted, "One of the extraordinary features of this epidemic is presented in the fact that natives of the city, both white and colored, have suffered severely, and many of them died from it." He also remarked, "This epidemic affected unacclimated negroes, of those who had never had Yellow Fever before, equally as generally as it did the white population, though not so severely."[80] His conclusions reveal his preoccupation with race as an explanatory factor in determining mortality, as he claimed, "Black vomit and other hemorrhages rarely occur amongst full-blooded negroes, though I have heard of a number of cases this year, and had one myself. Mulattoes and Quadroons are almost as liable to them as white people, and quite a number have died of hemorrhages this year. This difference between the Black and Mulatto must proceed from the mixture of races."[81] This sentiment was echoed in popular and medical depictions of yellow fever immunity that appeared from the 1850s through the turn of the century, as racial tensions escalated during the Civil War and the postwar era.

IMAGINING IMMUNITY AS EVIDENCE OF RACIAL DIFFERENCE

By the mid-nineteenth century, many doctors in New Orleans concluded that immunity was tied to race. In the Gulf South, and in colonial territories throughout the world, the nineteenth century marked a period of hardening notions of racial difference, supported by the growth of scientific racism. In New Orleans, a shift in ideologies of immunity reflected the growth of racial tensions that stemmed from political conflicts about the expansion of slavery in the 1850s. The development of ideas about race-based immunity to "tropical diseases" among physicians in New Orleans paralleled the growth of similar notions in the colonial Caribbean, Latin America, and British India. In fact, medical authorities considered their observations of racial immunity as evidence of racial difference. The hardening of racial dichotomies between whites and people of color in New Orleans corresponded to the intensification of racist ideologies in colonial contexts, as universalist ideas about the potential for the human body to acclimate were replaced by a belief in innate racial differences that separated the human species.

In the late eighteenth and the nineteenth centuries, colonial medical authorities identified yellow fever and malaria as diseases of "warm climates," and many considered these climates to be particularly unhealthful for "European constitutions." Numerous European medical authorities commented that Africans were not likely to contract malaria and yellow fever, which they associated with tropical environments. As physicians declared that Africans were immune to these fevers, planters used the idea to justify the use of African laborers on plantations throughout the Atlantic, the Caribbean, and the Gulf of Mexico. By the mid-nineteenth century, in colonial regions of the Atlantic, as well as in the antebellum South, medical writers and practicing physicians often made arguments supporting plantation slavery. They reasoned that since Africans were indigenous to semitropical and tropical zones, people of African descent could live and work comfortably in warm climates.[82]

During the mid-nineteenth century, ideas about immunity became increasingly connected with ideas about racial difference. Many scholars have shown the roots of nineteenth-century racial thought in the context of the European Enlightenment and the Scientific Revolution of the eighteenth century. Those concepts of race arose from the ideas of natural classification put forth by philosophers and scientists, including Charles de Secondat, baron de Montesquieu, Carl Linnaeus, Johann Friedrich Blumenbach, and Georges Cuvier, the latter described by Clifton Crais and Pamela Scully as "Europe's most revered scientist and the father of comparative anatomy."[83] Linnaeus, Blumenbach, and Cuvier applied Linnaean scientific classification systems to humans, emphasizing physical characteristics as markers of different racial types.[84] Cuvier famously dissected the body of Sara Baartman, a Khoikhoi woman whose body fascinated numerous European racial theorists, including Robert Knox and Joseph Arthur, Comte de Gobineau.[85] By the mid-nineteenth century, scientists in the United States and Britain utilized theories of racial inferiority to legitimate power structures, ranging from systems of slavery to colonial rule. Scientific and medical research, rooted in philosophies of racial types, connected the development of ideologies of racial difference held by naturalists and doctors based in Europe, in European colonies, and in the United States.

One of the most prominent racial theorists in the Gulf South region was Samuel Cartwright, who practiced medicine in Natchez and New Orleans. In 1851 he was appointed chairman of a committee of the Medical Association of Louisiana, which was "to report on diseases of the negro." Cartwright is perhaps most infamous for his theory of drapetomania, which he described as "the disease causing Negroes to run away."[86] Cartwright consistently cited Enlightenment thinkers in support of his views of racial difference. He claimed that many European scientists, including Blumenbach and Cuvier, "demonstrated, by dissections, so great a difference in the organization of the negro from that of the white man, as to induce the majority of naturalists to refer to him as a different species."[87] In his assessment of the unusually high numbers of black victims that he witnessed in the epidemic of 1853, Cartwright reasoned, "A number of the prognathous race died in the epidemic of New Orleans, 1853, more from panic, it is believed, than from the yellow fever of that year. Experience and observation prove that panic is very apt to kill a negro, but it is questionable whether the yellow fever *per se* has that power." He believed racial characteristics extended beyond physical and anatomical differences, arguing, "Science proves that the moral and intellectual diversities between the prognathous and Indo-European races, are actually greater than their physical."[88]

Josiah Nott was another prominent local doctor and racial theorist. In addition to researching the causes of yellow fever, Nott wrote extensively about ethnology and racial differences. A professor of anatomy at the University of Louisiana from 1857 to 1858, he combined his research on anatomical differences (including bones and physiognomy) with his readings of religious and historical texts and promoted his theories about racial inferiority to justify the enslavement of African Americans.[89] Nott was part of a larger group of doctors and naturalists who published broadly on racial difference and promoted theories of polygenism as evidence of fixed racial types.[90] Nott believed that Africans belonged in the tropics: "The black man was placed in Tropical Africa, because he was suited to this climate and no other." He emphasized the inability of humans to adapt (or acclimate) to different climates owing to their race, citing statistics indicating that blacks in Louisiana were healthier than blacks in the North. He described a process of racial degeneration among blacks in Massachusetts and Maine, claiming that both states had a higher proportion of individuals that he characterized as "insane" and "idiots" than Louisiana had. He believed that this difference was a result of the northern climate and the large population of "mulattoes," whom he called "hybrids," in northern cities.[91] Nott's views of race are also apparent in his studies of yellow fever. Despite his observations of yellow fever "attacking whites and blacks indiscriminately" during the epidemic of 1853, he argued that "negroes and mulattoes are exempt in a surprising degree from yellow fever." He further theorized that "the smallest admixture of negro blood, as in the Quarteroon or Quinteroon, is a great, though not absolute, protection against yellow fever." In a study on "the comparative influence of climate, endemic, and epidemic diseases on the races of man," he concluded, "I hazard nothing in the assertion, that one-fourth negro blood is a more perfect protection against yellow fever, than is vaccine against small-pox."[92] Thus, Nott and other proponents of theories that emphasized innate racial types used the notion of race-based immunity as proof of biological difference.

Connections between ideas about race among naturalists in the southern United States and Europe are evident in the work of the Swiss-born biologist Louis Agassiz, a student of George Cuvier, who began serving as professor of geology at Harvard University in 1847. While in the United States, he associated with American racial theorists, including Josiah Nott, George Gliddon, and Samuel Morton.[93] He wrote an introduction to Nott and Gliddon's *Types of Mankind* that supported polygenesist views of racial difference.[94] In 1850 Agassiz commissioned some of the earliest known photographs of slaves, on a South Carolina plantation. His work had two primary aims: "to analyze the physical differences between European whites and African blacks, [and] . . . to prove the superiority of the white race."[95] During the Civil War, he traveled to Brazil, where he took similar racialized photographs of Brazilians, attempting to categorize the diverse populations of Brazil into racial types.[96]

In the British colonies, a similar transition in medical views about acclimation and immunity occurred, simultaneously with its unfolding in the American South. Mark Harrison, in his analysis of British India and the Caribbean, has argued that between 1760 and 1860 ideas about acclimatization declined among British colonial medical authorities:

> Shifting power relationships in the colonies, together with new intellectual currents emanating from the metropole, wrought a profound change in the way Europeans came to see their bodies in relation to their subjects and the tropical environment. Anxieties created by the abolition of the slave trade, together with the hubris generated by the British conquest of India, focused medical attention more closely on apparent differences between the races. The guarded optimism about acclimatization that was characteristic of the eighteenth-century Enlightenment diminished as the perceived boundaries between races began to harden. Europeans came to regard themselves as exotica in foreign soil: feelings of superiority and vulnerability were two sides of the same imperial coin.[97]

This intellectual transformation mirrors the gradual abandonment of theories of Creole immunity and the professional acceptance of ideas of race-based immunity in New Orleans. Political tensions and tensions of empire influenced scientific theories of racial difference, which in turn shaped attitudes about disease, immunity, and climate. Shifting views of race in Louisiana paralleled the solidifying of ideas about racial difference in British colonial territories in the Caribbean and India, which developed alongside midcentury struggles surrounding the maintenance of colonial rule and the consolidation of empire. This process also corresponded to the growth of US imperialism, as the nation expanded westward into Mexico, California, and the Pacific Northwest.

Common threads in racial thought between medical authorities in colonial India, the colonial Caribbean, Brazil, and the American South demonstrate a global pattern in attitudes toward race in the emergent field of professional medicine. These intellectual currents were tied to escalating tensions over maintaining control over a racialized population, which peaked in the mid-nineteenth century. In South Asia, after the Indian Rebellion of 1857, the British Crown consolidated power across the region and ruled as the British Raj. In the mid-nineteenth century American South and British Caribbean, conflicts over slavery culminated in the American Civil War and gradual abolition in the islands.

In New Orleans, shifting ideas about racial immunity to yellow fever reflected the transforming social and political climate. In the period between 1817 and the Civil War, as yellow fever became increasingly common in the New Orleans, ideologies of Creole immunity, seasoning, and acclimation revealed the growth of tensions between native New Orleanians and newcomers from the eastern United States and Europe. During the period between 1850 and the Civil War, ideologies of race-based immunity reflected sectional and racial tensions. Racial conflicts grew during the Civil War and intensified during Reconstruction, as yellow fever spread deeper through the Lower Mississippi Valley.

4

Reconstituting the South

BUILT ENVIRONMENTS AND PUBLIC
HEALTH, 1861–1878

During the American Civil War, yellow fever failed to cause major epidemics in New Orleans, which was captured and occupied by federal troops beginning in the spring of 1862. After the war, yellow fever epidemics appeared with less frequency than in the antebellum years. Between 1865 and 1877, during the period of Union occupation known as Reconstruction, the city experienced only one major epidemic, in 1867. Minor outbreaks occurred in 1870 and 1873. The Civil War and the Reconstruction era in Louisiana and the Lower Mississippi Valley marked a period of structural changes to local political institutions and social systems, resulting from the abolition of slavery and military government. In addition, the region's environment underwent a period of physical reconstruction, as its residents adjusted and adopted new cultural attitudes about the environment, disease, and race.

Across the nation, the growth of modern medical institutions and the "Bacteriological Revolution" began after the Civil War and continued through the Reconstruction era. The widespread acceptance of medical knowledge about the deleterious impacts of microscopic bacteria shaped public health debates and practices during this period. As New Orleans rebuilt its civic infrastructure, the topic of yellow fever dominated medical research and public health reforms, which mandated antibacterial disinfection and quarantine to mitigate the threat of epidemics. Yellow fever was infrequent because of numerous factors, in addition to the enforcement of sanitation and quarantine. The demise of slavery and the illegal slave trade, the slowing of sugar production, economic stagnation, and a decline in immigration contributed to the prevention of severe epidemics.

In the summer of 1878, one year after federal troops left New

Orleans, the city experienced its worst yellow fever epidemic since 1853. It spread throughout the Mississippi Valley to hundreds of plantations, towns, and stations that had not previously confronted the disease. The severity and scope of the epidemic of 1878 can be attributed to ecological changes that enabled the growth of a large *A. aegypti* population in the Mississippi Valley and facilitated the spread of the yellow fever virus.

In the Gulf South, Reconstruction was more than a series of political reforms. Federal and private investors sought to rebuild the southern economy by funding numerous environmental engineering projects, aimed to expand commercial networks and integrate remote towns with major trade centers, especially New Orleans. These projects included the extension of land clearance and swamp drainage projects in lower Louisiana, large-scale engineering at the mouth of the Mississippi, and the construction and reconstruction of rail lines throughout the Lower Mississippi Valley. They constituted a substantive transformation of the region's built environment and enabled a series of demographic changes, as railroads facilitated postwar migrations and the flight of refugees during epidemics. Combined, these factors enabled the epidemic in New Orleans to spread through the region.

The Health of the City during the War

Historians frequently note that more soldiers died from disease than in combat during the American Civil War. Infectious diseases, including dysentery, pneumonia, and malaria, caused the largest number of deaths among soldiers, followed by smallpox, measles, and tuberculosis.[1] Recently, scholars have emphasized the role of disease in shaping military strategies and outcomes.[2] The Civil War and the Reconstruction era were a seminal period in the transition to modern medicine in the United States, marked by the professional and popular acceptance of public health and sanitation efforts.

Despite the prevalence of numerous diseases during the war, yellow fever did not spread in New Orleans. Although the city suffered from epidemics nearly every year since 1840, the disease was virtually absent between 1859 and the close of the war. Louisiana seceded from the United States in 1861, and by May of 1862 Union forces, led by David G. Farragut, had captured the city. Until the end of the war in 1866, federal troops occupied New Orleans and controlled access to the waterfront. Under the direction of Benjamin Butler, federal forces rigorously enforced sanitation and quarantine policies.

During these years of warfare and federal occupation, many residents speculated that Union forces would succumb to yellow fever when the "sickly season" began that summer.[3] Union officers and troops feared the fever, while Confederate natives of New Orleans expressed their desire for yellow fever to massacre the Union Army. According to numerous diaries and memoirs, many white residents "prayed that the fever would deliver the city from Union hands." Locals, including Irish immigrants, women, and children, taunted soldiers on the streets, confident that "Yellow Jack [would] grab them up and take them all away."[4] Confederate allies across the southern states also expressed this hope. A Virginia newspaper remarked that the Union would lose its control over New Orleans "if his Saffron Majesty shall make his usual annual visit to the city and wave his scepter in the hospitals there."[5]

Thus the war marked a brief shift in popular perceptions of immunity, as supporters of the Confederacy focused on the differences between bodies native to the North and the South, which they sometimes connected to climatic and environmental factors.[6] They believed that yellow fever would strike the city's Yankee occupiers, while they themselves would remain safe. White New Orleanians emphasized differences between themselves and Union soldiers, rather than focusing on the racial differences that had dominated discourses on immunity in the late 1850s. This ideology resembled notions of Creole immunity that had characterized popular beliefs about yellow fever immunity in the antebellum era. In May of 1862, Clara Solomon, a teenaged native of New Orleans, expressed in her diary her desire for a yellow fever epidemic. She believed that the fever's "appetite will be whetted by abstinence, & how many subjects will he fix upon. Why N.O. won't be large enough to bury them. . . . Already some have died from the effects of the sun! How can they stand it in the days to come!"[7] Her entry demonstrates an intimate understanding of epidemic patterns, as she observed that epidemics were more severe when the city had remained free from yellow fever for several years. Yellow fever failed to appear in New Orleans that summer, but the following year residents still believed that it posed a serious threat to the Union Army.

Union officers anticipated the threat of yellow fever in Louisiana and considered the region to be a "hostile environment."[8] Like local residents, they also believed that Union troops were more susceptible to yellow fever than natives. Captain Charles Boothby, while stationed in New Orleans, remarked that locals pointed to "ominous signs" and predicted an epidemic every season. However, he believed that Union officers had taken the necessary precautions to prevent the spread of the disease.[9] Further, many of the officers who led the invasion and occupation of New Orleans, including David Farragut, were yellow fever survivors and were not in danger of contracting the disease again.[10] In 1863 yellow fever appeared on a Union vessel anchored at New Orleans, causing more than one hundred cases; however, the fleet was quarantined and the fever did not spread from the port.[11]

Union troops in New Orleans not only feared the threat of yellow fever; they also sought to avoid contact with mosquitoes. Northern newspapers recommended that soldiers should take measures to protect themselves by using "musquito shields," "guards," or "bars."[12] Boothby wrote to his sister in Maine, "Do you know what a mosquito bar is? Well, it is an indispensable institution here." Boothby described the hooks and netting that he used to cover his bed, to prevent mosquitoes from entering during the night.[13] Although they did not associate them with fever, visitors and residents in New Orleans continually commented on the nuisance of mosquitoes and described their prevalence in the city.[14] Meanwhile, Clara Solomon, an enthusiastic supporter of the Confederacy, wrote that she "endeavored to kill as few mosquitoes as possible. For two reasons, the first being that we should be polluted by being touched by 'Yankee blood,' & secondly each one increases the number and aids in biting and tormenting them. I wonder how they like them!"[15]

Despite the presence of mosquitoes and nonimmune Union soldiers in the city, yellow fever failed to cause an epidemic, as many observers had predicted. The absence of epidemics in New Orleans during Reconstruction had enduring political and epidemiological consequences. It led to increased confidence in the efficacy of public health enforcement among local medical authorities and raised questions about the relative costs and benefits of disinfection and quarantine. Additionally, the absence of epidemics for more than seven years resulted in a lack of immunity among local children and newcomers, which ensured high death rates among these groups during the city's first postwar epidemic, in 1867.

Yellow Fever in Postwar New Orleans

Yellow fever reappeared in New Orleans at the close of the war as local businesses resumed their trade relations with Caribbean merchants, which allowed port traffic to and from cities where yellow fever was endemic. When local public health authorities regained control of the waterfront in the spring of 1866, they ignored the quarantine and sanitary regulations that Union soldiers had practiced regularly during the war. That summer, almost 200 fatalities were reported. The following year, a severe epidemic in New Orleans resulted in more than 3,300 deaths, including 200 Union soldiers. The fever spread to Memphis and several small towns in Louisiana, including New Iberia, St. Martinville, Lafayette, Opelousas, Washington, Alexandria, and Shreveport.[16]

The prevention of yellow fever epidemics dominated concerns and disputes over public health throughout the Reconstruction era. Several cases were reported in New Orleans each summer. Usually fewer than 100 deaths were reported each year, except during the outbreaks in 1870 and 1873, in which several hundred people died. In 1873 Shreveport suffered its most severe epidemic, with more than 750 deaths, while the disease claimed 226 lives in New Orleans. Throughout this period, officials reported cases of yellow fever at the port, usually onboard trade vessels from Caribbean cities, most commonly from Cuba (Havana and Matanzas). Although the opening of the port of New Orleans after the Civil War occasionally introduced the virus, the city enjoyed a long respite from major epidemics between 1867 and 1878.[17]

THE POSTWAR BACTERIOLOGICAL REVOLUTION

The Civil War marked a critical transition in medical knowledge and practice in the United States, as physicians focused on bacteriological research, institutional development, and public health policy. Though yellow fever did not pose a threat to soldiers during the war, the prevalence of other diseases had a profound effect on the army. In addition to infectious diseases such as diarrhea, dysentery, pneumonia, smallpox, measles, and tuberculosis, many wounded soldiers suffered from bacteriological infections, such as gangrene, because army doctors were not trained to disinfect their wounds. Physicians did not use antiseptics during the war, and it was not until the late 1860s that they recognized the existence of bacteria.[18]

Bacteriology, or germ theory, gained widespread acceptance among medical professionals in Europe and the United States in the 1870s, after the pioneering laboratory work of several European researchers, including Louis Pasteur, Robert Koch, John Tyndall, Joseph Lister, and others. Their investigations proved the existence of bacteria and demonstrated the role of bacteria as agents of disease, using microscopic examinations, test tube cultures, and animal experiments.[19] The Bacteriological Revolution in the United States began after the Civil War and had a significant impact on public health in the South during Reconstruction. Like their northern counterparts, medical authorities in southern states grew increasingly interested in bacteriology during the postwar era. However, southern doctors did not abandon their intellectual commitment to studying links between health, disease, and environmental conditions. Rather, they supplemented their broad views of disease ecology with ideas about microscopic disease-causing agents. Doctors expressed their support for microbiotic explanations of disease outbreaks, using the rhetoric of sanitation, cleanliness, and filth, as they had prior to the war and the rise of bacteriology. Deeply held ideas about the virtues of cleanliness and the dangers of filth led to widespread support for antibacterial disinfection, which local public health officials described as "cleansing."

PUBLIC HEALTH DEBATES

By the close of the war, arguments about the relative effectiveness of sanitation versus quarantine dominated public health debates. Many public health officials attributed the absence of epidemics during the war to policies enforced by the Union Army, which a local physician described as "the official usages and the armed discipline of the naval fleet in the harbor of New Orleans and up the river."[20] While nearly all medical authorities agreed that the systematic enforcement of public health procedures by the US military had prevented yellow fever epidemics, they disagreed about the effectiveness of disinfection requirements versus quarantine regulations. Many local elites, expressing concern for the commercial interests of the city, opposed the strict use of quarantine. Disinfection practices could be completed quickly and, unlike ten-day quarantine restrictions, did not significantly interfere with trade at the port. Thus, many local medical authorities argued that the enforcement of sanitary practices had saved the city from yellow fever, while a few insisted that the military's strict enforcement of quarantine had protected the city during those turbulent years.

Local physician E. D. Fenner believed that the absence of epidemic yellow fever during Reconstruction could be attributed to the "superior virtues of the local sanitary police." He argued that quarantine regulations during the war had not been strictly enforced and had not prevented yellow fever from entering the city. He personally witnessed several cases, noting that although yellow fever was present in the city, it had failed to cause an epidemic among soldiers and civilians. Fenner concluded that sanitary measures had prevented the fever from spreading from the waterfront into the city and that in the future, the city could remain free from yellow fever if officials continued to enforce the sanitary practices that were implemented during military occupation. He compared yellow fever in New Orleans to the plague in Cairo, likening the military campaigns of Union generals to the military programs initiated by Ottoman commander Mehmet Ali Pasha after he seized power in Egypt. He reminisced, "For all that precedes, it would appear that General Butler and Banks have done for New Orleans what the tyrant Mehemed Ali did for Cairo, and we may yet have occasion to mingle some thanks among the many curses that have been heaped upon their heads for their unnecessary severity upon the citizens of New Orleans."[21]

Another local physician, U. R. Milner, expressed more extreme views on the effectiveness of sanitation and the uselessness of quarantine during the war. Milner promoted local governance and opposed federal intervention in local affairs. In the aftermath of the Union occupation, his views reflected a common political view among local elites. His rhetoric demonstrates how officials used anxieties about outbreaks to centralize power by controlling public health policy: "The institution of quarantine originated in ignorance and fear, and became cemented by the love of power and personal aggrandizement, just as other pernicious political rings have been cemented and held together as heir-looms to be transferred to successors in a round of office, ostensibly for the public good, but, in fact, for the love of the paraphernalia of the office. It soon created the popular sentiment that the yellow fever is imported and contagious."[22]

In this view Milner is representative of many elite medical professionals who supported disinfection and opposed quarantine. Typically, physicians who believed that yellow fever was endemic to the Caribbean and imported to New Orleans each summer supported quarantine in addition to disinfection. Doctors who were opposed to quarantine argued that yellow fever was endemic to the Gulf Coast, that it was not contagious from person to person, and that therefore quarantine did not prevent epidemics. Milner argued that yellow fever was occasionally endemic and not contagious and could be abated by "extraordinary cleanliness." He praised the sanitary regime of Union officers and described how "scavengering [sic] and domiciliary hygiene, privies and garbage, stables and butcheries, damp and unventilated quarters, and the haunts of vice and debauchery, were all brought under police control." He concluded that "the relentless rigor and precision of a military government precluded the ordinary violations of quarantine regulations, while it gave peculiar certainty to the execution of sanitary regulations in the city."[23] His views reflected the commercial and political interests of local authorities by promoting a system of increased police intervention that would not disturb trade and commerce.

Though they had not identified the source of yellow fever, Union officers enforced measures that inadvertently decreased the threat of epidemics as well as bacteriological diseases, including cholera and typhoid fever. Although chemical disinfectants and cleansers did not affect the yellow fever virus, they helped to repel and kill *A. aegypti* mosquitoes and their eggs. The primary method of disinfection was the cleansing of ships, roads, and homes with coal tar acids (phenols, including carbolic acid), which killed bacteria and repelled mosquitoes, especially when used excessively.[24] Burning sulfur killed mosquitoes, while the disinfection of streets, gutters, and other receptacles of still water with coal tar acids destroyed their eggs.[25] Union-enforced quarantine regulations also helped to prevent yellow fever from spreading beyond the waterfront. Policies that focused on Caribbean vessels, while allowing a more lax quarantine for vessels arriving from North American ports, detained vessels that may have introduced infected persons or mosquitoes to the city. For example, Butler's quarantine policy directed officers to detain vessels that might be infected with yellow fever for forty days. He was particularly concerned about Spanish ships arriving from Cuba.[26] If these ships carried mosquitoes that had been infected with yellow fever in Havana, they would not have been able to infect humans after a period of ten to fourteen days. However, if the mosquitoes left the ship and entered the city, they could still transmit yellow fever to residents, particularly those who lived or worked near the waterfront. Passengers who carried yellow fever were infectious only for five to seven days, so even a brief quarantine would allow them to enter the city without posing a risk. As a result of the short incubation time of yellow fever, the rigorous enforcement of quarantine policy effectively prevented the introduction of infectious hosts. Because public health authorities did not enforce these practices in New Orleans before the war, they were not effective in preventing epidemics.

While some federal officials recommended the continued use of quarantine as a way of preventing the entry of yellow fever into the city, local public health authorities did not effectively monitor or enforce these procedures. In 1866 Congress authorized the use of federal public health officials for quarantine duty but could not fund the project. In 1872 Assistant Surgeon General Harvey E. Brown addressed commercial interests in his report on the state of quarantine in the South, arguing that a "properly-organized system of quarantine" would not interfere with the "interests of commerce" and instead would "prove really beneficial to the commercial prosperity of the ports where established." He criticized the efficacy of local and state quarantines in the South, arguing that they "lack in uniformity which is absolutely necessary to their efficiency, are not founded on rational views of the pathology of disease, and are generally defective in their administration."[27]

Despite federal recommendations, local medical authorities continued to loosen quarantine regulations, claiming that yellow fever had not caused a major epidemic in the city since 1867 because of the effectiveness of disinfection practices. Physicians and civic public health authorities promoted antibacterial sanitation practices, particularly the burning of sulfur and disinfection using carbolic acid, which Lister had successfully shown could be used as a postsurgical antiseptic spray and wound dressing in 1867.[28] In 1873 C. B. White, a local physician and the president of the Louisiana State Board of Health, described how the "energetic, systematic, and unsparing use of disinfectants began" when cases of yellow fever appeared on a vessel arriving from Havana. Roadways in New Orleans were "liberally sprinkled with crude carbolic acid by street sprinklers."[29] Samuel Choppin, who served as president of the State Board of Health from 1877 to 1880, championed germ theory during the late 1870s and attempted to "stamp out the disease by the profuse irrigation of the streets . . . with carbolic acid."[30] In 1876 White argued that "favorable results of quarantine may with fairness be attributed to the measures of disinfection practiced." The same year, G. W. R. Bayley, another member of the State Board of Health, who also served on the Chamber of Commerce of New Orleans, argued that "as a consequence of the successful sanitary results of disinfection, . . . quarantine restrictions upon commerce could, with safety to the public health, be now essentially modified." Following his appeal, the Chamber of Commerce and the Board of Health agreed that quarantine detention would be "reduced to merely that required for disinfection."[31]

Although medical researchers could not find the microscopic pathogen that caused yellow fever, they were aware of the general deadly effects of antibacterial cleansers. In 1875 local physician S. S. Herrick reported, "Testimony has been for years accumulating to the conclusion that [yellow fever] may be arrested and extinguished in infected localities by the use of agents destructive to low forms of life."[32] Many contemporary experts believed that sanitary policies helped to quell the threat of disease by cleansing areas of filth and unspecified germs. Though public health officials did not target mosquitoes, sanitary practices aimed at destroying "low forms of life" caused the destruction of adult mosquitoes and larvae throughout the city.

However, antibacterial disinfectants had no impact on the yellow fever virus. The lack of strict quarantine enforcement during epidemics enabled yellow fever to occasionally spread from the waterfront; however, since epidemics were not as severe as those of the 1850s, medical authorities that opposed quarantine viewed disinfection as a success. But public health measures were not solely responsible for preventing major epidemics. Combined with the effective end of the West African and Caribbean slave trade, a hiatus in sugar production, and the interruption of trade and immigration, which prevented the virus from appearing regularly via infected passengers and mosquitoes, public health policies aided in the suppression of epidemics in New Orleans during the Civil War and the Reconstruction era.

THE DECLINE OF SLAVERY, SUGAR, IMMIGRATION, AND YELLOW FEVER

In addition to the mitigating effects of disinfection and quarantine, the absence of severe yellow fever epidemics in Louisiana during Reconstruction is closely connected to the end of the illegal slave trade, the drop in sugar production (and the subsequent reduction in commercial activity at the port of New Orleans), and a substantial decline in European immigration. The decline of commerce and the halting of rapid growth essentially prevented the virus from repeatedly entering the city during the summer.

After the federal ban on the foreign slave trade in 1808, New Orleans emerged as a prominent center of the domestic slave trade. Despite its illegal status, the foreign trade in African and Caribbean captives continued through the antebellum era. Slaves often passed through New Orleans, and traders hid illegal slaves in secluded regions of southern Louisiana. During the 1840s and 1850s, most foreign slaves came through Texas.[33] During these years, epidemic yellow fever appeared for the first time in Galveston, where outbreaks continued through the Civil War and Reconstruction.[34] In the postwar era, the abolition of slavery in the United States resulted in the termination of the foreign slave trade. The abolition of slavery and the end of the illegal slave trade prevented the virus from entering the region by way of infected captives and mosquitoes on undocumented ships that came from regions where yellow fever was present.

The disintegration of Louisiana's sugar industry, and the impact of that shift on trade and commerce in New Orleans, may have also contributed to the decline of yellow fever epidemics during this period. During the war, the region effectively stopped producing sugar. Production dropped significantly in the immediate aftermath of the war, which "marked the end of a period of steady growth for the Louisiana sugar industry."[35] This decline can be attributed to the political and economic consequences of the Civil War and Reconstruction, as well as to global

changes in sugar production, including the rise of the beet sugar industry in Europe and California and the growth of industrial sugarcane
production in Cuba, Brazil, and Hawaii.[36] In New Orleans, the decline
in sugar production led to severe economic stagnation. Sugar had been
the region's most profitable export before the war, peaking in 1861 at
264,000 tons. Production reached one of its lowest points in 1864, at
less than 5,000 tons.[37]

The violence of war drastically altered the infrastructure of sugar
plantations in Louisiana. In addition to the destruction of the slave
labor system, the war caused severe physical damage on plantations and
bankrupted many planters. J. Carlyle Sitterson's description reveals the
extent of the devastation: "Sugarhouses and machinery were wrecked,
livestock driven away, agricultural implements lost or worn out, farm
buildings in bad repair, levees broken, leaving fields open to flood waters, and drainage ditches so filled up as to make successful cultivation
of cane impossible without extensive redigging."[38]

Without a reliable labor force, plantations could not recover from
this damage, and although production resumed after the war, it failed
to reach antebellum levels. Between 1866 and 1869 production doubled,
and in 1877 Louisiana produced about 73,000 tons, less than one-third
of the total produced in prewar peak years.[39]

Global sugar prices and demand for sugar increased after Civil War.
In the United States, sugar consumption increased from about 400,000
tons per year at the start of the war to more than 600,000 tons per year
in 1871. After the crash in Louisiana sugar production, consumers in
the United States found many alternatives. Despite increasing demand,
Louisiana sugar planters could not compete with the expanding beet
sugar industry and the productivity of cane plantations in Cuba, Hawaii, and Brazil. By the mid-nineteenth century, beet sugar production
emerged in Europe as a viable alternative to sugarcane that could be cultivated in temperate climates. German chemist Andreas Marggraf wrote
a study that detailed methods of extracting sugar from beets in 1747,
but large-scale beet sugar cultivation in Germany did not begin until
the 1830s, when low grain prices caused German planters, or "landed
gentry," to cultivate root crops. Owners of large estates in France also
began producing beet sugar at this time. In 1860 Germany and France
produced roughly 225,000 tons of beet sugar. Around this time Russia

and Austria-Hungry also began cultivating beets, and by 1875 the four regions produced more than 1.3 million tons combined.[40] In the United States, beet sugar cultivation in California grew slowly after the Civil War, and by the late 1880s it rivaled Louisiana's cane production levels.[41] Beet sugar production increased from 16.6 percent of global sugar production in 1858 to 34.1 percent in 1873. By 1893, beet sugar accounted for nearly 55 percent of the world's total sugar production.[42]

Though sugarcane production increased across the tropics, Cuba and Brazil dominated world markets. Since both regions depended on slave labor until the 1880s, well after slavery had been abolished in European colonies, they were able to produce sugar more efficiently and cheaply than sugar producers who relied on other forms of labor. During Reconstruction, Cuba remained the primary supplier of cane sugar to the eastern states, and the cane sugar was supplemented by beet sugar imported from Europe. In the 1870s, Hawaii supplied West Coast consumers with sugarcane; in addition, the beet sugar produced in California provided a modest amount of sugar to the US market by the late 1880s.[43] During this period, sugar production expanded in both Cuba and Hawaii. Refineries on the West Coast processed Hawaiian sugar, while Cuba supplied East Coast refineries.[44] The Civil War marked a turning point for the Hawaiian sugar industry, which grew steadily in the 1870s and 1880s. The Hawaiian industry really took off following the Reciprocity Treaty of 1875 and the abolition of slavery in Cuba (1880) and Brazil (1888), and by the time of Hawaii's annexation in 1896, it produced four times as much sugar as Louisiana.[45]

Changing immigration patterns also aided in preventing the yellow fever virus from causing epidemics in New Orleans. Between 1860 and 1866, European immigration to the city was interrupted because of the Civil War. Immigration resumed after the war but never again reached prewar levels.[46] Laboring immigrant populations continued to suffer the highest morbidity and mortality during outbreaks. Many native New Orleanians continued to blame immigrants for spreading yellow fever, often reasoning that they were susceptible to the disease because they lived in "poor" or "unclean" conditions. For example, in 1870, nearly six hundred yellow fever deaths were reported, most of them in a limited portion of the second district. Medical reports described most of the victims as Italians and added that the outbreak "prevailed among a class of people living under bad sanitary conditions, having no social intercourse with other classes, and extremely averse to apply for medical relief."[47] Under the rubric of sanitation and cleanliness, native New Orleanian physicians used mortality rates to rationalize the uneven results of postwar yellow fever outbreaks.

The Epidemic of 1878

One year after federal troops left the city, the Mississippi Valley experienced its most disastrous yellow fever epidemic, in terms of human lives lost and devastating economic impact. Many considered the epidemic to be the worst in the nation's history because of its scope and spread from New Orleans throughout the Lower Mississippi Valley. For the first time, yellow fever appeared in hundreds of towns and cities that had not previously encountered the virus. It reportedly caused nearly 5,000 deaths in New Orleans and a total of roughly 20,000 in the entire affected region. At the onset of the epidemic, about 40,000 residents, comprising nearly 20 percent of the city's population, fled. Many left the city by rail, causing the epidemic to spread rapidly, as they carried the contagion with them. Yellow fever quickly spread from New Orleans to Memphis, and widespread panic ensued. Within ten days of the public announcement of the presence of yellow fever in Memphis, 25,000 people, or more than half of the urban population, left the city.[48] Across the United States, more than 150,000 people fled their homes during the epidemic. Federal accounts estimated that economic losses in the nation during the epidemic totaled more than $30 million, with more than $15 million of that amount lost in New Orleans.[49]

Ecology and the Epidemic of 1878

The epidemic in New Orleans was the result of a conjuncture of political transformations that followed the end of Reconstruction in the United States and the end of the Ten Years' War in Cuba. Contemporary public health reports claimed that the epidemic of 1878 began as a result of one or two cases of yellow fever on the steamship *Emily B. Souder*, which arrived in New Orleans from Havana on May 23. However in 1878, at the close of the Ten Years' War, hundreds of refugees came to

New Orleans from Cuba. It is likely that many of these refugees would have avoided quarantine stations.[50] By 1877 conservative Democrats had regained control of the state legislature, which had been controlled by Republicans after the war and for most of the Reconstruction era. The Republican government supported federal policies that enfranchised African Americans, while Louisiana Democrats contested their power. Post-Reconstruction political changes shaped the composition of public health boards, allowing local medical authorities, including Samuel P. Choppin, P. S. Carrington, and G. Farrar Patton, to regain control of local public health policy. Months before the epidemic, Congress passed the Quarantine Act of 1878, a "weak law" that "made no appropriation for any government activity, and . . . prohibited federal infringement on the prerogatives of state and local health authorities."[51] Thus, the coincidence of the end of the Ten Years' War in Cuba and Reconstruction in 1878 enabled refugees to enter New Orleans without delay, and without passing quarantine. By April, officials failed to systematically enforce quarantine and sanitation laws, and as a result many unrestricted vessels entered New Orleans, including ships carrying fruit and refugees from the Ten Years' War.[52] Patton noted that "during the months of April and May a steady stream of people from Havana, where yellow fever was on the increase, poured into New Orleans by several lines of steamers."[53]

The scale and severity of the epidemic in the Lower Mississippi Valley resulted from a series of ecological transformations, which encouraged the growth of the region's *A. aegypti* population and accelerated the spread of the yellow fever virus. Significant changes to the built environment included the engineering of water management projects, the construction of railroads, and development in small outposts along rail lines. Additionally, immunological factors that were tied to demographic changes, including postwar migrations, population growth, and the flight of refugees during epidemics, enabled unusually high mortality. Finally, weather and climatic patterns, especially the impacts of the 1877–78 El Niño episode, may have exacerbated the severity of epidemics.

WATER MANAGEMENT

Management of the Mississippi River has been a primary concern for inhabitants of New Orleans from its settlement to the present day. From the colonial period through the nineteenth century, under the governance of France, Spain, and the United States, state and private interests invested in water control projects, with several aims. Primarily these projects aimed to control flooding to facilitate agricultural production, and to clear swamps to provide more space for agriculture and suburban development. Additionally, local developers often sought to drain swamps because they believed that low-lying wet environments were unhealthful. Throughout the antebellum era, residents associated wetlands with "noxious and deadly miasmas" that they believed were the cause of numerous fevers, including malaria, and cited health as an impetus for draining and clearing swamps.[54]

It is very likely that the fever residents associated with the wetlands was indeed malaria, since still water in swamps and bayous provided ideal breeding spaces for *Anopheles* mosquitoes. By the early nineteenth century, residents often noted that the Mississippi Delta was a "very unhealthy" region, particularly in the summer.[55] While it is unclear exactly when malaria became endemic in the lowlands of the Mississippi Valley, numerous mid-nineteenth-century observers described its ubiquitous presence. In addition to noting the presence of fevers, observers often commented on the preponderance of mosquitoes in swamplands. Over the course of the nineteenth century, the growth of plantations surrounding swamps brought humans in close proximity to *Anopheles* mosquitoes. Changing the course of the Mississippi made the stagnant water situation more severe in the valleys. Before, "the river's natural pattern of advancing and retreating over the valley kept water moving, but with the construction of levees and drainage ditches, even though the total water surface area was reduced, the remaining water sat still," providing greater breeding spaces for *Anopheles* mosquitoes. Throughout the Lower Mississippi Valley, residents often acknowledged the presence of malaria in wetlands and the relative absence of yellow fever. Local medical reports frequently described wetlands as "malarious" and nearby towns as "healthy."[56]

Although yellow fever did not frequently spread to Memphis along river routes from New Orleans before 1878, it is likely that the city's *A. aegypti* population grew significantly between the 1830s and 1870s.[57] During this period, Memphis became increasingly connected to New Orleans via steamships, and development in the city and surrounding plantations provided ample breeding spaces for *A. aegypti*. Growth of the urban mosquito population resulted from a combination of environmental factors, including deforestation and the spread of plantation agriculture, water control projects, and urban growth, by a process similar to the one that enabled the proliferation of *A. aegypti* in New Orleans in the early nineteenth century.

Urban, suburban, and rural development was enabled by greater investments in swamp drainage and clearance projects. Swamp reclamation in the Lower Mississippi Valley gained momentum in the 1870s. In response to heavy floods, the federal government had passed the Swamp Land Acts of 1849 and 1850, which granted federal wetlands to state governments with the stipulation that they would invest in levee construction and land reclamation projects, drying these lands for settlement and agriculture. However, these projects did not materialize until the late 1870s because of financial constraints. Reconstruction-era investments in surveying and controlling the Mississippi prompted a surge in the building of levees, dredging, draining swamps, and clearing snags along river routes.[58] The slow and steady reconstruction of plantations and urban centers facilitated the spread of *A. aegypti* throughout the region, providing ripe conditions for when the virus was reintroduced.

In addition to altering the physical environment, Reconstruction-era water control projects fostered the growth of trade and traffic in New Orleans and facilitated an increase in traffic from the Caribbean into the city. In 1875 construction of a major engineering project began at the mouth of the Mississippi River, where it reached the Gulf of Mexico. Federal interests in revitalizing the southern economy aimed to connect the eastern and western United States by building regional trade networks, in addition to connecting southern cities to global markets. The Mississippi River served as a central access point, connecting the western United States with vessels that passed through New Orleans traveling to and from European and Caribbean ports.[59] The largest outlet from the Mississippi into the gulf, the Southwest Pass, would often get blocked by sandbars, causing delays to vessels entering or leaving New Orleans.[60] Larger ships relied on dredging or on towboats, which were often slow and unreliable. This sparked interest in finding more efficient alternatives, such as building a canal.[61] Economic imperatives encouraged cooperation between local and federal authorities as they considered various ways of opening the mouth of Mississippi.

It was at this time that James Eads, a civil engineer with experience in managing the Mississippi, proposed a plan to build a system of jetties, or "artificial riverbanks," which were "designed to narrow the streams, keeping [the river's] current powerful and its channel deep, [which would] pry open the river mouth."[62] In 1875 Congress approved Eads's plan. After a severe flood in 1874, Congress initiated a series of public health programs that provided relief for flood victims; hired a committee of engineers to work on reclamation of the floodplain; and invested in engineering the mouth of the Mississippi to open it to large, ocean-going vessels.[63]

Construction lasted about four years, until 1879. The jetties opened the Mississippi to a huge increase in river traffic and an increase in the size of vessels that could access New Orleans. As the project neared its completion and the passes opened in 1877, one of its engineers wrote, "Prior to the construction of the jetties the commerce between New Orleans and foreign countries was carried on by vessels which could not load deeper than eighteen to nineteen feet, and then they ran great risk of detention for an indefinite time before getting to sea. These facts prevented many vessels from coming to this port." He explained that these vessels "were with great difficulty towed through the narrow ditch dug by the government dredges at the mouth of the Southwest Pass, or were delayed for days while the bar was blocked with other vessels. Now [they] can pass in or out with safety."[64] Supporters of the project raved about the "commercial benefits" of the jetties and the substantial increase in the number of steamships that were able to enter New Orleans without delay. Resident engineer E. L. Corthell noted that "since opening the pass to navigation in 1877, and the discontinuance of work by the government dredge boats at Southwest Pass in August of that year, there had been a considerable increase in the number of vessels crossing the bar, especially of steamers, and also a great increase in draft." The number of steamships entering New Orleans increased from 587 in 1877 to 840 in 1879, and included one hundred large steamers.[65]

Of course, the opening of the jetties coincided with the outbreak of yellow fever in 1878. In fact, construction of the jetties was delayed by the epidemic in mid-July. By August, most of the workers were dis-

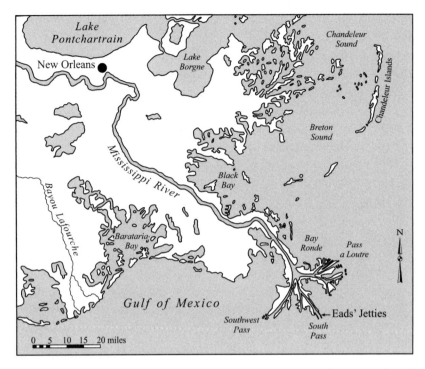

FIGURE 9. Eads's jetties opened the mouth of the Mississippi to larger vessels and increased river traffic. (Drawn from "Mississippi Jetties" and Corthell, pl. 2. Cartography by Mary Lee Eggart.)

charged. Those who were sick went to New Orleans or St. Louis. About half of the remaining population contracted yellow fever.[66] People who fled epidemics, either to avoid getting sick or because they needed hospital care, were able to rapidly migrate throughout the Mississippi Valley on newly built railroads.

RAILROADS

In 1854 A. P. Jones, a Mississippi physician, ominously predicted the connection between the growth of rail lines and the spread of yellow fever. He warned that "when the lines of railroads are completed from New Orleans to the various points contemplated, yellow fever will be seen periodically, if not annually in all the inland cities, villages, and rural districts, having direct and rapid communications with that city, from the base of the Alleghenies to the base of the Rocky Mountains."[67] Prior to the 1850s, yellow fever epidemics in New Orleans rarely spread beyond coastal and river routes, but the construction of rail lines in the 1840s and 1850s enabled the virus to infect towns and plantations that were connected to the city by rail. The reconstruction and expansion of railroads in the Mississippi Valley in the 1870s, and the subsequent growth of small outposts along rail lines, enabled yellow fever to spread to rural and inland regions in 1878.

The construction of rail lines in the Lower Mississippi Valley in the 1870s constituted a major alteration to the region's built environment. As late as 1856, there was still not much track in Louisiana, Mississippi, and Tennessee. In the eastern Mississippi Valley, a few railroads were constructed in the 1850s, including a line from New Orleans to Grand Junction, Tennessee (completed in 1860), and a line from Memphis to Grenada, Mississippi (completed in 1861). However, Union troops destroyed much of these tracks within a few years, during the war. They were rebuilt in the 1870s, alongside new long-distance rails. During the postwar period, the federal government, with support from local parties, subsidized the construction of most of the long-distance railroads built in the western Mississippi Valley.[68] Memphis emerged as a major hub, as Democrats elected in 1870 rebuilt rail lines and began constructing new lines to Selma, Alabama, and Paducah, Kentucky.[69]

In New Orleans, a series of developments that heightened communication between the port city and its hinterland facilitated the spread of yellow fever. The first major shift was in 1867, when the "city council gave the New Orleans, Opelousas, and Great Western Railroad 125 feet of the waterfront, opposite the French Quarter." Next, the "state legislature granted the New Orleans, Mobile, and Chattanooga line the right to build a terminal on the riverbanks" and also allowed the railroad to "lay double track along much of the waterfront." At the same time, "the city council made a similar grant to the New Orleans, Jackson, and Great Northern line, meaning . . . a second set of double track . . . along the waterfront."[70] Ari Kelman argues that in fact, because of the lack of port traffic owing to the federal blockade during the war, which rerouted trade, traders in the Mississippi Valley had "grown relatively comfortable with railroads during the war." A contemporary federal account noted that, "thanks to the embargo war, railroads gained in four years an advance on the Mississippi which under ordinary favorable circumstances it would have taken them twenty years to have secured."[71]

Thus, for the first time, there was contact between incoming river traffic and outgoing rail traffic, allowing carriers of yellow fever, including humans and mosquitoes, to move quickly from New Orleans into the Mississippi Valley. In 1874 the New Orleans, Jackson, and Great Northern Railroad merged with the Mississippi Central Railroad, creating the New Orleans, St. Louis, and Chicago Railroad. By 1878 there was heavy traffic along this route, as well as along the line from New Orleans to Jackson, Tennessee, which later became part of the Illinois Central Railroad.[72] By 1878 inland areas throughout Louisiana, Mississippi, and Tennessee had become connected to New Orleans by rail lines. At the start of the Civil War, there were just 335 miles of track in Louisiana; this amount doubled by 1880.[73] In 1853 Mississippi had just three rail lines; by 1878 the state had more than a thousand miles of railroads.[74] Dozens of towns, cities, and outposts located along the newly built rail lines reported the presence of yellow fever for the first time in 1878. The epidemic spread along the Chicago, St. Louis, and New Orleans Railroad, the Louisiana-Texas Railroad, the New Orleans and Mobile Railroad, and many others. Railroad towns were especially at risk partly because of lax quarantine enforcement at railroad stations. Prior to 1878, since yellow fever had mostly spread to river ports, public health authorities associated the spread of epidemics with ships. As a result, they focused on the enforcement of disinfection and quarantine at river ports.[75] This had serious consequences because of the role of the railroad in enabling people to flee epidemics. After the epidemic of 1878, the correlation between railroad traffic and yellow fever was apparent to some. A doctor in Grenada, Mississippi, described a morbid scene of "corpses rotting" on the rail platform and the closure of all businesses except coffin and drug sales. He wrote, "The cars swept swiftly by. The railroad, which had brought death, now brought bread to feed the dying, and coffins to bury the dead."[76]

REFUGEES AND DEMOGRAPHY

The flight of local people from epidemics was a common response throughout the nineteenth century, and refugees often played role in spreading the virus as they left cities on dirt roads, by river, and by rail.

In 1879, in an address to the New Orleans Medical and Surgical Association, Dr. John Dell Orto described how locals who believed that their children were immune to yellow fever "saw their infants, their boys and young girls dying with symptoms similar to those of foreigners" and "were seized by such a panic, as to cause an exodus unheard of in the history of epidemics in New Orleans."[77] More than sixty-five thousand refugees fled from New Orleans and Memphis. By 1878 new, expanded rail systems made it possible for greater numbers of people to flee epidemics, traveling greater distances at greater speeds, when they were still able to transmit the virus if bitten.[78] The loose quarantine enforcement at most railway stops made it possible for them to seek refuge in many towns and cities throughout the Mississippi Valley.

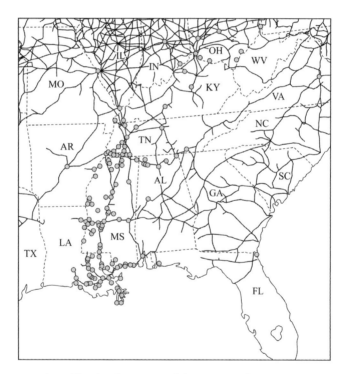

FIGURE 10. The epidemic of 1878 spread from New Orleans to Memphis to hundreds of other cities, towns, plantations, and small outposts via newly constructed rail lines. (Compiled from *Conclusions of the Board;* Augustin; Spinzig, *Yellow Fever;* Patterson. Cartography by Mary Lee Eggart.)

White southerners fled to small towns that they considered "safe,"
like Holly Springs and Dry Grove, Mississippi. Not only did these towns
elect not to establish quarantines, but private homes and hospitals wel-
comed and treated victims of yellow fever. In Holly Springs, located
along the Chicago, St. Louis, and New Orleans Railroad, local relief
groups actually "invited refugees from infected towns to come and wait
out the epidemic." Similarly, Dry Grove, Mississippi, a "remote and secluded" village located ten miles west of the New Orleans Railroad and
eighteen miles south of the Vicksburg and Meridian Railroad, served
as a destination for refugees. Reverend W. K. Douglass described Dry
Grove as "a mere cross-roads hamlet" of about "one hundred souls," both
"white and colored," which "had been sought by persons desiring to escape from threatened railroad towns." He explained that "applications
for places for refuge were received by the people of Dry Grove at the very
time when the pestilence, walking in its own darkness, was laying its
hands on its victims." By September nearly all of the doctors and nurses
who attended the sick had contracted the fever, and Douglass recalled
that "there was not in the neighborhood of Dry Grove a man who was
not ill himself or bound to the bedside of the sick in his own house-
hold."[79] Because the virus spread to areas that had never been exposed
to yellow fever, it gained access to a huge nonimmune host population.
The large numbers of refugees during the epidemic, combined with the
speed of their arrival in small, remote towns, caused thousands of people to encounter yellow fever for the first time. The lack of immune populations in these regions enabled the virus to spread quickly, resulting
in higher mortality rates than in cities that had previously come into
contact with yellow fever.

Further, the epidemic of 1878 was particularly devastating to African
Americans because of demographic changes in the Mississippi Valley
during Reconstruction. In addition to those who lived on plantations
and in towns that had not previously confronted yellow fever, black residents in urban areas encountered the virus for the first time. By the
1870s New Orleans and Memphis became home to a large proportion
of nonimmune African Americans. Between 1865 and 1878, roughly
23,000 African Americans migrated to New Orleans, nearly doubling
the city's "colored" population, and more than 17,000 settled in Memphis between 1860 and 1870.[80] These cities experienced higher mortal-

ity than ever before as a result of the postwar migrations of freed African Americans.

CLIMATE

A final factor that may have increased the severity of the epidemic is the change in climatic and weather patterns resulting from the strong El Niño episodes of 1877–78. J. R. McNeill has argued that in the Caribbean and in the American South, several "politically important" epidemics occurred during El Niño years, as changing rainfall patterns "provided helpful but by no means necessary conditions for yellow fever epidemics."[81] A few climatologists have made this argument about the 1878 epidemic in the Mississippi Valley, based on evidence from scientific surveys of tree ring data, ice cores, and fossil pollen sedimentation in coastal basins, lake beds, and coral reefs. These studies indicate warmer temperatures and increased rainfall during these years, which would have resulted in the proliferation of mosquito populations.[82] Historical evidence supports this view, as data collected by contemporary physicians and meteorologists reveals exceptionally high temperatures and precipitation during these years. After the epidemic, physician Carl Spinzig, a German immigrant who practiced in St. Louis, collected data on average temperatures and rainfall in the 1870s to show the relationship between meteorological changes and the occurrence of yellow fever. He argued that the "prevalence and subsidence of yellow fever is on a parallel with the increase, prevalence, and subsidence of summer extremes."[83]

In New Orleans, what might have been a smooth narrative of the rise of yellow fever over the course of the nineteenth century was interrupted by the Civil War and the subsequent decline in development between 1861 and 1866. Those years are characterized by a decline in sugar production, economic growth, trade, immigration, urban development, water control projects, and railroad construction. The Reconstruction era marked a series of transformations, which included the rebuilding of environmental and cultural landscapes as well as the reconstruction of social and political structures. During this period, the rebuilding of New Orleans resulted in significant growth and development, not only surrounding the city, but throughout the Lower Mississippi Valley. Ecological changes, including significant alterations to the built environment, enabled the outbreak of yellow fever in 1878 to spread throughout the region, causing the nation's most disastrous epidemic. The devastation caused by the epidemic of 1878, and a subsequent epidemic in 1879, sparked a series of transformations in social, political, and cultural attitudes about race and immunity, which are the subject of chapter 5.

5

Degrees of Resistance

REIMAGINING RACE, HEALTH, AND THE ENVIRONMENT, 1878–1905

The yellow fever epidemic of 1878 in New Orleans spread throughout the Mississippi Valley, causing outbreaks across the eastern United States. This epidemic was part of a global pandemic, as yellow fever outbreaks appeared across the Atlantic, in cities from Brazil to tropical West Africa, including Rio de Janeiro, Freetown, Dakar, and Saint-Louis-du-Sénégal.[1]

In the American South, the devastation caused by the epidemic of 1878, and another outbreak in 1879, marked a series of shifts in cultural, social, and political ideas about yellow fever in relation to attitudes about race, identity, and public health. In New Orleans, and the Gulf South broadly, three key changes occurred. First, the epidemic marked a period of shifting views about racial immunity. The hardening of racial boundaries within society led medical authorities to solidify their racial ideas about yellow fever immunity. Second, the epidemic marked a gradual transformation in medical perspectives, toward an emphasis on bacteriological explanations of disease causality. Third, medical professionals pursued programs that reflected a growing faith in public health, manifested in the support of medical institutions, including research organizations and public health boards.

The epidemic caused locals to rethink their attitudes about yellow fever immunity in a broad sense. Throughout the antebellum era, contemporary physicians and untrained observers had imagined immunity and resistance to yellow fever based on numerous individual categories, including race, nativity, creolism, age, gender, and temperance. In addition to these categories, contemporaries viewed certain environments and geographies as immune, including highlands, inland regions, and remote towns that appeared to be safe during epidemics. The devastation of the 1878 epidemic and its impact on peoples and places thought to be immune or exempt caused many to rethink their views about the causes, patterns, and prevention of yellow fever. It made some question the effectiveness of disinfection, yet at the same time it prompted a series of public health reforms and research programs. However, medical authorities failed to identify the role of mosquitoes in spreading yellow fever, and thus they promoted old methods, primarily quarantine and disinfection, until the turn of the century. Despite the severity of the 1878 epidemic in remote regions and among categories of peoples that residents considered safe or immune, late-nineteenth-century physicians emphasized race in their studies of epidemiological and immunological patterns.

Postwar Racial Reconstruction

Between the 1850s and the turn of the century, Louisiana underwent a period of racial polarization, perpetuated by increasing political conflicts surrounding the Civil War and emancipation and the ensuing racial violence during the Reconstruction and Jim Crow eras. Though racial bifurcations escalated throughout the nation following the war, the realignment of racial identification in New Orleans was uniquely divisive among the Creole population. Almost immediately after the war, a unified white identity developed among many Louisianans who had previously identified along cultural lines. White Creoles, European immigrants, and American migrants from the eastern United States exhibited a racial solidarity that distinguished them from Creoles of color and former slaves, whom they categorized as "colored" or as "negroes." As a distinct racial identity grew among whites, a unified identity grew among nonwhite Louisianans. Rebecca Scott has argued that "however great the social gaps between the *gens de couleur* and field slaves in the pre-war period, the necessity of an alliance had . . . become evident, as Louisiana became a focus for the national struggle over civil rights."[2] Post-Reconstruction segregation policies, particularly the lack of schools for people of color, led black New Orleanians to form racially exclusive social bonds. During the 1870s and 1880s, "black Americans and creoles . . . transcended ethnic boundaries" as nonwhites of varying ethnic and religious backgrounds formed social bonds through schools, church, and benevolent associations.[3] Despite an overall trend toward racial polarization, however, cultural identities continued to be contested and redefined throughout the 1880s and 1890s. For example, Francophone natives who identified as whites struggled to define the "Creole" category as exclusively white, while Anglo-American journalists and authors depicted them as a mixed race.[4]

The emergence of secret white supremacist organizations immediately after the war, most notably the Ku Klux Klan (1865) and the Knights of the White Camelia (1867), led to the intensification of organized racial violence in the region. During Reconstruction, local conflicts, often accompanied by violence against "Republican officeholders and their African American allies," led to the establishment of a state militia "composed of black volunteers, some Irish immigrants, and a certain number of white Confederate soldiers willing to enlist under General James Longstreet, now a Republican and a proponent of regional reconciliation."[5]

Violent racial conflicts escalated during this period, manifested in riots such as the Memphis Riots of 1866 and the Colfax Massacre of 1873.[6] During the Colfax Massacre, described by Eric Foner as the "bloodiest single instance of racial carnage in the Reconstruction Era," a white militia killed more than 150 blacks who were occupying a courthouse in Grant Parish.[7] By the spring of 1874, the vigilante White League emerged as an openly militant white supremacist organization. Unlike members of the Ku Klux Klan and the Knights of the White Camelia, White Leaguers did not hide their identity. A few months after the establishment of the White League, black and white Republicans organized a local militia in the bayou parishes (LaFourche and Terrebonne) surrounding New Orleans. Democrats characterized this organization as a "negro militia."[8] The physical presence of local militias and militant white supremacist groups exacerbated racial riots and violence, which characterized the final years of Reconstruction.

Medical elites, including Dr. Stanford Chaillé, a professor in the Medical Department of the University of Louisiana who served as president of the New Orleans Board of Health, publicly denied the violence of white supremacist organizations. In 1877 he testified before the US House of Representatives Committee on Louisiana Affairs against accusations that "whites" used violence, intimidation, murder, maiming, mutilation, and whipping to prevent "colored citizens" from voting. In his testimony, he described the state's majority of "white voters" and indicated a sense of political unity among "white citizens." Chaillé categorized the white population as including "native born" and "foreign born" whites and never used the term "Creole." In his assessment of why the "colored" population suffered greater mortality than the white population, he revealed his views of racial inferiority. Although he claimed that greater mortality among the black population could be attributed to "ignorance, improvidence and inferior hygienic conditions rather than any race-peculiarity," he concluded that "while some few intelligent negroes have improved since the war as to health, productiveness, etc., ... the majority, which contains a large number who are grossly ignorant, improvident and brutal, has deteriorated since emancipation, and certainly ... their average condition as to health, etc., is inferior to the whites."[9]

RESPONSES TO THE EPIDEMIC OF 1878

In the Mississippi Valley, reactions to the 1878 epidemic reveal a communal sense of horror and confusion, since many had never witnessed a yellow fever epidemic and had believed the disease was confined to urban areas along the Gulf Coast. When yellow fever came from New Orleans to Vicksburg in August, a local nurse commented, "It is like a terrible dream."[10] Jackson local J. L. Power, who organized relief work in Mississippi, wrote, "No one but an eye-witness can realize the confusion and desolation, and destitution, consequent upon the present scourge."[11]

The 1878 epidemic marked a period of postwar reconciliation between whites in the northern and southern United States. Edward Blum has shown how the epidemic evoked feelings of religious and racial unity among white Americans, who viewed it as a redemptive moment for southern whites. He argues that "although left out of most studies of Reconstruction, the outbreak stood as a pivotal moment in postwar national reconciliation and the marginalization of African Americans." He contends that as "northern and southern whites reveled in their new-found solidarity, they also joined together to neglect the medical needs of southern blacks."[12]

Following the epidemic, numerous institutions provided relief to southern yellow fever sufferers and their families. In New Orleans, more than forty benevolent organizations formed relief committees for this purpose. Among them were the Orleans Central Relief Committee, the YMCA, the St. Theresa Society, the Howard Association, the Masons, the Odd Fellows, the Fireman's Charitable Organization, the German Benevolent Association, the Algiers Relief Committee, and others. Local organizations did not have the funds to handle the size of the epidemic, so they relied on donations from the federal government and from charitable organizations and private donors located in neighboring states, the Northeast, and Europe. Local chapters of fraternal organizations, including the Masons and the Odd Fellows, raised funds throughout the nation.[13]

On December 6, 1878, a group of New Orleans citizens gathered at the Varieties Theatre to publicly express gratitude to the "heroic efforts of the physicians, and nurses, charitable associations, and clergy" that had "so generously befriended them during the epidemic of Yellow Fever which had scourged their city through the long, baleful summer of 1878."[14] The proceedings emphasized that the victims of the epidemic included many children, widows, and poor residents: "How many orphans rescued from suffering and death—how many widows comforted—how many of the poor, who were dependent on daily labor for daily bread, rescued from despair and starvation—no earthly record will ever show." They also expressed thanks for the support they had received from throughout the nation, stating that "across the broad expanse of a vast continent, from North and South, and East and West, the tributary streams of beneficence rolled in one unebbing tide of overflowing generosity. Into the valley of the shadow of death in which we walked, it poured its life-giving waters, fresh from the gushing springs of human affection. Never has any people before been recipients of so grand a charity; never can its impressive lesson of humanity be forgotten."[15]

In addition to numerous private organizations, the federal government provided rations for New Orleanians, including sugar, coffee, tea, rice, flour, and bacon. By September the federal government had provided more than fifty thousand packages of rations to yellow fever sufferers, which were distributed by the aforementioned charitable groups.[16] However, these organizations did distribute these rations to all peoples. The federal government's instructions mandated that only "those persons having yellow fever in their families and who were destitute" could receive support. The chairman of the Orleans Central Relief Committee remarked that "this resolution prevented us from relieving many." To enforce this policy, officials "required the persons applying for relief to produce doctor's certificates showing yellow fever, and detailed statements from reliable persons that the parties were destitute." This practice reveals the role of local doctors in regulating the dispersal of federal supplies. The type of people that the committee sought to relieve is evident in the chairman's description of a destitute widow. He "found her in need of the necessities of life, and sick. She was the owner of the property, but her tenants were too poor to pay; she could not mortgage or sell, and could only cry for help."[17] While reports show that ten thousand individuals received federal rations, more than twenty-seven thousand cases of yellow fever were reported in the city.[18]

Southern physicians emphasized national reconciliation and racial solidarity in published records of the epidemic, quoting publications from major cities in the northern United States and Europe, such as the *New York Times* and the *London Standard*. These newspapers "published editorials eulogistic of the courage and endurance of the people of the South during the epidemic," demonstrating their support for the southern states.[19] Often such editorials described their feelings toward southern people in racial or ethnic terms. An article reprinted from the *London Standard*, titled "Heroism of the Southern People in War and in Pestilence," stated, "There may be among the various nations of Aryan family one or two who would claim that they could have furnished troops like those which followed Lee and Johnston, Stewart and Stonewall Jackson; but we doubt whether there be one race beside our own that could send forth its children in hundreds to face in towns desolated by the yellow fever the horror of a nurse's life and the eminent terror of a martyr's death."[20] Ideas about racial difference shaped the ways in which medical professionals and other white observers interpreted the impact and meaning of the epidemic, despite evidence of African American victims.

EVIDENCE OF BLACK SUSCEPTIBILITY

Anecdotal and official evidence from postwar yellow fever epidemics in the Lower Mississippi Valley challenges perceptions of racial immunity to yellow fever. Empirical data collected by residents and members of benevolent organizations reveals a high percentage of nonwhite individuals, identified variously as "negroes," "mulattoes," or "colored." In 1867, a yellow fever epidemic began in New Orleans after the fever had been absent from the city for eight years. When it spread into the rural parishes of southern Louisiana, Mary Gay, who lived on St. Louis Plantation in Iberville Parish, wrote that the fever was "brought there by a negro from New Iberia."[21] By September of 1867, the Freedman's Bureau in Louisiana reported that doctors had treated 5,918 freedmen. State reports claimed that freed people in New Orleans and other communities along the Mississippi and Bayou Teche were suffering from "diseases of a malarious origin."[22] However, it is more likely that they contracted yellow fever during the epidemic. Since the fever did not commonly appear in rural communities around Bayou Teche and other neighboring regions prior to 1867, many residents encountered the disease for the first time. Because they were not immune, the epidemic was able to spread quickly throughout the bayou country surrounding New Orleans.

Following the 1867 epidemic, homeopathic physician William Henry Holcombe of New Orleans wrote that "within the memory of all living physicians, the yellow fever never attacked the native creole population, never extended beyond the suburbs of cities or towns, never attacked the same person a second time, never occurred in the pure negro race, and rarely seized upon children. Now it attacks children, negroes, creoles, and acclimated persons indiscriminately." Holcombe's alarming depiction of the epidemic, contradicting common ideas about immunity, reveals the ways in which locals reacted to their observations of higher mortality and greater impacts of the disease. Many of his conclusions are based on his haphazard observations rather than empirical data, and they reflect the general attitude of panic among residents of New Orleans. He also claimed that "a first attack is no certain security against another, and the second attack is sometimes the worse of the two."[23] During the epidemic of 1878, numerous observers noticed a similar shift in the disease's victims. They described how the fever attacked a large number of Creoles and children, in addition to causing unprecedented high mortality rates among nonwhite populations. The lack of immunity among black Americans is evident in Memphis, which served as a primary urban destination for many freed people in the 1870s. Between 1860 and 1870, the city's black population grew from 3,000 to about 20,000, representing roughly 30 percent of the city's population of 65,000.[24] Within about a week after the epidemic began, the majority of the city's white population fled. The remaining population consisted mostly of those who did not have the means to leave. Of these, about 5,000 individuals, mostly whites, entered refugee camps located outside of the city. By mid-September, fewer than 20,000 people remained in the city, with a black majority of about 14,000 people.[25] One local, who did not sympathize with the freed black population, remarked: "The day's record . . . is horrible. The few new cases are not a tithe of those which have occurred. Negroes will not work, will not leave town, but lie about and draw rations, and then get sick and become a burden intolerable. They give their sick no care, and seem to think they must be fed on idleness and nursed with greatest care."[26]

The next day the author recounted being awakened and "informed by the landlady that she had just discovered a house in the immediate vicinity in which were three colored men—one dead, the other two delirious with fever" and mentioned several other cases of fever among "mulattoes."[27] It was not uncommon for white residents to criticize blacks for remaining in the city and acquiring rations. Another account depicted a line of "closely-packed" men and women waiting for rations from the Citizen's Relief Committee, noting, "there were all shades of black, but not one white man or woman. . . . The blacks will not leave the city and work in the fields so long as they can obtain free rations, and the whites don't have the heart to drive them out."[28]

As the fever claimed more victims, corpses accumulated in Memphis, because of the lack of undertakers and burial space. Numerous contemporaries described in detail the presence of decaying corpses on the streets. A local physician wrote: "The question of disposing of the dead is becoming a serious one. . . . It has even been suggested to burn the dead if they cannot be buried more promptly, as corpses are known to have lain unburied for forty-eight hours, burdening the air with odors, and becoming so revolting that people have fled the neighborhood."[29]

High mortality rates made it impossible to count bodies. For example, a burial corps organized by the Citizens' Relief Committee found more than sixty unburied bodies. A local lamented how many bodies "were put away in the trenches . . . where paupers and the unknown sleep peacefully together."[30] Mass burials and cremations resulted in the absence of victims in official records, including a large number of families who could not afford to bury their dead. A local survivor reporting from Camp Jo Williams, a refugee camp for whites about five miles south of Memphis, reported, "Colored families living within a few hundred yards of our hospital, who have not visited the infected district at all and kept aloof from our camps, have sickened and died."[31] The author also noted, "The negroes, five thousand, are still in the city. No appeal will drive them from the certain death which awaits them. The pest has gotten among them, and Heaven only knows who will bury their dead."[32]

The chaos and panic produced by the epidemic heightened racial tensions in many cases but occasionally fostered interracial cooperation and appreciation. In Memphis, a lack of access to basic resources led to "petty thieving," mostly of necessities such as food, clothing, wood, and coal. Observers also described social chaos, manifested in public "lewdness and drunkenness." A group of white residents falsely accused a group of "negro male nurses" of the "wholesale rape of white women." However, some sources commented on the bravery of people of color during the epidemic, noting that they were susceptible to yellow fever. For example, J. M. Keating, an Irish immigrant and local newspaper editor who remained in the city during the epidemic, commended black soldiers, nurses, and policemen, who "were deferential and respectful to the white race"; he described the "devotion" and "courage" of nine black soldiers who died of yellow fever.[33] Physicians who worked with the Howard Association medical corps praised the work of R. H. Tate, the first black doctor to practice in Memphis, who came from Cincinnati to provide medical care during the epidemic. He treated many patients whom he identified as "colored," before he died of yellow fever three weeks after his arrival in Memphis.[34]

In addition to anecdotal accounts, federal reports reveal a significant number of cases and deaths among nonwhite residents in Alabama, Mississippi, and Tennessee. The federal "Board of Experts," a committee created to investigate yellow fever after the epidemic, compiled data from across the affected region. In several instances, reports show a substantial percentage of victims that they identified as "colored." For example, in Alabama, federal reports indicated a large proportion of "colored" cases, even in areas where the white population constituted a significant majority. The white population was almost twice the "colored" population in Decatur, a town of about 1,200 people located at a railroad crossing on the Tennessee River. When yellow fever arrived, many residents fled, with the aid of the Howard Association of Memphis, and the town was left "almost depopulated." Of the 250 reported cases, 168 were designated as "colored" and 64 were white. According to the report, the epidemic had resulted in the death of 25 whites and 21 "colored" persons. In Florence, Alabama, another small town with a white majority, located at a railroad junction about a mile from the Tennessee River, the disease caused a small epidemic, with records of 24 white and 26 "colored" deaths.[35]

Data collected in Mississippi reveals numerous victims of color. For example, in Bolton, Mississippi, a town of 200 people, 168 cases were reported. The Board of Experts' report noted that of 110 "colored" cases, 24 died and of 34 white cases, 10 died. The former governor Albert G. Brown's plantations in Mississippi reported 5 white and 16 "colored" cases, resulting in 1 white and 3 "colored" deaths.[36] In Port Gibson, a town of about 1,500 people that served as the county seat of Claiborne County, reports identified substantially more "colored" than white cases. In the last week of August, 50 deaths occurred, and by September, "silence reigned the streets." A local observer lamented, "Every home was a hospital; the dying and the dead were all around and about us. Corpses, just as the victims died, wrapped in sheets and blankets, and hurriedly encoffined, were stealthily lifted out of doors and sometimes out of windows, and buried in haste at sunrise, after dark by dim lanterns, and frequently lay all night long in the graveyard, unburied." Out of 291 "colored" cases, 22 died, and of 133 white cases, 30 died. Another local account, from Port Gibson, reported that mortality rates of whites and blacks were "about equal."[37] In Vicksburg, on the Mississippi River about four hundred miles north of New Orleans, yellow fever infected more than 60 percent of the total population; of 3,000 white cases, 641 were reported dead, and of 2,000 "colored" cases, 231 were reported dead. The population of Water Valley, a post village located along the Mississippi Central Railroad, was evenly divided by race in 1878, and records indicate more "colored" than white victims.[38] In King's Point, a landing town on the Mississippi, one local account indicated that by late September, "a malarial or mild yellow fever occurred, which seemed to take in every one, especially colored people."[39]

Reports from Tennessee, which had a substantially higher percentage of white residents than Mississippi, Alabama, or Louisiana, showed that although observers noticed numerous cases of yellow fever among nonwhites, the proportion of white deaths reported was significantly higher than "colored" deaths. In Brownsville, Tennessee, one-fourth of the town's population fled when they heard news of the yellow fever in Memphis, and of the remaining 1,000 residents, there were 162 "colored" cases and 102 white cases. Almost 30 percent of the residents of the railroad town of Grand Junction, Tennessee, fled when they heard about the presence of the fever. It infected nearly 75 percent of the small town's remaining residents, which amounted to 102 white and 83 "colored" cases. Of these, 56 white and 18 "colored" deaths were reported.[40] The data in these reports reveals the recorded presence of nonwhite yellow fever victims, which medical professionals simultaneously acknowledged and overlooked in their analyses of immunity and resistance.

POSTWAR IDEAS ABOUT RACE AND IMMUNITY

Despite substantial evidence of nonwhite victims, US medical authorities insisted that race was a factor in determining yellow fever resistance. This inconsistency can be attributed to the lack of official death records of many "colored" victims, combined with the racial preconceptions of disease resistance among medical officials. The federal Board of Experts explicitly addressed the problems that they encountered while trying to collect data. They admitted that the data compiled in their report was incomplete and contained many approximations, noting, "As to some places, it is known that the total number of cases and deaths exceeds the figures given, because the reports from which these figures are taken were written prior to the disappearance of the disease; and, as to nearly all places, it is not doubted that the total cases and deaths . . . were much more numerous than reported."[41] The difficulty of obtaining vital statistics was a result of the lack of organization among medical authorities during the epidemic, the undocumented number of refugees and persons who fled at the onset of the epidemic, and the lack of burials and accounting of black victims. It is probable that official records failed to account for a greater proportion of nonwhite deaths, since they generally did not receive the same level of professional care as white patients.

Perhaps the most compelling explanation for the persistence of ideas of race-based yellow fever resistance in the late nineteenth century is the statistical discrepancy caused by the large influx of European immigrants, combined with the continued use of statistical evidence derived from incomplete data. While reports often neglected to account for deaths of the nonwhite population, they often included detailed counts of mortality among the European immigrant population. Native people of color in southern cities constituted a higher percentage of the population than in the northern United States and western Europe. Further, the bulk of the South's immigrants came from western Europe and had not been previously exposed to yellow fever. In New Orleans especially, immigrants made up the majority of yellow fever victims. Medical authorities categorized these individuals as whites, thereby presenting an unbalanced representation of white yellow fever victims.[42]

General statistics derived from the data collected by the Board of Experts showed higher death rates among whites, partially owing to the absence of death records of black yellow fever victims; thus, the statistical data that medical authorities collected during the epidemic was skewed. For example, in the small village of Terry, Mississippi, located on the Chicago, St. Louis, and New Orleans Railroad, C. J. Hester recounted that the first case occurred four miles outside the town, at the home of the former governor. Eliza Grayson, described as a "mulatto girl," caught the fever and died after a bout of black vomit. Members of her family were infected, including her mother, who died, and her brother, who survived. The ex-governor and his acquaintance Colonel Dabney both contracted the disease and survived. The doctor who came to take care of them caught the fever and died shortly thereafter. Out of the ten cases that Hester described, there were five deaths, and at least two would have been classified as "colored" in official records.[43] It is also likely that Eliza Grayson's mother, who did not survive the sickness, was of African descent. However, federal reports neglected to record these cases and in fact reported zero deaths in Terry. It is probable that such lapses in official reports were not uncommon.

The lack of complete records, combined with the medical researchers' preconceptions of racial difference, led them to emphasize connections between race and yellow fever resistance and conclude that race was a determining factor of disease susceptibility. Records collected by federal public health authorities altered local systems of classification and skewed statistical data. For instance, the Board of Experts categorized yellow fever victims as either "colored" or "white" and did not include "mulattoes" in their report. In its discussion of race-based resistance from yellow fever, the board concluded that "amongst the several races of men, the European or white race affords the greatest susceptibility to yellow fever and affords the highest ratio of deaths to cases" and that "the susceptibility of the black race is much less, and amongst them, the ratio of deaths is much lower." Despite the use of a binary classification system in their statistical data, the report included a closing note about the higher susceptibility of "mulattoes," which they described as "an intermediate between that of the whites and blacks," depending on their racial composition. The board contended that "Asiatics" were as susceptible as "whites," since witnesses reported a large number of deaths among Chinese immigrants in the southern states.[44]

Like federal authorities in the United States, medical authorities in British colonies argued that race determined an individual's susceptibility to yellow fever, despite the contrary evidence in their reports. While in British Guiana during the 1860s, British colonial medical officer Izett Anderson noted cases of yellow fever among immigrants and natives. He recalled cases among "visitors from the country" and records of "upwards of 100 cases of well marked yellow fever in black immigrants from Barbados" in 1866, in addition to attacks among long-term residents of the colony, including "creoles," persons of "color," and "negroes." However, he concluded that "as a rule the black and coloured races are but little liable to contract the disease" and that natives of Sweden, Norway, and Russia were most susceptible.[45]

In contrast to views of yellow fever resistance among US and British authorities, evidence from Caribbean observers reveals the susceptibility of blacks. Global traveler and writer Lafcadio Hearn, who lived in New Orleans for ten years after Reconstruction, argued against popular perceptions of immunity of the "black race." He maintained a view of inheritable immunity that combined the concept of race with evolutionary rhetoric to analyze high death rates among Africans. While visiting Martinique in 1887, he argued, "It has been generally imagined that the physical constitution of the black race was proof against the deadly climate of the West Indies. The truth is that freshly imported Africans died of fever by the tens of thousands; the creole-negro race, now so prolific, represents only the fittest survivors in the long and terrible struggle of the slave element to adapt itself to the new environment."[46]

In Cuba, physician and researcher Carlos Finlay, before conducting his pioneering research on the role of the mosquito as a carrier of the yellow fever virus, observed higher mortality rates among blacks than among whites. However, he used this evidence to show the superior ability of whites to acclimate to the Cuban climate, in an effort to encourage white settlement in Cuba. In the 1870s, he published several articles that promoted theories of acquired immunity and rejected ideas of racial immunity. He presented data showing that black Cubans experienced higher mortality rates than white Cubans and argued that this was evidence that the "black race" had more difficulty acclimating than European newcomers and native Cubans.[47] Finlay studied yellow fever during the Ten Years' War, as the slave trade declined and European immigration increased. His observations are confirmed by contemporary descriptions of yellow fever in the slave barracoons on the Flor de Sagua plantation, according to the account of former slave Esteban Montejo, who escaped captivity in 1868.[48] Despite his contradictory views about immunity, Finlay's views of racial superiority mirrored the views of physicians in the United States. Regardless of what they observed, doctors turned to race to explain their observations. While Finlay argued that different rates of mortality served as evidence of the superiority of whites, doctors in Louisiana interpreted differential rates of immunity as evidence of racial difference.

As postwar views of race-based resistance to yellow fever solidified in the southern United States, physicians in New Orleans abandoned previously held beliefs of Creole immunity. In 1881 New Orleans physician H. D. Schmidt commented, "Although the customary assertion that native-born or long acclimated persons enjoy immunity from an attack has now been sufficiently proved as unfounded, it cannot be denied that, in most instances, acclimatization greatly ameliorates the severity of the attack." Schmidt came to this conclusion based on the high susceptibility of "unacclimated persons, especially in those who have lived in northern latitudes, beyond the yellow fever zone." He also linked immunity to geographic origin and ethnicity, noting, "It has become a general rule, corroborated by all writers, that the nearer a person has been born and lived to the North Pole, the more liable he is to be attacked by the disease, and the smaller his chances will be for recovery." However, he acknowledged that his observations during the epidemic of 1878 disproved this assertion. He maintained that "the French, Italian, and Spanish population of New Orleans suffered equally as much, *if not more,* from the disease than that of Teutonic or Anglo-Saxon origin; even the Negroes did not remain exempt."[49]

Popular perceptions of race-based resistance appeared throughout the South. Sam Small, known as "Old Si" in the Atlanta *Constitution,* parodied the subject, revealing the simplicity of perceived black resistance literally as a matter of color:

> Well, I'se a tuff citizen for enny complaint ter tackle, an' I managed ter be dar yit when ole yaller jack flung up de fite; but I d'clar' ter grashus, now, dat d'seze don't hanker much arter niggers, kase he don't often win de fite tell he gits a feller turned yaller, an' niggers don't turn yaller wuff er cent; but whenebber he gits er white man lyin' out looking like er chromo of er mustard patch in bloom, dere's gwine ter be er hole in de semeterry groun' nex' day, sho!![50]

The medical history of freed African American populations during yellow fever epidemics remains an understudied area. While many scholars have examined plantation records to assess African American experiences with disease in the South, these sources focus on enslaved individuals who lived on plantations, rather than free people who lived in cities. As a result, it excludes the large population of free people of color, especially during the postwar period. From the 1870s through the twentieth century, most medical professionals ignored evidence of black yellow fever victims. Ideological preconceptions, supported by incomplete statistical data, led many nineteenth- and twentieth-century medical elites to believe that blacks were immune to tropical fevers. Notions of racial difference, immunity, and resistance continued to inform and shape the historiography of yellow fever in the twentieth century.

Combining Environmental and Bacteriological Perspectives

Changing social, political, and cultural dynamics of the postwar era shaped medical ideas both about racial immunity and about the environment. Prior to the Bacteriological Revolution of the 1860s and 1870s, the dominant framework for understanding disease was broadly environmental; physicians understood a region's health in connection with numerous ecological variables. As shown in chapter 3, medical researchers in the Gulf South studied connections between local environmental conditions and the absence or presence of disease and often attributed epidemics to miasmas, stagnant water, and filth. The rise of bacteriology catalyzed medical development throughout the world, influencing many researchers to study diseases by identifying microscopic organisms in the blood and organs of infected patients, rather than observing more general environmental trends.

Beginning in 1867, as bacteriology, or "germ theory," attracted the attention of physicians, they supplemented their environmental views of disease etiology by searching for microscopic causes of yellow fever. The ideology of germs pervaded yellow fever research in New Orleans. Local physician H. D. Schmidt, a pathologist at Charity Hospital, wrote that "in the beginning of 1867, the germ theory, which, not long before, had commenced to attract the attention of medical men, had also taken root in my mind, inducing me . . . to search for the germs in the very numerous specimens of black vomit which I then examined."[51] Schmidt's transforming views reflected a growing faith in bacteriology among medical professionals, along with a shift in their research, as they began to focus on microcausal factors rather than broad ecological patterns.

By the 1870s bacteriology dominated epidemiological research, and medical authorities around the world abandoned miasmatic theories and instead searched for microscopic germs. Nancy Tomes has shown how the discovery of germs, defined as "any microscopic organism capable of causing human or animal disease," caused an ideological transformation in American society. Knowledge of the existence and potential threat of germs shaped human social behavior, eliciting widespread concern about disease contagions and the maintenance of domestic sanitation and public health. Gradually, as more physicians, politicians, and families began to believe in the "gospel of germs," they changed their everyday behavior and made decisions based on the knowledge that sanitary scientists produced.[52] From the 1870s through the 1890s, the concept of invisible germs, or microscopic bacteria, materialized in

American medical science as a result of a combination of successful developments in laboratory technology and disease prevention in Europe and the northern United States.[53] The ideology of germs shaped both medical research and public health policies. As scientists shifted their focus to germs, they failed to recognize the etiology of nonbacterial diseases, including yellow fever and malaria, which were most pervasive in the southern states.

While many medical professionals in the South accurately identified the epidemic patterns of yellow fever, they acknowledged that they did not have the microscopic technology to view the disease-causing agent. In 1876 Galveston physician Greensville Dowell echoed Josiah Nott's ideas about the cause of yellow fever, as he speculated that yellow fever was caused by an insect that was not large enough to detect with a microscope: "There must be some cause, specific and *sui generis*, that produces it. This cause I have assumed is animalcular or fungotic (microscopic), and partakes of the nature of the grasshoppers of Egypt and the western prairies, or the smut in cereals; but these are too small to be observed with any instruments we now have, and so far have eluded demonstration; but if we compare the effects of cold and heat on gnats and mosquitoes, it will not be difficult to believe it is of the same nature, as it is controlled by the same natural laws."[54]

Though his theory of the "animalcular" agent was technically incorrect, because he conflated the virus and the insect host, Dowell's observations reflected an accurate assessment of the yellow fever's ecological patterns. In 1878 a New Orleans nurse also reasoned that yellow fever–causing germs were "of animalcular origin . . . generating and spreading over surfaces like grasshoppers or caterpillars, and being introduced into the human blood. If they exist, the most powerful microscope has hitherto been unable to discover them. One fact that points to their existence is that the same extremes of heat and cold that kill other insects also kills yellow fever, whose contagion cannot exist and becomes inoculable at 32º and 212º."[55] Although medical researchers in the South recognized that patterns of yellow fever transmission closely resembled the patterns of insects and drew a connection between stagnant water and fever, they did not try to find a culpable insect species.

Perceptions of disease outbreaks in the Gulf South and the Carolina

Lowcountry represented a mixture of environmental and bacteriological perspectives, echoing antebellum ideas about environmental conditions and fevers. In 1867 a witness in Charleston wrote, "Complaints of these fevers have been very general in those sections caused no doubt in great measure by stagnant waters emitting their poisonous vapors & greatly increasing a malarial condition of Atmosphere."[56] After the 1878 epidemic, Joseph Jones, a professor at the University of Louisiana, who served on the Louisiana State Board of Health, modified his views on the nature of yellow fever. He transitioned from emphasizing climatic and atmospheric conditions to arguing that "heat and moisture, and surrounding climatic conditions . . . caused the development of a certain poison . . . [which] may be conveyed by minute forms of plant or animal life." Jones then began looking for this poison in the blood of yellow fever victims, under a microscope.[57]

For most of the nineteenth century, like European visitors and doctors who practiced in tropical regions, southern doctors drew connections between environmental conditions and diseases that they linked to warm and wet climates, particularly fevers. They linked the presence of disease with local conditions, such as atmosphere and temperature. During Reconstruction, which coincided with the global rise of bacteriology, local physicians and residents continued to debate the causes and prevention of disease and gradually turned their focus toward bacteriological explanations and solutions. The 1870s marks a transitional period in medical thought among physicians in the Gulf South, characterized by a shift from an emphasis on the environmental perspectives to the widespread acceptance of bacteriology and, eventually, growing support for federal public health enforcement. As southern physicians became increasingly interested in bacteriology during Reconstruction, they opposed federal authorities by advocating disinfection over quarantine. This changed after the epidemic of 1878, which marked a new period of renewed faith in bacteriology and the growth of public health and research institutions. The epidemic of 1878 challenged many local ideas about the causes and prevention of yellow fever, and the altered views were expressed in responses to the outbreak of yellow fever in 1879.

Bacteriology and Public Health after 1878

The devastation of the 1878 epidemic transformed prevailing perceptions about yellow fever, among the general public as well as medical professionals and policymakers. Prior to 1878, people who fled epidemics in New Orleans were invited to seek refuge by traveling upriver, to Memphis and other cities and towns that claimed to be "safe," such as Holly Springs and Dry Grove, in Mississippi. Their belief in the health of their environment, very likely combined with commercial interests that precluded the enforcement of quarantine, made residents in these small communities think they were not at risk. A resident of Holly Springs, lamenting the epidemic, wrote: "The people of [Holly Springs] were so confident that their location and the purity of their atmosphere rendered them safe, that they did not establish quarantine. When refugees from Memphis and Greenville brought yellow fever there, some uneasiness, and anxiety, existed, but the patients had either died or were convalescent, and all apprehensions had ceased. But the fatal seed was germinating while the citizens were thus lulled into a sense of security, and on the first day of September the whole city was thrown into consternation by the discovery that forty-six cases had almost simultaneously been developed."[58]

The epidemic of 1878 instigated radical changes in how locals understood the relationship between epidemics and local environments. Residents who believed they were safe from yellow fever because of their location reconsidered this notion, as a Memphis philanthropist explained: "The notion that prevailed throughout the country, and that still has hold on many otherwise well-informed persons, that there is a yellow fever zone, beyond the limits of which the dreaded disease can not flourish, had a great deal to do in the encouragement of a hardihood which, during 1878, cost Holly Springs and other places every life that was lost by yellow fever."[59]

When yellow fever reappeared in 1879, local governments established strict quarantine along rail lines, attempting to prohibit the entry of yellow fever refugees. Throughout Tennessee and Mississippi, local public health boards formed to enforce quarantine and disinfection. Public health officers conducted daily inspections to prevent future outbreaks. Around Memphis, local armed quarantine patrols, aimed at pre-

FIGURE 11. "Arrest of Yellow-Fever Refugees by the Safety Patrol of Memphis," from *Frank Leslie's Illustrated Newspaper,* August 23, 1879. (Philip S. Hench Walter Reed Yellow Fever Collection, University of Virginia.)

venting residents from fleeing during epidemics, arrested and detained yellow fever refugees.[60]

In addition to public health institutions and benevolent organizations that provided care for yellow fever victims, the severity of the 1878 epidemic led to the establishment of numerous state organizations that focused on preventing future outbreaks. These new public health systems included local boards of health and federal research programs. Generally, doctors and other residents responded to the epidemic by supporting the enforcement of public health measures, including disinfection as well as quarantine, which had previously been ignored for economic reasons. From the end of Reconstruction through the turn of the century, debates about the effectiveness of sanitary measures and quarantine remained a central conflict among medical authorities. Many historians of public health in the South have made this argument.[61]

Following the epidemic, Congress allowed "limited quarantine powers" to the Marine Hospital Service. Southern public health officials outside of New Orleans urged Congress to impose national quarantine regulations in New Orleans. Tennessee state representative Casey Young argued that "only a national quarantine, administered by a national board of health, could effectively exclude yellow fever."[62] In response to the possibility of federal quarantine in New Orleans, local medical authorities organized boards to address yellow fever prevention. These private organizations, including the New Orleans Parish Medical Society (1878) and the New Orleans Auxiliary Sanitary Association (1879), promoted sanitation and "limited quarantine" as the best mode of preventing yellow fever and other diseases.[63]

In December of 1878, Congress authorized the federal Board of Experts to investigate yellow fever and cholera in the southern states. The board, which organized in Memphis, was composed of twelve medical authorities from various cities in the United States, including Boston, Albany, Memphis, Savannah, Jackson (Mississippi), and Mobile. Three members were from New Orleans: Stanford Chaillé, Dr. S. M. Bemiss of the University of Louisiana, and Col. Thomas S. Hardee, a sanitary engineer. Many southern medical authorities claimed that the mandates of the federal board were intrusive to state-governed boards, whose foremost consideration was the local commercial interests. They criticized the board because it did not include more physicians from southern port cities, particularly Charleston and New Orleans, arguing that it functioned "under the leadership of the determined and managing apostle of quarantine."[64] Despite unresolved disputes among the board members about the nature and prevention of yellow fever, they agreed on a list of public health recommendations. The board recommended preventive measures such as the surveillance of ships, the strict enforcement of quarantine, disinfection of clothing and baggage, and the cleansing of bodies upon arrival. The board also emphasized the isolation and segregation of sick persons and the establishment of "camps of refuge" outside of cities and towns where yellow fever had been epidemic in previous years. In general, the board's recommendations did not reflect their field observations, which showed that disinfection and sanitary reform were ineffective. For example, the board demonstrated the failure of chemical disinfectants in open air but nevertheless concluded that research and experimentation in disinfection practice "should be liberally encouraged."[65]

By March of 1879, Congress had created the National Board of Health to assist with quarantines in southern ports. However, that board did not have the authority to effectively regulate local commercial activity. The board appointed twenty-five sanitary inspectors, with seventeen stationed in Memphis and New Orleans. The inspectors were instructed "to act as an advisor or instructor, but never as possessing positive authority, unless such authority may be temporarily conferred to do so." The board maintained that it was "more important that [inspectors] exert all the moral influence possible in order to effect the best results."[66]

In April of 1879, the National Board of Health approved the establishment of the Havana Yellow-Fever Commission, chaired by Chaillé. Other members included George Miller Sternberg, a US Army physician and prominent bacteriologist, who served as secretary of the board; Dr. Juan Guitéras (John Guiteras), a pathologist and histologist; and Thomas Hardee, a sanitary engineer.[67] The establishment of the commission marked an early iteration of cooperation between Cuban and North American public health officials and medical researchers, which resulted in the acceptance of the mosquito vector theory by the close of the nineteenth century.

6

"Mosquito or Man?"

IMPERIALISM AND THE RISE OF
TROPICAL MEDICINE, 1878–1912

By the late nineteenth century, the transition from miasmatic theory to bacteriology was nearly complete among mainstream scientists and public health officials. However, by the turn of the century, researchers around the world also came to recognize the role of mosquitoes in carrying malaria and yellow fever and began promoting mosquito eradication campaigns. This discovery paved the way for the rise of the field of tropical medicine, which focused on controlling numerous nonbacteriological diseases, including many parasites and diseases hosted by insects.

Efforts to manage and eradicate so-called tropical diseases were tied to the growth of late-nineteenth-century imperialism, as European empires claimed territories throughout most of Africa and much of Asia and as the United States emerged as a dominant power in the former colonies of Spain in the aftermath of the Spanish-American War. By the end of the nineteenth century, US imperialism extended beyond continental expansion and the forcible relocation of Native Americans and became tied to commercial interests in the Caribbean, Latin America, and the Pacific, primarily in tropical regions that could produce crops including sugarcane, bananas, and coffee. In the early twentieth century, the United States emerged as the preeminent global power in colonial and postcolonial spaces throughout the tropics, commanding control of territories through military conquest and economic domination in sovereign countries.

In 1900, at the close of the Spanish-American War, the US government appointed the US Army Yellow Fever Commission, which led a series of successful mosquito eradication campaigns in Havana (1901), followed by operations in Veracruz (1903), the Panama Canal Zone

(1904), and New Orleans (1905), eliminating the threat of yellow fever epidemics in these regions. The success of these campaigns depended on the use of military force in areas that the United States and British Empire controlled. The relationship between imperialism and antimosquito operations was a global phenomenon. Collaborations between military and medical authorities enabled the triumph of public health campaigns aimed at eliminating yellow fever in the tropical Atlantic until the 1950s. At the same time that the United States started to enforce mosquito eradication, public health boards, focused on antimosquito policies, emerged in Panama, Brazil, and the British Caribbean. Public health institutions, including the US Public Health and Marine Hospital Service, the London School of Tropical Medicine, and the Department of Public Health in Brazil, cooperated to research and control tropical diseases. They promoted public health programs directed toward mosquito-borne diseases, which formed the basis of early studies of tropical medicine. The apparent success of eradication campaigns at the turn of the century ushered in an era of mosquito control measures in territories held by American corporations in Latin America, including parts of Panama, Honduras, Costa Rica, and Guatemala.

In 1905, after the successful eradication of yellow fever in New Orleans through the enforcement of mosquito control measures, local business leaders promoted research in the emergent field of tropical medicine, which enabled the economic dominance of US corporations in Latin America. New Orleans emerged as the center of research on tropical medicine in the United States, as private investors who were interested in controlling tropical diseases on plantations in Latin America funded the founding of the Tulane School of Hygiene and Tropical Medicine. Alongside the famous United Fruit Company (based in Boston), two New Orleans companies established competitive plantation economies in the region: Vaccaro Brothers (which later became Standard Fruit) and Cuyamel Fruit (which later became part of United Fruit and moved its headquarters to New Orleans).[1] These companies achieved economic dominance by effectively controlling the threat of yellow fever, malaria, and other tropical diseases throughout the region, notably in Honduras, Costa Rica, Guatemala, Puerto Rico, and Cuba.

Thus, the field of tropical medicine developed in the US South and Central America as well as in territories controlled by Britain, France, and Brazil. Across the globe, the study of tropical medicine was facilitated by the growth of empires and the maintenance of racial hierarchies. Researchers emphasized connections between the tropical environment and what they classified as "tropical diseases." Ideas about the tropics were rooted in the nineteenth-century notion of a racialized environment, in which doctors emphasized the importance of "conquering" tropical diseases as the key to the conquest and control of tropical environments and peoples.

From Miasmas to Mosquitoes

In the late 1870s, bacteriology dominated global medical research and public health policy, including studies of yellow fever. In 1881 Cuban physician Carlos Finlay published his compelling research on the role of mosquitoes in transmitting yellow fever, but US medical authorities remained reluctant to accept his theory until the American occupation of Cuba following the Spanish-American War. Historians often frame the eradication of yellow fever in North America as an accomplishment achieved by Walter Reed and the US Army Yellow Fever Commission (known as the Reed Board), a group of four men who investigated and experimented with Finlay's mosquito theory in 1900, and by the subsequent enforcement of mosquito control measures under William Crawford Gorgas and the US Public Health and Marine Hospital Service.[2]

In 1881 Finlay identified the *Culex* mosquito as the carrier of yellow fever.[3] Finlay, a Cuban native whose parents had emigrated to the island from France and Scotland, studied in England, Scotland, France, and Germany before attending medical school in the United States. In 1853 he enrolled at Jefferson Medical College in Philadelphia, as that city emerged as the center of medical research in the antebellum United States between 1840 and 1860.[4] Between 1846 and 1860, the majority of medical students in Philadelphia came from the southern United States, and Finlay studied alongside these men.[5] After he graduated in 1855, Finlay began researching yellow fever and its transmission. During the 1860s and 1870s, his methods reflected contemporary medical ideology, and his early research reflected the mainstream understanding of miasmatic theory. In 1865 he measured the "alkalinity" of the atmosphere as a cause of yellow fever and other diseases, and several medical authorities in the United States and Britain accepted his ideas.[6] Finlay began investigating the role of mosquitoes as a second host for yellow fever shortly after consulting with several bacteriologists who came to Cuba as part of the federal US Havana Yellow-Fever Commission, created in response to the epidemic of 1878 in the Mississippi Valley. The commission included George Sternberg, who later became surgeon general of the Marine Hospital Service and appointed the Reed Board. While in Cuba in 1879, Sternberg consulted with Finlay, but neither considered the role of the mosquito while working together. Both focused on investigating a bacteriological cause.[7] After consulting with a team of North American bacteriologists, including New Orleans physician Stanford Chaillé, Finlay "altered the direction of his research towards the idea of an independent vector."[8] By 1880 Finlay identified this vector as the *Culex* mosquito and began conducting experiments in Havana.[9]

Despite his accuracy in describing the mosquito-transmission theory and identifying the host species of mosquito, medical authorities throughout the Americas and Europe did not accept Finlay's theory for twenty years. From 1880 to 1900, bacteriologists around the world searched for a yellow fever germ. In Brazil, Domingos Freire declared that he had discovered an organism in the blood of yellow fever patients, which he named *Cryptococcus xanthogenius* in 1885.[10] After his failed inoculations, several bacteriologists in the region erroneously claimed to have found the bacterium, including João Baptista de Lacerda of Brazil, Manuel Carmona y Valle of Mexico, and Paul Gibier of France, who had searched for Freire's bacterium in Cuba.[11] During this time Sternberg traveled to Brazil and Mexico, hoping to find a yellow fever germ, and he revisited Cuba in 1889. In Havana, Carlos Finlay had also attempted to find a yellow fever germ in the blood and "blister serum" of yellow fever patients. In 1896 Italian bacteriologist Giuseppe Sanarelli convinced many medical researchers that he had isolated the yellow fever germ, which he named *Bacillus icteroides*.[12] Sternberg and others spent four years researching Sanarelli's findings before considering the mosquito theory that Finlay had proposed more than fifteen years earlier. The US Army Yellow Fever Commission's interest in mosquitoes was likely connected to the publicity generated by the success of Patrick Manson and Ronald Ross's research (initially conducted during the late 1890s in China and India, respectively), which revealed the role of *Anopheles* mosquitoes in spreading malarial *Plasmodia* to humans.

However, even after the board's acceptance of the theory, contemporary physicians and medical officers often pointed to problems in Finlay's "science," while acknowledging his theoretical contribution to the field. For example, assistant surgeon Joseph Goldberger, who, under the auspices of the Marine Hospital Service, studied yellow fever and mosquitoes in the southern United States, Mexico, and the Caribbean until 1905, wrote that Finlay "made his experiments without system—in a measure haphazard, and consequently the mode of propagation of the disease was not proven for twenty years after he suggested it," and he lamented that it was "a great pity that he fell short in applying strictly scientific methods in his studies."[13] US Army surgeon William C. Gorgas, of Mobile, Alabama, who directed mosquito eradication campaigns in Cuba and Panama after 1900, recalled that members of the Reed Board worked closely with Finlay but "were rather inclined to make light of his ideas." Eventually, after many lengthy discussions, they gradually came to accept his mosquito theory.[14]

While early-twentieth-century medical researchers saw problems in Finlay's science, historians have shown how political, social, and economic factors affected the course of yellow fever research in Cuba and the United States. Nancy Stepan argues that "political and economic factors were more important in the lag than any supposed shortcomings in Finlay's science." These factors included the wars of independence fought in Cuba between 1878 and 1898 and the subsequent US intervention in the Spanish-American War. Between 1880 and 1898, "many sanitation scientists who emerged as leaders in sanitation after 1902 in the first Republic of Cuba were in exile or abroad for political or professional reasons," including Aristides Agramonte, who served on the Reed Board. Stepan argues that because of the war and chaotic conditions on the island, Spanish authorities did not prioritize medical research or sanitation, despite the danger that yellow fever posed to foreign soldiers.[15] In fact, it was due to US involvement in the Spanish-American War that the United States became increasingly interested in yellow fever and altered the course of yellow fever research.[16]

The Spanish-American War and the War on Mosquitoes

By the spring of 1898, the United States had entered a military conflict that began as a Cuban revolt to gain independence from Spain in February of 1895. The Cuban-Spanish conflict threatened US political and economic interests by disrupting trade and military control of the island, which was often called the "key" to control of the Gulf of Mexico. The war also interfered with the possibility of the construction of an interoceanic canal through Panama, an idea that increasingly attracted entrepreneurs in the United States during the 1890s.[17]

The United States defeated the Spanish in just three months, with fewer than four hundred casualties of war. However, more than twenty-five hundred American soldiers died from yellow fever during the war, causing yellow fever control to become a priority among members of the army medical board.[18] Between 1899 and 1900, military officers continued to enforce quarantine and sanitary reform, which included cleansing, disinfection, and fumigation.[19] The US Army's occupation of Cuba promoted yellow fever research because of the threat of the disease to officers stationed on the island. The threat of yellow fever caused the federal government to adequately fund yellow fever research, which the board then carried out systematically in Havana.

In terms of institutional and scientific developments, several reforms occurred in the aftermath of the Spanish-American War. Major organizational and educational reforms included the organization of the Army Nurse Corps, the Department of Military Hygiene at the US Military Academy, and the Army Medical Reserve Boards. The Marine Hospital Service established boards designed to target tropical diseases, focused on typhoid fever and yellow fever in the Americas. In May of 1900, army surgeon general Sternberg appointed the US Army Yellow Fever Commission to investigate yellow fever in Cuba, under the direction of Walter Reed of Virginia, who was a professor of bacteriology and clinical microscopy at the Army Medical School at the time. This board consisted of Reed and three other members: James Carroll, a Canadian bacteriologist; Jesse Lazear of Baltimore, a bacteriologist who had begun studying malarial parasites in the 1890s; and Cuban physician Aristides Agramonte, who oversaw autopsies and pathological research.[20]

The Reed Board did not go to Havana with the intent of eradicating mosquitoes. The board researched the cause of yellow fever, while advising public health officers to enforce sanitary policy, particularly cleansing and disinfection. Initially, the board conducted a series of bacteriological investigations, including a lengthy disproval of Sanarelli's findings.[21] Reed appointed army medical officer W. C. Gorgas, who had yellow fever immunity and had been stationed in Cuba since the beginning of the war, as chief sanitary officer in Havana. Gorgas wrote that when they arrived in Havana in 1898, "the military authorities concluded that this was the opportunity which the United States [had] been awaiting for the past two hundred years. Thinking that yellow fever was a filth disease, they believed that if we could get Havana clean enough, we could free it from yellow fever. It was felt that if we could eliminate Havana as a focus of infection, the United States would cease to be subject to epidemics." By late summer, Gorgas believed that "Havana had been cleaner than any other city had ever been up to that time." However, he noted that "yellow fever had been steadily growing worse than since we had taken possession of the city, and in 1900 there were a greater number of cases than there had been for several years."[22]

While most medical researchers continued to search for a microscopic yellow fever–causing germ, Jesse Lazear began conducting mosquito experiments, using eggs that he had obtained from Finlay. After infecting himself and James Carroll with yellow fever, Lazear died in September of 1900.[23] Reed was in Washington at the time. After Lazear's death, Reed became convinced that the mosquito was the yellow fever vector and decided not to inoculate himself when he returned to Cuba. By November, Reed established Camp Lazear in Quemados, an isolated area southwest of Havana. His team included several Cuban physicians, including Carlos Finlay, Juan Guitéras, and A. Díaz Albertini. The researchers at Camp Lazear systematically tested Finlay's mosquito-transmission theory on paid volunteers, who were soldiers and newly arrived Spanish immigrants.[24] The experiments at Camp Lazear, which lasted only a few months, resulted in the funding and enforcement of mosquito eradication campaigns in Havana, led by Gorgas, who became known for eradicating yellow fever in the city for the first time in nearly two hundred years.[25] The eradication of yellow fever in Cuba at the turn of the century can most accurately be described as a collaboration between Finlay and a group of North American and Cuban bacteriologists, fiscally and militarily supported by the US government.

The Military-Medical Complex
and the Rise of Tropical Medicine

In 1902 the US Public Health Service expanded and merged with the Marine Hospital Service, forming an organization known as the US Public Heath and Marine Hospital Service. Essentially, the federal bureau acquired a military component.[26] This merger enabled the service to enforce public health measures within the nation and overseas; it also facilitated military campaigns during this period of imperial growth, as the United States expanded its territory into tropical and subtropical regions in Cuba, Puerto Rico, Mexico, the Panama Canal Zone, Guam, Hawaii, and the Philippines.[27]

These tropical environments were capable of producing agricultural commodities that were difficult or impossible to grow in the United States. The territories that the United States acquired after the Spanish-American War produced a substantial portion of the world's sugarcane, and the territories acquired by US corporations in the early twentieth century could be used to cultivate other profitable crops and procure natural resources. From the beginning of the Reconstruction era through the turn of the century, Cuba had been the primary supplier of sugar to the United States. After the Civil War, Hawaii emerged as an important source of the nation's sugar. Capital investment in colonial and postcolonial spaces throughout the tropical world from the turn of the century through the 1940s enabled American companies to produce vast quantities of consumer products, including sugarcane, fruits, coffee, rubber, beef cattle, and timber.[28] In their efforts to control these regions and build plantations, American imperialists and capitalists contended with numerous diseases, including yellow fever and malaria. Managing the risk of disease was vital to maintaining control of these tropical environments.

The development of research institutions focused on tropical diseases, and subsequent mosquito eradication enforcement, involved transnational collaborations across the Atlantic. At the turn of the century, European medical researchers from England, France, and Germany began establishing schools of "tropical medicine," including the Liverpool School of Tropical Medicine (1898) and the London School of Tropical Medicine (1899). Specialists conducted research in Brazil (in Pará and Rio de Janeiro). When the Reed Board began investigating the role of mosquitoes in the propagation of yellow fever in Havana in 1900, the Liverpool School of Tropical Medicine appointed several doctors to study the disease in Pará. By the end of the following year, a French coalition began an expedition to study the transmission of yellow fever in Brazil and established its headquarters in Rio de Janeiro, and by 1904 the Hamburg School of Tropical Medicine sent doctors to study the disease in Brazil, also based in Rio. In 1905, the Liverpool School of Tropical Medicine had reestablished its Yellow Fever Laboratory in Pará under the direction of new physicians.[29]

The growth of a national military-medical complex, in which the federal government relied on military support to implement and enforce sanitary measures, was integral to the successful eradication of yellow fever in locales throughout the tropical Americas. Having military support played an essential role in the implementation of new sanitary measures. Only a large, intrusive, and coercive public health force could systematically destroy mosquitoes and mosquito habitats. After the triumph of the US Army Board in Cuba and Panama, military involvement and the establishment of military institutions grew and continued to practice sanitary policies in territories outside of the nation. Federal imperial interests, alongside commercial interests, in the tropical Caribbean and Central America led to the growth and development of public health and medical research institutions in the United States, including the US Public Health and Marine Hospital Service (1902), the American Society of Tropical Medicine (1903), and the Walter Reed Army Medical Center (1909), as well as the School of Hygiene and Tropical Medicine in New Orleans (1912), the nation's first such institution.

IMPERIALISM AND ERADICATION CAMPAIGNS

Over the first decade of the twentieth century, as news of the success of Reed's commission in Cuba traveled throughout the region, public health authorities in the tropical Atlantic led antimosquito campaigns. The campaigns usually included a military component, which systematically enforced antimosquito measures by public health officials. A national yellow fever board enforced mosquito eradication in Brazil, while US and British boards and US private corporations operated in Panama, Mexico, Belize, Honduras, Costa Rica, Guatemala, the southern United States, Puerto Rico, and numerous other Caribbean islands.

Research Sites in Puerto Rico and Mexico

The US Marine Hospital Service had begun sending officials to Mexico and Puerto Rico to conduct yellow fever research in 1900, focusing on the study of *Stegomyia* mosquitoes. Between 1900 and 1903, laboratories in Washington analyzed specimens collected by public health officers stationed in cities including Ponce, Puerto Rico; Tampico and Ve-

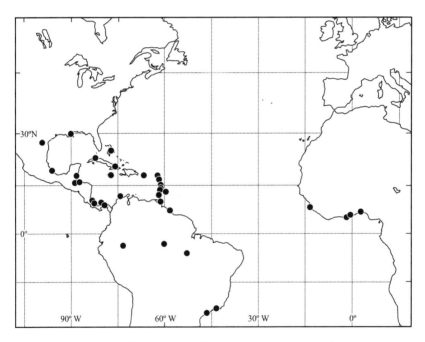

FIGURE 12. Key sites of mosquito-eradication campaigns targeting *A. aegypti*, c. 1900–1906. (Compiled from Boyce, *Health Progress and Administration; Mosquito or Man?; Yellow Fever and Its Prevention; Yellow Fever Prophylaxis;* Stepan, *Beginnings of Brazilian Science*, 88–89; and from the annual reports of the United Fruit Company, 1912–15. Cartography by Mary Lee Eggart.)

racruz, Mexico; and Laredo, Texas.[30] Many officers who were stationed in these areas conducted research rather than overseeing eradication campaigns. Officers who had acquired immunity to yellow fever could safely work in these regions, collecting mosquitoes and observing their breeding and biting patterns. Scientists in Washington who received the mosquitoes could run tests in a controlled environment, allowing them to find effective methods of eliminating breeding spaces and killing the mosquitoes, in addition to developing technologies to protect humans while traveling or sleeping. By 1904 the US Public Health and Marine Hospital Service was advising public health officers to burn pots of sulfur to kill mosquitoes, but the service had determined that "the disinfection of baggage and passengers' effects to prevent infection from yellow fever [was] no longer required." Officials redefined and systematically enforced quarantine regulations, which focused on destroying mosquitoes and their breeding spaces and removing sick passengers, rather than just detaining and cleansing ships.[31]

Mosquito Brigades in Brazil

Public health authorities in Brazil successfully eradicated yellow fever for several years by engaging in practices similar to those followed by the Reed Board. The "young, virtually unknown" Oswaldo Cruz, after his appointment as director of Brazil's federal Department of Public Health, by March of 1903 had sent a representative to Havana to observe the work of American authorities in Cuba; by April he had organized the new Serviço de Prophylaxia da Febre Amarella (Yellow fever prophylaxis service).[32] The service operated by dividing Rio into sanitary districts, policing suspected areas, destroying mosquitoes, and identifying and isolating yellow fever patients. It formed "anti-mosquito brigades," one of which "consisted of 1,500 men to wage relentless war upon all the breeding places of the *Stegomyia*." In addition to destroying breeding spaces, brigades attempted to kill mosquitoes using sulfur and pyretheum.[33] By the end of the year, "the brigades of 'mosquito killers' became a familiar sight in the city."[34] Incidences of yellow fever decreased from 1903 until the disease was absent from the city in 1909. Mosquito brigades also successfully removed the threat of yellow fever in Santos.[35]

Mosquito Control in the Panama Canal Zone

The success of Reed's board prompted US representatives to seriously consider the construction of an interoceanic canal through Panama. Prior to 1900, the prospect of building a canal raised concerns about yellow fever epidemics, which commonly occurred in the Canal Zone, bordered by Colón on the Atlantic and Panamá City on the Pacific. French engineers had repeatedly attempted to build a canal through the isthmus since 1880, but their efforts were unsuccessful in large part because of the presence of yellow fever. Impediments to the French project included labor shortages because of yellow fever deaths, in addition to environmental obstacles owing to the rocky landscape, tropical storms, and malaria.[36]

After the Spanish-American War, federal officials and local entrepreneurs in the United States became increasingly interested in the prospect of the canal, which would give traders in the Gulf of Mexico direct and rapid access to goods from Asia. After the United States pledged to build the canal in 1902, Patrick Manson, who served as medical adviser to the British Colonial Office at the time, warned that without the strict enforcement of antimosquito measures, yellow fever could cause devastating epidemics in Asia. He emphasized the disruption of trade that yellow fever would cause if it "broke out in distributing centres such as Zanzibar, Aden, Bombay, Calcutta, Colombo, Singapore, Batavia, Bangkok, Saigon, Hong Kong, Shanghai, or Yokohama."[37] Despite his concerns, Manson was optimistic about the ability of US officials to contain the disease. He applauded the success of the Reed Board and advised public health officers in the Canal Zone "to stringently enforce destruction of all mosquitoes, their eggs, and their larvæ in all ships, before these ships are allowed to clear from the Pacific end of the Canal, or from other ports on the Pacific side of the American Yellow Fever District." He concluded that quarantine was unnecessary because the journey from Panama to Asia took more than two weeks, and in this time sick individuals would no longer be infectious.[38] In the fall of 1902, Sternberg relieved Gorgas of his duty in Havana and placed him in charge of sanitary work on the Isthmus of Panama. During the year prior to the commencement of the building of the Panama Canal, Gorgas went to

Egypt as representative of the US Army to the first Egyptian Medical Congress, where he was directed to "examine into what had been the sanitary conditions during the construction of the Suez Canal," more than thirty years earlier.[39]

The eradication of yellow fever in the Canal Zone, directed by Gorgas beginning in 1903, elicited support for the construction of the canal among federal representatives and local commercial and public heath boards. The prospect of a canal especially drew the support of the Board of Trade in New Orleans, which declared in 1904 that Panama "holds the key to the commercial situation of the great nations, and when our Government shall have completed the gigantic obligation it has assumed, and the canal is open for traffic, there will be thrust upon us an opportunity which, if not taken advantage of to the maximum, will mean our commercial undoing." The board asserted that the Republic of Panama was "today the centre of the world's greatest activity" and considered New Orleans to be "the gateway to the South and the Mississippi Valley at this period of the world's progress."[40] Members of the Board of Trade emphasized the importance of yellow fever control and affirmed the success of the Reed Board. They reported, "Dr. Gorgas has had wonderful experience with health matters in Havana, and was instrumental in eliminating yellow fever in Cuba, and on the Zone, where the regulations, health conditions, and the control of the sanitation, health laws, and hospital service, are absolutely under his control, he expects to be equally successful," and petitioned the Louisiana State Board of Health to cooperate with the US Public Health and Marine Hospital Service.[41]

Between 1903 and 1908, Gorgas enforced policies that aimed to protect citizens from mosquitoes and prevent breeding, such as prohibiting the collection of stagnant water by screening cisterns, policies enforced by house-to house inspections and fines for those who failed to comply with public health mandates.[42] The United States began construction in 1904, one year after Gorgas's mosquito eradication campaign successfully removed the threat of yellow fever in the Zone. Paul Sutter has shown how the work of American entomologists, especially L. O. Howard, facilitated the growth of state institutions that enabled the "commercial and military expansion of the United States into tropical Latin America and the Asian Pacific." Despite entomologists' role in "celebrating their apparent sanitary conquest of the tropics," some of them noted

that mosquito breeding was often a result of ecological changes resulting from human construction projects.[43]

Scientists and public health officers, including Howard and Gorgas, often discussed their successes in racial terms that echoed nineteenth-century medical ideas about race and immunity. Henry Rose
Carter of the US Public Health Service advocated racial segregation
among canal construction workers to prevent malaria from spreading
to nonimmune populations. Howard asserted that mosquito control in
the Canal Zone made it "possible for the white race to live healthfully in
the tropics."[44] Gorgas argued that public health efforts in tropical zones,
ranging from the Amazon to the Congo, would benefit "the white man"
and enable "a large emigration . . . from the present civilized temperate
regions to the tropics."[45]

Yellow Fever Eradication in New Orleans

Though their methods were not entirely effective in preventing major
epidemics, public health authorities in the US continued to enforce
practices such as the disinfection and fumigation of vessels, aimed at
killing microscopic germs, until 1905, when an outbreak appeared in
New Orleans for the first time since before the Spanish-American War.
The success of the US Army Yellow Fever Commission in Cuba and Panama had convinced local medical officials that mosquitoes carried yellow fever and transmitted it from human to human and that epidemics
could be prevented by declaring a war on mosquitoes.

In 1905 rumors of the presence of yellow fever in the southern United
States prompted the Public Health and Marine Hospital Service to send
officers to investigate in cities throughout Louisiana, Mississippi, Alabama, Georgia, Texas, and Florida.[46] In addition to carrying out government research, public health officers were ordered "to conduct a campaign of education among the medical profession and laity . . . upon the
importance of screening all cases of febrile diseases from the access of
mosquitoes until a positive diagnosis is made, and upon methods for the
destruction and prevention of the propagation of these insects."[47]

As early as 1900, a few local medical authorities in New Orleans had
already started investigating the habits of mosquitoes in the city and
advocating mosquito eradication policies, but campaigns prior to 1905
were for the most part ineffective. In 1901 the Orleans Parish Medical

Society appointed a commission to study the breeding habits of mosquitoes in the city, and by July the Board of Health of New Orleans had issued a circular with details of the breeding patterns of the mosquitoes, advising citizens to oil and screen cisterns and warning them that mosquitoes laid eggs in broken bottles, tins, and unused tubs. However "little heed was paid to anti-mosquito measures," because "apathy took place, householders raised objections, and precautionary measures were neglected."[48] The 1901 campaign failed because of a lack of enforcement. However, local investigations of the breeding habits of New Orleans's mosquitoes, in addition to studies conducted in Puerto Rico and Mexico at this time, provided valuable information for public health authorities in 1905.

On July 21 public health authorities announced that yellow fever was officially present in New Orleans. Representatives from the city and state boards of health, health officers from surrounding states, and the Public Health and Marine Hospital Service, agreed to enforce mosquito prevention campaigns in addition to quarantining incoming port traffic.[49] The success of the 1905 campaign can be attributed to the cooperation of federal, state, and local organizations, including the Public Health and Marine Hospital Service, the Orleans Parish Medical Society, the Citizens' Volunteer Ward Organization, and several other local media and educational campaigns.[50] The systematic enforcement of mosquito eradication policies, directed by Public Health and Marine Hospital Service officers, effectively removed the threat of yellow fever from the city by engaging in "general warfare against all mosquitoes, except swamp." The service employed more than twelve hundred men and placed each ward under the supervision of an army surgeon, instructed to discover and isolate early cases of yellow fever, kill all *Stegomyias*, and ensure that each ward was "equipped with its forces of inspectors, oilers, screeners [and] fumigators."[51] Medical officers used practices similar to those employed in Cuba, Brazil, and Panama, including the screening and oiling of cisterns and fumigation using sulfur, pyrethrum, and steam.[52] Screening and oiling cisterns proved to effectively decrease the proliferation of mosquitoes, and many residents advocated the policy. Young proponents of the campaign wore buttons that read, "My cisterns are all right; How are yours?" Every week, officials organized a "mosquito killing day" throughout the city, on which they encouraged the entire population to kill the mosquitoes in their homes by means of fumigation practices.[53]

In 1905 members of the Liverpool School collaborated with the US Public Health and Marine Hospital Service and enforced eradication campaigns in Central America, including British and Spanish Honduras, Belize, and adjacent republics, at ports that supplied fruit to the United States and often passed through New Orleans.[54] Within a few years, they began yellow fever operations in British Caribbean colonial possessions, including Barbados, St. Lucia, Demerara, Trinidad, St. Lucia, Grenada, and Jamaica.[55] British colonial officials worked with local authorities and enforced education campaigns, in addition to a "war against insect pests in the West Indies," which consisted of "a progressive policy of extermination waged against the *Stegomyia*" and various antilarval measures aimed at eliminating open stagnant water containers. British public health officials in Caribbean colonies advocated a policy that was based on the success of the US Yellow Fever Commission. British pathologist Rubert Boyce, who assisted in the public health expeditions to British Honduras and New Orleans and was a founding member of the Liverpool School of Tropical Medicine, declared, "A policy of this kind is bound to bear fruit, as it has already done in New Orleans, Cuba, Panama, Brazil, Mexico, etc. etc., and I am convinced, bring about the total eradication of yellow fever."[56] By 1910 Boyce remarked, "Yellow fever is not to-day regarded as the inevitable penalty of our desire to go to tropical lands; it is to-day the penalty of ignorance and superstition." The success of public health campaigns in New Orleans, Central America, and the Caribbean served as an example to promote similar policies in imperial territories throughout the British Empire.[57]

Corporate Imperialism

The American Empire of the twentieth century operated more by asserting economic dominance than by formal political control. Thus, in the United States, institutions of tropical medicine developed as a result of "corporate colonialism" and imperialism in Central America and the Caribbean.[58] By the early twentieth century, local authorities in New Orleans believed that the threat of tropical diseases constituted an issue of national importance and advocated research and public health measures. The rise of tropical medicine was important not only for public health in the southern states, but also for private, corporate interests in Central America. In fact, private corporate funding for medical research in Latin America, focused on tropical diseases, formed the basis of the establishment of the School of Hygiene and Tropical Medicine in New Orleans. As public support for the 1904 yellow fever eradication campaign arose after the US Public Health and Marine Hospital Service demonstrated the success of mosquito control measures in Cuba, Puerto Rico, Mexico, and the Panama Canal Zone, private investors became increasingly interested in supporting research to prevent and eradicate tropical diseases. Private interests were instrumental in the growth of local institutions as investors began acquiring land in Central America.

In 1912 Samuel Zemurray, an entrepreneur who had recently purchased vast amounts of plantation land in Honduras, funded the establishment of Tulane University's School of Hygiene and Tropical Medicine.[59] Zemurray, known as "Sam the Banana Man," immigrated to the United States from Russia in 1892 and within a few years had settled in New Orleans. Along with another entrepreneur, Ashell Hubbard, he contracted with the United Fruit Company before purchasing five thousand acres of land in Honduras and establishing the Cuyamel Fruit Company in 1910. In December 1910 he organized and financed a military coup to reinstate Honduras's deposed president Manuel Bonilla so that he could secure tax exemptions for his company. John Soluri has shown how Zemurray's operations and US intervention in Honduras "set the stage for a veritable bonanza of concessions approved by Bonilla during his first year in office," including two railroad concessions to the United Fruit Company.[60] Thus, the collusion of the US government with private interests sparked the founding of the nation's first school of tropical medicine in New Orleans.

Upon the establishment of Tulane's Department of Tropical Medicine, the United Fruit Company donated an additional twenty-five thousand dollars.[61] Within a few years, the company had effectively removed the threat of yellow fever from its territories. The Medical Department of the United Fruit Company reported that yellow fever had been endemic on its plantations in Panama until 1903, when the company began directing its efforts "toward the destruction of all mosquitoes." By 1906 it reported no cases of yellow fever in Panama.[62] One year later, the company claimed that owing to "sanitary improvement," Port Limón, Costa Rica, was transformed from a "miserable swamp, infested with yellow fever," into a "modern city, second to none in beauty and cleanliness."[63] By 1915 the company reported that yellow fever was not present on its properties in Guatemala and Honduras.[64] A contemporary account of the operations of the United Fruit Company described its role in the "health conquest of the tropics," highlighting collaborations between US corporations and imperial medical researchers in Asia, Africa, and Central America:

> Scientists and physicians with experience in Java, India, the tropical sections of Africa, and elsewhere responded to the call to assist American enterprise in this pioneer industrial invasion of the tropics. It was this paucity of our knowledge concerning tropical diseases which impelled the United Fruit Company to suggest and later to give substantial financial assistance to the founding of a department in Tulane University for the exclusive study and investigation of maladies peculiar to the coastal regions of the Caribbean, and much of the advancement since accomplished has been due to the discoveries made and the remedies applied by those sent out by this university.[65]

The corporate funding that enabled the establishment and growth of Tulane's School of Hygiene and Tropical Medicine supported research on yellow fever, in addition to numerous other diseases that were prevalent in Central America, including malaria.[66] In New Orleans, local medical institutions were funded and founded not only for the purpose of improving local health conditions, but also to support the growth of economic and imperial enterprises in Latin America.

The narrative of triumph and conquest of tropical diseases in contemporary accounts obscures some of the causal links between imperial projects and the growth of diseases in tropical Latin America. Because of the expansion of American corporate control, the lowlands of Central America underwent a series of ecological changes, similar to those that contributed to the rise of yellow fever in Louisiana and the Lower Mississippi Valley in the nineteenth century. The establishment of plantations and port cities required extensive land clearance, deforestation, and drainage, creating new habitats for mosquitoes. Additionally, the construction of transportation infrastructure enabled the expansion of mosquito habitats and provided *A. aegypti* with new populations of laborers and other newcomers to feed on. Large-scale projects such as the building of the Panama Canal and smaller ventures such as the building of railroads in Honduras, Guatemala, and Panama increased the risk of yellow fever epidemics. American capital was integral to funding much of the land clearance, water control, and railroad construction throughout Central America.[67]

The Roots of Tropical Medicine

Medical researchers studied diseases of warm climates throughout the colonial era, before the professional field of tropical medicine emerged in the late nineteenth century. Studies of diseases that were particular to "warm climates" preceded the bacteriological era and in fact merged with miasmatic theory. The notions of diseases associated with "warm climates" and "tropical diseases" were both grounded in the idea that tropical environments presented challenges that did not threaten populations in temperate zones. Medical authorities considered ecological differences between tropical and temperate climates not only in terms of temperature and rainfall, but also in regard to differences in culture, race, and social behavior. Many doctors who studied diseases of warm climates or tropical medicine also studied race, and in most cases the racial preconceptions of doctors are evident in their research.

Historians often connect the development of the field of tropical medicine with the growth of powerful colonial regimes and the expansion of the British Empire in Asia and Africa. Numerous scholars have also shown linkages to the growth of institutions in Latin America and the Philippines, as a consequence of American imperialism.[68] While many scholars have found the roots of tropical medicine in colonial medical regimes in India, North Africa, East Asia, the Caribbean, and South America, the antebellum United States is absent from this discourse.[69] However, public health regimes directed toward the study of tropical medicine in the United States also fit this pattern, as they developed in the South, centered in New Orleans and supported by imperial and corporate interests. Subtropical regions like New Orleans inhabited a space between the tropical and temperate zones, and contemporaries viewed the city as a liminal space in terms of race, culture, and society as well.

The institutionalization of research on tropical medicine in the US South is particularly significant because of the pervasiveness of tropical diseases in the southern states and the presence of those diseases until the twentieth century. Further, because of the prominence of racial slavery and federal expansionist policies directed toward Native Americans, the history of diseases of warm climates in the United States developed in the context of colonialism and empire. In addition, the rise of US imperialism and corporatism in Latin America and the Pacific at the turn of the century encouraged the development of tropical medical institutions and the success of the so-called conquest of yellow fever.

The field of tropical medicine that developed in European medical institutions between 1890 and 1912 reflected a long history of colonial medical research directed toward diseases of warm climates. Many historians have considered British colonial physician Patrick Manson, who researched the role of parasitic organisms and mosquitoes in malaria and founded the London School of Tropical Medicine in 1899, as the founder or "father" of tropical medicine.[70] During the late 1890s, while working in Xiamen (Amoy), Manson researched the role of the *Anopheles* mosquito in the transmission of malaria. Also at this time, Ronald Ross, who worked as an officer in the British Indian Medical Service, studied the *Plasmodia* parasites that cause malaria while stationed outside of Hyderabad. Just as Manson and Ross conducted research in British imperial spaces, the team of US army surgeons credited with the discovery of the etiology of yellow fever conducted experiments in American imperial spaces.

Douglas M. Haynes, in his study of Patrick Manson and the "conquest of tropical disease" in the British Empire, argues that imperialism was the driving force behind the rise of tropical medicine. He contends that "the history of tropical medicine is more than a story about disease in the tropical world. It reveals the critical role of imperialism in constituting British medicine and science in the nineteenth and twentieth centuries. The health care needs of the formal and informal British empire contributed to the growth, as well as the institutional development, of the profession at home."[71] Haynes states that malaria "posed the single greatest challenge to the expansion of European colonies."[72] Similarly, yellow fever presented the greatest threat to the expansion of the United States in the Caribbean, despite the presence of malaria in the region.

The health care needs of American soldiers stationed in Cuba during the US occupation were a critical factor in the establishment of medical institutions and organizations aimed at eliminating yellow fever.

Since European medical interventions in colonial territories in Africa, Asia, and the Americas began centuries before the Mansonian period, scholars have challenged the narrow definition of tropical medicine as a field that emerged in the context of late-nineteenth-century imperialism.[73] Manson defined tropical diseases as diseases of high atmospheric temperature, using the term "tropical" in a meteorological sense rather than a geographical sense. He associated insect-borne diseases, including yellow fever, malaria, dengue fever, elephantiasis, sleeping sickness, and kala-azar (black fever or visceral leishmaniasis) with environmental conditions that bred insects, particularly rain and high temperatures. For this reason, the diseases could appear in temperate and subtropical geographical zones during the summer. Manson classified more than forty diseases as tropical, including bacterial infections and diseases that he labeled as of an "undetermined nature," such as pellagra and beriberi, which were caused by vitamin deficiencies.[74] Though the tropical climate was not a cause of many of these diseases, Manson labeled them as tropical diseases because they were commonly found in tropical geographies. This pattern, of linking diseases of poverty and malnutrition with climate, continued through the postwar era and the twentieth century. In the United States, medical authorities identified tropical diseases with the warm climate of the South, including yellow fever, malaria, and pellagra. David Arnold argues that understanding the "revolutionary significance" of developments in the study of tropical medicine in the late nineteenth century, which included advances in the fields of bacteriology, parasitology, immunology, and microscopy, along with the "innovative combination of laboratory research and experimentation (often conducted in metropolitan institutes) with field observations in tropical countries, and the targeting of specific diseases (notably malaria, but also sleeping sickness and yellow fever) for both laboratory research and public health campaigns," requires an analysis of pre-Mansonian forms of tropical medicine.[75] This is certainly the case in the United States, where the origins of the field of tropical medicine developed in the warm, wet environment of southern Louisiana.

Health, Environment, and Race in Louisiana
and the Lower Mississippi Valley

In Louisiana, the study of ailments that later became known as "tropical diseases" began during the colonial period. Arnold argues that "medicine was a conspicuous element in the process of European exploration and colonization virtually from the outset" and that early tropical medicine was characterized by a sense of "otherness" that Europeans linked to tropical regions.[76] French colonists and American settlers had similar views of Louisiana's landscape, climate, and culture. In the early eighteenth century, the first French colonists to settle in coastal Louisiana associated fevers with the rain and heat of summer months, as well as with vessels arriving from Havana. French colonists noted that Canadian settlers were more likely to contract fevers in Louisiana.[77]

In the early nineteenth century, after the Louisiana Purchase, American newcomers often linked fevers to the warm climate of summer. In 1804 Governor Claiborne wrote, "Louisiana is a beautiful country, and rewards abundantly the Labour of man;—But the Climate is a wretched one, and destructive to human life."[78] The presence of fevers distinguished the southern United States from the rest of the nation, particularly during the period of continental expansion in the nineteenth century. During this time, the American South closely resembled European colonies in the tropics, characterized by a system of racial subjugation and plantation labor in a warm climate. Conceptions of disease being linked to the warm climate of the South resembled European views of disease in colonial territories. The process of settlement and expansion in the Mississippi Valley, in addition to that in the Arkansas and Missouri territories, caused anxieties about the foreign disease environment among settlers. Conevery Bolton Valenčius argues that the climate in these regions "heightened many migrants attention to the effects of change of place, since they feared the enfeebling effects of hot climates."[79]

Throughout the antebellum period, residents continued to draw connections between climate and culture in the South. In addition to a sense of "otherness," early tropical medicine was characterized by "the power of localism, manifested through the particular medical needs

and social composition of the local inhabitants, the impact of indigenous practitioners on Western traders and travelers, the use of local
drugs and different topographies to counter disease, the growth of local
medical services and even local schools of thought and practice."[80] In
colonial Louisiana, settlers "eulogized Indian medicine men and drew
enthusiastic pictures of the perfect health of the natives," despite frequent outbreaks of smallpox that killed large proportions of populations
in villages along the Mississippi and surrounding bayous.[81] Local observations and understandings generated a "science of localities—one in
which being on an ill-defined frontier or in the swampy backwaters of a
distant American territory could be turned into an advantage . . . moreover, as the sectional crisis of the questionably united States deepened,
medical geography slid easily into an argument for Southern nationalism."[82] In part, Southern nationalism developed in response to conceptions of the region as part of a different environment than the temperate
northeastern states.

In addition to anxieties about disease, southern physicians expressed
their concerns about race. Valenčius explains that "taking seriously antebellum newcomers' concern for the intimate ties between personal
and environmental well-being thus provides skeptical modern observers a way to understand the experienced physical dimensions of slippery
racial definitions and white preoccupation with them."[83] The growth of
a free black population in the 1840s and 1850s intensified racial tensions among medical professionals in the South. In Louisiana, perceptions of race shaped medical research and civic policy. The racial and
ethnic diversity of New Orleans blurred racial distinctions and caused
many scientists to emphasize ideologies of racial difference. In the antebellum period, the "logic of white Americans . . . was simple. They did
not belong in hot places; black people did." The concept of "whiteness"
in America was "most powerful in opposition to black."[84] By the 1860s,
Americans of European descent viewed themselves as white Americans,
and scientific theories of racial difference (including anatomy, physi-
ology, and psychology) commonly asserted the inferiority of nonwhite
races.

Ideas about health and illness in the southern states revolved around
settlers' conceptions of race and ecology in the Gulf South and in newly
acquired lands west of the Mississippi. Settlers and migrants often de-

scribed their perception of the West as a "new country" that was "young, unspoiled, and uninhabited." Migrants from the eastern United States encroached on regions inhabited by Native American nations in the Missouri and Arkansas territories, supported by national military campaigns to remove Native Americans. The contradiction between the image of the new country and the brutal realities of Indian removal reveals the complexity of national identity during this period. Western expansion continued after the Civil War and played a role in reconciliation between the Union and former Confederate states. Cecilia O'Leary demonstrates how militarism against the Plains Indians in the 1870s and 1880s played a role in national reconciliation. She argues that "without the enthusiasm of a popular imperialism first generated by the Indian wars and later dramatically consolidated by the Spanish-American War, the impetus for cultural reunification would have been significantly delayed."[85] Links between late-nineteenth-century expansionist policies in Native America and imperialism at the turn of the century are evident in Walter Reed's career prior to his direction of the US Army Yellow Fever Commission. Reed worked as an army physician, stationed in various points in US states and territories including Alabama, Nebraska, and the Arizona Territory. Described as a "frontier doctor," Reed provided medical care to US soldiers, settlers, their families, and Native American captives. Between 1887 and 1890, Reed oversaw the medical care at Mount Vernon Barracks in Alabama, where the US government held Apache captives including military leader Geronimo. In 1890 Reed provided medical care to wounded soldiers at Fort Keogh, Montana, after the Sioux Massacre at Wounded Knee.[86]

The history of yellow fever eradication campaigns at the turn of the century reveals links between imperialism and the rise of tropical medicine. Ironically, the ecological conditions created by imperial expansion, including the construction of plantations, railroads, and waterways, increased the risk of yellow fever in many tropical environments. Rather than evaluating the role of ecological change in compounding epidemics, medical authorities focused on proximate causes of the disease. Medical knowledge regarding the role of the mosquito explained the mysterious patterns of yellow fever and led public health officials to focus on a new enemy: the mosquito. Attempts to study yellow fever in tropical regions continued in the first half of the twentieth century and remained linked to colonial and imperial regimes in Latin America and West Africa. Despite global efforts to control the disease, outbreaks of yellow fever increased in tropical Africa, and sylvan yellow fever became endemic among primate populations in the tropics of South America.

Epilogue

YELLOW FEVER, PAST AND PRESENT

The global map of yellow fever transformed profoundly between the nineteenth and twenty-first centuries. In the nineteenth century, epidemic yellow fever, characterized as an "urban disease," prevailed in tropical and subtropical port cities throughout the Atlantic and occasionally caused outbreaks in temperate ports in North America and Europe. By 1905 epidemics had ceased in temperate regions. Between 1905 and 1950, cases of yellow fever had declined around the world, and medical authorities asserted that it was a "conquered" disease.[1] However, within ten years, epidemics were no longer confined to port cities in the tropical world. After 1950, the incidence of yellow fever increased in tropical Africa and South America, and the disease appeared for the first time in East Africa. Over the course of the twentieth century, researchers in Brazil, Columbia, Nigeria, and Uganda found that yellow fever appeared more frequently in nonurban spaces, particularly tropical forests and savannahs.

Yellow fever epidemics declined in the early twentieth century as a result of the enforcement of mosquito control measures in the years between 1910 and 1930; mass vaccination programs in colonial Africa and South America followed in the 1930s and 1940s. Cases of yellow fever increased after 1950 because of the decline of immunization campaigns and mosquito eradication measures in the aftermath of national independence movements in those regions. The transformation and decline of global mosquito eradication campaigns, which had begun using DDT in the 1940s and gradually stopped using it in the 1960s and 1970s, contributed to the "reemergence" of yellow fever, as cases escalated in tropical regions of both Africa and South America during the 1980s and 1990s.[2]

In addition to the decline of vaccination and mosquito control programs, ecological changes in tropical Africa and South America, including increased deforestation, agricultural intensification, and urban growth have increased the risk of yellow fever, especially in tropical Africa. Research conducted in the twentieth century that identified two additional cycles of yellow fever (sylvan and intermediate) reveals the significance of environmental change in the growth of epidemics and endemic zones. In the 1930s researchers discovered that additional species of both mosquitoes and primates hosted yellow fever in tropical forests. They identified cases in the forests of tropical Africa and South America as sylvan yellow fever, also known as sylvatic or jungle yellow fever. "Sylvan" distinguished this form of the disease from its epidemic (or urban) form, which was characterized by epidemics in port cities, spread by the city-dwelling *A. aegypti* mosquito. Epidemics in tropical forests were not seasonal; the disease remained present in these regions for long periods of more than a year at a time, and as a result researchers have categorized sylvan yellow fever as endemic in Africa and the Americas. In the 1990s researchers identified a third, "intermediate" cycle of yellow fever, in addition to its urban and sylvan cycles. They classified the intermediate or "savannah" yellow fever cycle as the one found in "most savannah areas where there is some human activity," and they termed these regions "zones of emergence," because they "reflect the mechanism by which yellow fever evolved from the sylvan cycle to become an important human disease."[3] As the threat of sylvan and intermediate yellow fever has increased in tropical Africa and South America, environments and nonvaccinated populations remain at risk if they encounter the virus.[4]

The Decline of Yellow Fever, 1905–1950

The success of the US Army Yellow Fever Commission, led by W. C. Gorgas, in eradicating yellow fever in Havana, Veracruz, and the Panama Canal Zone, led to increased confidence among public health officials in the early twentieth century that the disease could be globally eradicated. After World War I, researchers from the United States, Britain, France, Brazil, and South Africa studied the disease more extensively in tropical regions of Africa and Brazil. French and American organizations, including the Institut Pasteur and the Rockefeller Foundation, conducted research in colonial West Africa during the 1920s. These groups dominated global etiological research and public health policy in regard to yellow fever, and they were able to carry on their research by cooperating with colonial regimes that controlled most of Africa in the early twentieth century. In 1918 the Rockefeller Foundation formed the Yellow Fever Commission, led by Gorgas, and in 1925 it organized the West African Yellow Fever Commission and established laboratories in Nigeria and Ghana. The West African commission initially focused on isolating the disease-causing organism and studying regional epidemics.[5]

In 1927 both French researchers in Senegal and American researchers in Nigeria isolated the yellow fever virus and began searching for a vaccine. By 1930 scientists in both regions had developed vaccines that successfully prevented outbreaks among immunized individuals. In Senegal, French scientists developed what became known as the French neurotropic vaccine (FNC) or Dakar vaccine, which they isolated from a yellow fever patient named Francoise Mayali and tested on monkeys.[6] In Nigeria, American researchers associated with the Rockefeller Foundation's West African Yellow Fever Commission identified what became known as the Asibi strain of the virus. In Lagos, A. F. Mahaffy isolated the virus by injecting the blood of a twenty-eight-year-old yellow fever patient from Ghana, named Asibi, into more than thirty rhesus monkeys. All but one of the monkeys died from yellow fever. The commission's team conducted autopsies on the dead monkeys, isolated the virus, and struggled to find a vaccine. In 1930 Max Theiler, a South African researcher associated with the Rockefeller Foundation, used the virus obtained from Asibi to develop a vaccine, which became known as "17D," and by 1937 mass vaccination campaigns began in Brazil and West Africa.[7]

International efforts to control yellow fever were largely successful in eradicating urban epidemics across the Atlantic, particularly after scientists isolated the virus and developed vaccines. Mass vaccination policies, combined with mosquito control measures aimed at city-dwelling *A. aegypti* mosquitoes, met with success in controlling yellow fever in urban spaces. However, in the 1930s scientists began to identify increasing numbers of yellow fever cases in undeveloped rain forests. In 1932 a group of yellow fever researchers in Brazil, led by Fred L. Soper and funded by the Rockefeller Foundation, found cases of yellow fever in nonurban regions where *A. aegypti* mosquitoes were not present.[8] The virus was carried by multiple species of *Haemogogus* and *Sabethes* mosquitoes in South America, including *H. leucocelaenus, H. capricorni, H. janthinomys, S. chloropterus,* and many more. These mosquitoes are closely related to *Aedes* mosquitoes. Various species of *Aedes* mosquitoes host the virus in African forests. Among those, *A. africanus* is spread throughout the endemic zone; *A. bromeliae* and *A. keniensis* are present in East Africa; and *A. furcifer taylori, A. luteocephalus,* and *A. opok* are found in West Africa.[9]

Currently, outbreaks of yellow fever in forested regions of Africa and South America occur in several species of monkeys. In addition to the numerous species of wild mosquitoes that can carry sylvan yellow fever, several species of monkeys can serve as primate hosts. In the tropics of South America, researchers have found the virus in various species of howler monkeys (*Alouatta*) that usually exhibit symptoms and die from the disease. In tropical Africa, numerous genera of monkeys host the virus, including *Colobus abyssincus* in East and Central Africa and several species of *Cercopithecus*. In most cases, African monkeys do not display signs of infection, with the exception of the lemur *Galago senegalensis* in East Africa. This species is common in other parts of Africa, but scientists have found that it exhibits symptoms only in East Africa.[10] This research suggests that yellow fever may have been present in some forests of West Africa or West Central Africa prior to the twentieth century and was later introduced to the jungles of East Africa.[11]

The identification of sylvan yellow fever led to a new series of concerns about how to control the disease in nonurban environments, since mosquito and monkey eradication in these regions was not a viable option. Until the 1930s, scientists believed that humans were the only mammalian host of yellow fever and did not distinguish between urban and sylvan yellow fever. The discovery of sylvan yellow fever led medical authorities to believe that "while control of urban yellow fever remained both possible and effective, there could be little thought of global eradication of the disease."[12] Despite the presence of sylvan yellow fever, the eradication of urban yellow fever led public health authorities to believe that the virus was no longer a major threat to human populations.

Reemergence: 1950 to Present

In 1951 George Strode and his associates at the Rockefeller Foundation published a comprehensive textbook on yellow fever, which described the "conquest" of yellow fever by public health measures. At this time, after the implementation of mass immunization programs that had begun in 1942, yellow fever had "virtually disappeared from colonial French West and Equatorial Africa."[13] During this period, however, epidemics continued in regions that did not enforce mass vaccination campaigns, including the British colonies in Ghana and Nigeria.

Yellow fever reemerged in parts of West Africa and South America in the 1950s, and the disease has continued to appear in epidemic and endemic form into the twenty-first century.[14] In the 1950s, several large-scale yellow fever epidemics occurred in French West Africa, Nigeria (1950–52), and Central and East Africa, including the Belgian Congo (1958–59), Sudan (1959), and Ethiopia (1959).[15] In the early 1960s, yellow fever caused a severe epidemic in southwestern Ethiopia, which lasted for two years and affected roughly 10 percent of the population.[16] Epidemics continued during the 1970s and 1980s in West and West Central Africa.[17] In Latin America, epidemics reappeared in the Panama Canal Zone in 1950 for the first time in more than forty years, followed by outbreaks in Costa Rica (1951) and on the Guatemala-Mexico border (1957).[18] Enforcement of mass vaccination campaigns in Latin America has remained largely confined to urban campaigns in Brazil, which began in 1938 and continued through the early 1950s.

Scholars argue that in Africa, yellow fever increased between 1955 and the present owing to several factors, including the decline in funding and enforcement of mass vaccination campaigns, the inability of public health efforts to control yellow fever among nonhuman primates, and increasing urbanization, which has led to an increase in *A. aegypti* populations and large populations of nonimmune humans. Public health officials replaced routine vaccination campaigns with emergency vaccination campaigns, which public health authorities put into effect only when they identified an official outbreak.[19] This has led to increasing numbers of nonimmune individuals at the onset of an epidemic.

From a global perspective, incidences of yellow fever have increased after 1980. Current reports show that in tropical Africa and South America, yellow fever infects up to 180,000 persons per year, causing between 29,000 and 60,000 deaths. In West Africa, where nearly 90 percent of yellow fever cases occur, researchers have attributed the reemergence of the disease to the decline in efforts to control its sylvan form, as well as to urban growth and expansion.[20] Since no measures were taken to vaccinate the monkeys that hosted yellow fever and transmitted it to humans in these regions, the virus could not be effectively controlled. Urban growth in Africa has led to a growing percentage of nonimmune individuals in cities, which, themselves, are estimated to be growing in number at a rate of 4 percent per year. In 2008, reports showed forty-three cities with populations greater than 1 million and estimated that by 2015, more than seventy cities would have populations exceeding 1 million. More recent data from the United Nations confirms a trend of urban and rural growth in African countries.[21]

Scholars have described twentieth-century patterns of reemergence in Africa and the Americas as a consequence of increasing urbanization and its impact on *A. aegypti* populations. Research on mosquito populations shows that the risk of urban yellow fever's returning to Africa and tropical America has recently increased.[22] Some argue that the disease could emerge in regions that have not yet been affected, including parts of Asia, Australia, and Oceania.[23] In Africa, major epidemics occurred throughout the 1990s among unimmunized populations in Cameroon (1990), Ghana (1993–94, 1996), Liberia (1995, 1998), Gabon (1994), Senegal (1995, 1996), Benin (1996), and Kenya (1992). Scientists have attributed the reemergence to "breakdowns in vaccination and mosquito control programs" in these regions.[24] The US Centers for Disease Control currently reports endemic yellow fever zones across sub-Saharan Africa that extend from the west coast across the continent, affecting more than thirty nations from Mauritania to Tanzania. The endemic zone includes East African regions that did not experience major epidemics until the 1950s, in the Sudan, Ethiopia, and Somalia.[25] Reports show significantly fewer cases in South America; most cases have occurred in the Amazon basin and surrounding grasslands, appearing in parts of Brazil, Paraguay, Argentina, Bolivia, Peru, Ecuador, Columbia, Panama, Venezuela, Guyana, Suriname, and French Guiana.[26] More recently, the World Health Organization has reported concerns about outbreaks of yellow fever in Angola and the Democratic Republic of Congo, after confirming hundreds of cases that persisted in 2015 and 2016 despite "extensive vaccination campaigns."[27]

Scientists have described the emergence of yellow fever in East Africa as an "enigma." They explain that patterns of the disease are difficult to understand and interpret because of its "unpredictable focal periodicity, lengthy inter-epidemic periods, and precarious potential for large epidemics.[28] The epidemic in Ethiopia (1960–62) was the largest epidemic thus far reported worldwide, and recent outbreaks in Kenya (1992–93) and Sudan (2003 and 2005) have raised concerns about the possibility of urban outbreaks in the future. Since vaccination programs have not been enforced on populations in East Africa, yellow fever "will continue to emerge unpredictably and remain an imminent public threat," it is claimed.[29]

Data from the World Health Organization shows that the most common outbreaks of yellow fever in Africa are through the intermediate transmission cycle.[30] The increased occurrence of intermediate yellow fever in the late twentieth and the twenty-first centuries reveals the role of ecological transformations in creating endemic zones. These recent environmental changes parallel changes that occurred in the eighteenth century, when contemporaries began recording the appearance of yellow fever in coastal West Africa. The emergence and impact of epidemic yellow fever grew during a period of global colonial development in the eighteenth and nineteenth centuries. Similarly, deforestation and urban expansion during the mid to late twentieth century caused sylvan and intermediate yellow fever to expand in developing regions of Africa and South America.

Deforestation in Latin America, brought about by urban development, global demand for timber, and food production, has led to an increase in yellow fever cases in the Amazon rain forest. The clearing of land for pastures to raise cattle for beef, as well as farmland to grow soy, has had a devastating impact on rain forests since the 1960s.[31] William Coleman has argued that yellow fever affected forest-dwelling humans only when they came into contact with mosquitoes that lived in the forest canopy, which commonly occurred during the felling of trees.[32] The

173

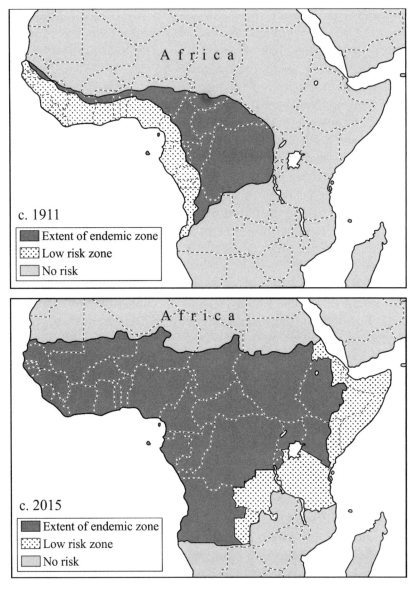

FIGURE 13. Spread of yellow fever across Africa in the late twentieth century. Yellow fever escalated in East Africa in the 1950s, after global health authorities proclaimed that it was a "conquered disease." (Compiled from Boyce, "History Of Yellow Fever"; Monath, "Yellow Fever"; CDC, "Areas with Risk of Yellow Fever"; and Jentes et al. Cartography by Mary Lee Eggart.)

ecological impacts of deforestation and urban growth have contributed to an increase in cases of yellow fever in these regions, among unvaccinated native populations and loggers.

The threat of urban yellow fever in temperate and subtropical cities in the Americas, including parts of the United States, Mexico, the Caribbean, and Central America, has grown in the past fifty years because of the lack of effective control over the *A. aegypti* population.[33] Between 1970 and the turn of the century, "dramatic changes in the distribution of the urban vector, *Ae aegypti,* have occurred in the western hemisphere. Whereas this mosquito was previously eradicated from most yellow fever endemic countries, it has reinfested these areas and is now widely distributed"[34] The *A. aegypti* currently occupies regions that extend from forty degrees from the equator in both hemispheres, from Asia to the Americas, and researchers predict that its range will increase with global warming.[35] As a result, yellow fever and other viruses spread by *A. aegypti* (including dengue, chikungunya, and Zika) are now a threat in regions that were not previously at risk.[36]

Rather than enforcing mosquito eradication within the nation, twentieth-century US public health authorities focused on eradicating the disease in South America and Africa. DDT campaigns met with much resistance and were not used in the United States and Puerto Rico. Public health efforts effectively exterminated these mosquitoes in tropical ports outside of the United States and diminished their population in the 1930s and 1940s. However their numbers increased when these measures ceased to be enforced, particularly after 1960.

In New Orleans, the absence of yellow fever in the twentieth century can be attributed to strict control of the port and mandatory vaccinations of individuals who arrived in the United States from regions where yellow fever was present. Mosquito control measures, which experts held responsible for the eradication of yellow fever in the early twentieth century, have not been enforced since the development of the vaccine. The urban *A. aegypti* population has grown since the 1930s and currently resides in temperate, subtropical, and tropical urbanized regions across the globe. The population of *A. aegypti* in New Orleans and surrounding regions, which have become increasingly urbanized since the 1960s, continues to grow without restriction.[37]

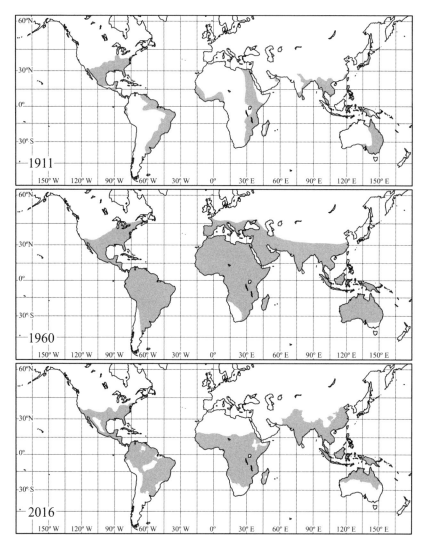

FIGURE 14. Documented *A. aegypti* populations grew over the twentieth century despite mosquito control programs. (Compiled from Boyce, *Yellow Fever and Its Prevention*; Christophers; and CDC, "Estimated Range." Cartography by Mary Lee Eggart.)

Ecology and Unintended Consequences

The relationship between humans and the rest of the natural world is a continual process, which J. R. McNeill has described as a "cotillion of co-evolution."[38] The history of ecological change exposes the power of humans to alter landscapes, water systems, and the evolution of other species, in addition to transforming human history. The narrative of the rise of yellow fever in New Orleans reveals the unintended consequences of human endeavors and demonstrates how ecological changes mold cultural and geopolitical landscapes. Examining how human actions influenced nonhuman agents, including viruses, bacteria, parasites, and mosquitoes, which spread a variety of diseases, exposes how humans shape disease ecology by altering environments, thereby causing epidemics and creating endemic zones. In nineteenth-century New Orleans, yellow fever molded socioeconomic and cultural structures locally and affected the course of medical research and public health policy globally.

This study indicates the impact of human actions in the emergence and rise of urban yellow fever in the nineteenth century, but further studies are necessary to gain understanding of the rise of sylvan yellow fever in the twentieth century. The factors discussed in this book (including Atlantic slavery, sugar production, maritime commerce, and urban development) are responsible for the growth of urban yellow fever in the Atlantic world during the seventeenth through the nineteenth centuries. Similar factors, combined with the sporadic use of DDT and other pesticides, might be responsible for the rise in sylvan and savannah yellow fever in the twentieth century.[39]

The impacts of twentieth-century yellow fever control methods included the growth of insect populations and other diseases. Sporadic pesticide use in tropical regions has caused the evolution and immunity of insects. Scientists have found links between insecticides (such as DDT) and cancer. The use of DDT and other insecticides, including permethrin and temephos, often results in mutations that cause resistance to these pesticides in mosquito populations. Researchers have determined that resistance to DDT is most common, even in mosquitoes that have been exposed to other pesticides. The development of pesticide resistance occurs among yellow fever–carrying *Aedes* as well as malaria-carrying *Anopheles* mosquitoes.[40] Laboratory tests in the late 1950s have shown carcinogenic effects of DDT, which became widely publicized after Rachel Carson's *Silent Spring*. Experiments on mice in the late 1960s indicated links between DDT and liver tumors.[41] More recent studies continue to show possible carcinogenic effects of DDT and other pesticides that have become more commonly used as insects have become resistant to DDT. Researchers have warned about the potential of pesticides as a cause of prostate and breast cancer, in addition to pancreatic cancer, neuropsychological dysfunction, and reproductive disorders.[42]

Numerous studies have also found problems with vaccination campaigns. Early mass immunization campaigns have contributed to higher incidences of other diseases, such as encephalitis. During the Nigerian and Central American epidemics of 1951–52, the FNC vaccine was found to cause postvaccinal neurotropic diseases (particularly encephalitis) and was discontinued in 1971. However, the vaccine remained in use through 1982 in West Africa, resulting in cases of encephalitis there.[43] Twenty-first-century biologists describe the widely used 17D vaccine (Asibi) as "one of the safest and most effective vaccines yet developed," and public health authorities enforce its use among travelers and in mass immunization campaigns.[44] However, it may also have adverse effects, including immediate hypersensitivity, neurotropic and viscerotropic diseases, and death, which have been reported as common among infants, rare among children, and most common among adults over age sixty.[45] That vaccine is still the most effective method of prevention, but it is in short supply. A 2001 study of yellow fever indicated that "current vaccine supplies are marginal, emphasizing the vulnerability to an unexpected emergency such as the occurrence of urban yellow fever in coastal Brazil, the USA, or Canada."[46] More recently, researchers have concluded that "many questions remain about yellow fever disease, the etiological agent, and even about its natural transmission cycle. The threat of urban outbreaks and long-distance introductions is increasing."[47] Questions about how to contain and prevent future outbreaks remain because of the complex evolutionary mechanisms of the disease vectors.

Unintended consequences of human development led to the emergence of epidemic yellow fever in the Atlantic World. Similarly, unintended consequences of technologies used to control and eradicate yellow fever have led to new problems, such as the ubiquitous use of chemical pesticides and larvicides. It is beyond the scope of this study to expound the scientific studies that have led some scholars to consider the ill effects of global disease control policies. Long-term impacts of human innovations can be viewed only from a historical perspective.

Notes

INTRODUCTION

Epigraph: Hearn, "——!——!! Mosquitoes!!!" Also quoted in LaBarre, 47.

1. Tregle, quoted in Kmen, xi.
2. Starr, xxii.
3. Hutson, 2–3, 14; Bronner, 147.
4. Hutson, 5, 14.
5. Ibid., 5; A. Oakey Hall, 23.
6. Dowler, "Researches," 275–77; Alexander, 2:30.
7. Peirce F. Lewis, 16–18.
8. Contemporary European observers made these connections upon visiting tropical regions in the eighteenth and nineteenth centuries, often focusing on the detrimental effects of tropical climates on Europeans. Medical professionals increasingly emphasized the same connections in the early twentieth century, as they established the professional field of tropical medicine. See Lind (1768 and 1811); James Johnson; Scheube. Several historians have elaborated on relationships between ideas of tropicality, the categorization of tropical diseases, and the emergence of the field of tropical medicine. See Stepan, *Picturing Tropical Nature;* Valenčius; Harrison, *Climates and Constitutions;* and *Medicine in the Age.*
9. J. R. McNeill, *Mosquito Empires,* 2.
10. Stowe, *Doctoring the South,* 6; Valenčius, 232–35.
11. Peirce F. Lewis, 5.
12. Gwendolyn Midlo Hall, 35, 157.
13. Domínguez, 30, 46.
14. Dowler, "Review," 67; Campanella, *Geographies of New Orleans,* 207–8; Logsdon and Bell, 132–34; Domínguez, 123–26; Brasseaux, Fontenot, and Oubre, 3–4; see also the essays in Kein.
15. The term "creole" was frequently used throughout the colonial Caribbean and Latin America, as well as in island colonies in the Atlantic and Indian Oceans.
16. Kein, xiii–xv.

17. See Cable, *Creoles of Louisiana*, 3–4; Cable, *Grandissimes*. See also Dowler, "Review," 67.

18. Thernstrom, 247.

19. Boyce, "History of Yellow Fever (Concluded)," 301; Valenčius, 79–81; Stowe, *Doctoring the South*, 5.

20. Savitt, *Medicine and Slavery*, 241; Patterson, 861–62; Coelho and McGuire, 94; J. R. McNeill, *Mosquito Empires*, 46. For a comprehensive account of historiographical debates on the question of inheritable immunity to yellow fever, see Espinosa, "Question of Racial Immunity."

21. Curtin, "'White Man's Grave.'" For an exchange between Kiple and Watts on this subject, see Sheldon Watts, "Yellow Fever Immunities"; Kiple, "Response to Sheldon Watts"; Sheldon Watts, "Response to Kenneth Kiple."

22. The ambiguity of racial identity in the United States further complicates studies of racial immunity. For example, Melbourne Tapper has shown that "sickling today is viewed as a black-related disease not simply because the majority of people suffering from the disease are blacks, but because various medical sciences in tandem with anthropology have represented it as a disease of 'black people' since the turn of the twentieth century." Medical authorities classified sickle-cell anemia as a race-related disease; when they encountered sickling in white patients, "what was ultimately at stake . . . was not sickling (the clinical entity) but the racial purity (the degree of nonblackness) of these bodies." In addition to sickling, nineteenth- and twentieth-century medical discourses on pellagra, tuberculosis, and AIDS have linked these diseases with blackness. Tapper, 10–13; Marks, 34–37; see also Gamble; Harrison-Chirimuuta.

23. Arnold, *Imperial Medicine and Indigenous Societies;* and *Warm Climates and Western Medicine.*

CHAPTER ONE

1. The term "epidemic" refers to a large-scale outbreak, rather than the presence of isolated cases or endemic yellow fever. Yellow fever could become endemic, or seasonally endemic, in tropical and subtropical zones that could sustain a large enough population of primates and mosquitoes.

2. Scholarship that demonstrates the role of yellow fever in shaping Atlantic history includes J. R. McNeill, *Mosquito Empires;* Crosby, *Columbian Exchange;* Sheldon Watts, *Epidemics and History.*

3. Curtin, "Epidemiology"; *Disease and Imperialism;* and "Disease Exchange across the Atlantic," 329; see also Crosby, *Columbian Exchange;* and *Ecological Imperialism;* William McNeill, *Plagues and Peoples;* J. R. McNeill, *Mosquito Empires.*

4. Curtin et al., 215; Curtin, "'White Man's Grave,'" 99; Patterson, 862.

5. Webb, *Humanity's Burden*, 32–41, quotation on 32; See also Packard, *Making of a Tropical Disease*, 26–27.

6. Webb, *Humanity's Burden*, 58–63; Packard, *Making of a Tropical Disease*, 23, 35–37.

7. In 1881 Carlos Finlay identified this mosquito as the *Culex*, while researching the role of mosquitoes in transmitting yellow fever in Havana. In the United States, researchers initially identified the species as *Culex fasciatus*. Entomologists have since reclassified this mosquito numerous times. By 1901 medical authorities in the United States referred to the species as *Stegomyia fasciata* (*S. fasciata*). Until the 1950s medical researchers and etymologists continued to identify it as *S. fasciata*, or sometimes *S. calopus* (before 1930). In this book it is identified as *A. aegypti*. See Finlay, "Inoculations for Yellow Fever"; "Mosquito Hypothetically Considered"; and "Yellow Fever: Its Transmission," 395–409; see also Gorgas, 16–17; Agramonte, 219; Howard, Dyar, and Knab, 293–94. Until the mid-twentieth century, the urban *A. aegypti* was the primary mosquito host of the yellow fever virus; however, since the 1950s, scientists have identified numerous other species of *Aedes* mosquitoes in Africa, in addition to several species of *Haemogogus* and *Sabethes* mosquitoes in South America, that host the virus, as the disease has become more common in tropical forests and savannahs.

8. Similar symptoms of dengue fever and chikungunya include abrupt high fever, severe joint and muscle pain, and headaches. Barrett and Monath; Monath, "Yellow Fever" (1999); and Yellow Fever: Victor, Victoria?"; Vainio and Cutts; McGrew, 165–75, 356–64.

9. Webb, *Humanity's Burden*, 66–79.

10. The existence of *P. knowlesi* is not included in most historical accounts. See Packard, *Making of a Tropical Disease*, 22–27; Webb, *Humanity's Burden*, 3. For information on *P. knowlesi*, see Putaporntip et al.; Singh et al.; Fong, Cadigan, and Coatney.

11. Yellow fever spread to East Africa in the 1950s. Details are included in the epilogue.

12. Galbraith and Barrett, 757–58; David R. Hill, 246.

13. Curtis, Mills, and Blackburn, 493; Slosek, 249–51.

14. Wilson, 269; Goodyear, 12; Christophers, 57; see also recent reports on *A. aegypti* by the World Health Organization, *Dengue*, 61; and the CDC, "Estimated Range." These reports list flower vases, potted plants with saucers, animal water containers, hollow fence posts, tree holes, and rock holes as larval habitats.

15. Carpenter and LaCasse, 52, 57.

16. Cooper and Kiple, 1102.

17. Galbraith and Barrett, 756.

18. Patterson, 855; Goodyear, 6.

19. Curtin, "'White Man's Grave,'" 96.

20. Sheldon Watts, "Yellow Fever Immunities," 956.

21. Chastel, 665; Christophers, 77; Coelho and McGuire, 94, 103; Horn, 129–30; McCandless, 140.

22. Webb, *Long Struggle against Malaria*, 3–5, 23, 39.

23. Humphreys, *Malaria*, 9–10, 12.

24. Slosek, 249; Finlay, "Mosquito Hypothetically Considered"; Wilson; Gorgas, 121. Note that the standard spelling of "Vera Cruz" (Mexico) in the nineteenth century has changed to "Veracruz." I use the modern from throughout, except when quoting nineteenth-century sources.

25. Gorgas, 120–21.

26. Keating, 13.

27. The outbreak in Guadeloupe in 1635 was called "*coup de barre*" and may have actually been yellow fever; see Carter, *Yellow Fever*, 196; Boyce, *Yellow Fever and Its Prevention*, 14, 48–49. Boyce believed that yellow fever was endemic to both the Americas and West Africa.

28. Sheldon Watts, *Epidemics and History*, 228–29; Bloom, 2–3.

29. Coleman, 18–19; Carpenter, 19.

30. Guerra, "Aleixo De Abreu."

31. Several sources claim earlier outbreaks of yellow fever that began in the late fifteenth century, during the period of European colonization in the eastern Atlantic islands and the Gulf of Guinea coast. They cite outbreaks in the Canary Islands (1494–1512), the Cape Verde Islands (1510–15), Benin (1520), and São Tomé (1558). See Augustin, 178, 189–90, 344–45.

32. Boxer, 100–103.

33. Guerra, "Aleixo De Abreu," 64–65; Augustin, 353. See also Webb, *Long Struggle against Malaria*, 7.

34. Schwartz, 188; J. R. McNeill, *Mosquito Empires*, 65; Boxer, 152.

35. Curtin et al., 227.

36. Ibid., 229–30.

37. Searing, 59.

38. The officer was mistaken in his identification of tigers, since they are not present in Africa. Lind (1811), 30.

39. Ibid.

40. Ibid., 31.

41. Ibid., 41–42.

42. Ibid., 88.

43. Ibid., 31.

44. Ibid., 41–42.

45. Headrick, 61, 69–70.

46. Lind (1811), 135–36.

47. Carter, *Yellow Fever*, 255–57.

48. Lind (1811), 42–45; Robertson, 15–16.

49. Robertson makes a point of mentioning that he did not observe the "vomiting of matter like the grounds of coffee." Robertson, 16.

50. Schotte; Augustin, 257.

51. Schotte, 36–37.

52. Ibid., 39–40; See also Carter, *Yellow Fever*, 257.

53. He notes that "the Europeans suffered much more by it, in proportion, than the mulattoes, and those much more, than the blacks." Schotte, 40.

54. Ibid., 36–46.

55. Reys, 3, 69.

56. La Roche, 61; Augustin, 260; Carter, *Yellow Fever*, 202.

57. Billy G. Smith, 2, 69.

58. Ibid., 111.

59. Ibid., 97, 156.

60. Carpenter, 9. It is possible that yellow fever appeared to be more virulent because of the El Niño episode of 1789 to 1793. See Billy G. Smith, 168, 188.

61. Augustin, 150–51.

62. Boyce, *Yellow Fever and Its Prevention*, 65.

63. Ibid., 48–49.

64. Ngalamulume, "Keeping the City Totally Clean," 193.

65. Lind (1811), 47.

66. La Roche, 61; Augustin, 260.

67. Ngalamulume, "Keeping the City Totally Clean," 188.

68. Ibid., 191.

69. Ibid., 192.

70. Quoted in Dutroulau, 15; see also Thévenot.

71. Ross, 5.

72. Carter, *Yellow Fever*, 72, 270; Boyce, *Yellow Fever and Its Prevention*, 181. Carter's views of race are evident in his claim that "in pure-blooded negroes, yellow fever is of low mortality, almost a non-fatal disease."

73. On yellow fever immunity among Africans as evidence of West African origin, see Cooper and Kiple; Kiple and Higgins, 237–48. On the existence of inherited or unexplained resistance (i.e., lower death rates) to yellow fever among "blacks" or African Americans more generally: Powell, 97–98; Kiple and Kiple, "African Connection," 211; Carrigan, "Yellow Fever," 59–60; Kiple and Higgins, 237–48; Kiple and Coneè Ornelas, 73.

74. Curtin, "Epidemiology"; Kiple and Kiple, "African Connection," 211; Kiple, *African Exchange*, 59–60; Kiple and Higgins, 237–48.

75. Eric Hobsbawm conceived of the "long nineteenth century," as an analytical time frame, from 1789 to 1914, marked by the ages of revolution, capitalism, and empire. This period also coincides with the prevalence of epidemic yellow fever in the Atlantic.

76. Patterson, 857; Augustin, 868.

77. Bloom, 4–5; Bloom notes that the epidemic in Lisbon was introduced via ships coming from Rio de Janeiro, where the disease first appeared in 1849; Coleman, 19.

78. Manning, 19; Curtin, *Tropical Atlantic*, 16–20; David Eltis, Trans-Atlantic Slave Trade Database, http://slavevoyages.org/assessment/estimates.

79. Searing, 46.

80. The female *A. aegypti* feeds on human blood, while both males and females feed on fluids containing sugar.

81. Bloodgood, 201; US Navy Department, 22; Carpenter, 37–38; Hargis, *Ship Origin of Yellow Fever*, 6.

82. Curtin, *Rise and Fall*, 73.

83. Jason W. Moore, 421; J. R. McNeill, *Mosquito Empires*, 48; David Watts, 39.

84. J. R. McNeill, "Yellow Jack and Geopolitics," 205.

85. Goodyear, 13.

86. Ibid., 11.

87. Christophers, See also de Meillon, 57, and Eliason, 289.

88. Goodyear, 12.

89. Diseases that emerged in the Caribbean included many that were common in Europe, the Mediterranean, and sub-Saharan Africa.

90. Goodyear, 13–14; Dunn, 49–62.

91. Sheldon Watts, *Epidemics and History*, 228.

92. Dunn, 303–4; Ligon, 11–12.

93. Curtin, *Rise and Fall*, 73.

94. After the devastating epidemics of 1685–92, yellow fever was unrecorded in Brazil until 1849. It might have become endemic among primate populations in the eighteenth century, as expeditions in the Tietê River reported its presence in forests in 1800. The 1849 epidemic began in Salvador and spread to Recife, Natal, Belém, Santos, and Rio de Janeiro. After this epidemic, yellow fever escalated throughout Brazil. See Cooper, 675; Dean, 102–3; Peard, *Race, Place, and Medicine*, 21. On the establishment, decline, and revival of the Brazilian sugar industry, see Schwartz, 161–64.

95. Keating, 13; Carter, *Yellow Fever*, 184–85.

96. Jackson, 126.

97. Keating, 13.

98. Dunn, 303.

99. Although the *Oriflamme* left from Bangkok, it is likely that it became infected with yellow fever in Pernambuco, where it stopped during the severe epidemic of 1685–92. There was no yellow fever in Siam. See Heagerty, 1243; Carpenter, 8–11; Carter, *Yellow Fever*, 196.

100. Carpenter, 9; Pym, 3–4; see also Billy G. Smith, 156, 170.

101. Blane, 316, quoted in Coleman, 5; and Sheldon Watts, *Epidemics and History*, 213.

102. Holcombe, *Yellow Fever*, 5.

103. Even after the United States banned the importation of African slaves in 1808, an illegal slave trade from the Caribbean continued, and New Orleans emerged as a center of the domestic slave trade. See Obadale-Starks, 3, 29.

104. LaChance, 101.

105. Alexander, 2:233.

CHAPTER TWO

1. The French "Old City," or Vieux Carré, occupied the space that is now commonly known as the French Quarter.

2. Colten, *Unnatural Metropolis,* 2. See also Colten, *Southern Waters,* 41–42.

3. Ari Kelman has described how the phrase "Mississippi Delta" has a common cultural usage that includes places that are technically in the river's floodplain, such as Memphis and Jackson. However, the "Mississippi Delta" as a geological region includes only the area south of the Red River. This region includes most of what is now the southern section of the present state of Louisiana, also called "lower Louisiana." See Kelman, *River and Its City,* 3.

4. Ibid., 4.

5. Ibid., 22.

6. Ibid., 4.

7. Kolb and Van Lopik, 9.

8. Brasseaux, "Image of Louisiana," 153–54.

9. Gwendolyn Midlo Hall, 128–30.

10. Usner, 557, 558.

11. Aiken, 205; see also Le Gardeur, "Origins of the Sugar Industry," 7.

12. Sitterson, *Sugar Country,* 13; Follett, 10; Le Gardeur, "Origins of the Sugar Industry," 4.

13. Follett, 10; see also Sitterson, *Sugar Country,* 18.

14. One arpent is 192 feet. Under the French arpent system, land grants typically included twenty-five arpents along the river and forty arpents back from the river. See Hilliard, 258; Stubbs, 648; see also Trudeau.

15. Conrad and Lucas, 3; Forstall, 53.

16. Josef Solís began making tafia in the 1790s. See Conrad and Lucas, 6; Stubbs, 648; Le Gardeur, "Origins of the Sugar Industry," 1.

17. Gwendolyn Midlo Hall, 277; John Hebron Moore, 590.

18. Usner, 558.

19. Ibid.; Din, 17. Terre-aux-Boeufs was also known as Tierra de Bueyes (Land of cattle). This area is now part of St. Bernard Parish.

20. Kelman, *River and Its City,* 23.

21. Le Gardeur, "Origins of the Sugar Industry," 9.

22. Fraginals, 17, 74–76.

23. Funes Monzote, 66–67.

24. Curtin, *Tropical Atlantic,* 16–20; and *Rise and Fall,* 79–81.

25. Sheldon Watts, *Disease and Medicine,* 225; Mintz, 99–100; Curtin, *Rise and Fall,* 146.

26. J. R. McNeill, "Yellow Jack and Geopolitics," 210–11; Dubois and Garrigus, 37.

27. J. R. McNeill, "Yellow Jack and Geopolitics," 210; Sheldon Watts, *Disease and Medicine*, 236.

28. "Cary's Account of the Yellow Fever of 1793," quoted in Carpenter, 13; Billy G. Smith, 188; Sheldon Watts, *Disease and Medicine*, 236.

29. This date is contested; while most sources claim that de Boré first granulated sugar in 1796, others date the event to 1794–95. See Dessens, 79–81; Stubbs, 649–50; Sitterson, *Sugar Country*, 3.

30. It is probable that de Boré, who was elected the first mayor of New Orleans in 1803, became known as the pioneer of the Louisiana sugar industry because his grandson Charles Gayarré (1805–1895) was one of the most prominent Louisiana historians of the late nineteenth century; Le Gardeur, "Origins of the Sugar Industry," 1.

31. Arthur and Huchet de Kernion, 414; See also Friedrichs.

32. Le Gardeur, "Origins of the Sugar Industry," 21.

33. Letter from Pontalba to Miró, quoted in ibid., 10.

34. Le Gardeur, "Origins of the Sugar Industry," 14.

35. Planters used the fresh cane to seed new cane by placing the cane flat in rows about two inches below the ground.

36. Quotation in Stubbs, 650. Most sources (including Stubbs) claim that Méndez purchased Solís's estate in 1791, but the actual date of sale was May 17, 1794. See Le Gardeur, "Origins of the Sugar Industry," 13.

37. Sitterson, *Sugar Country*, 118.

38. Barton, *Cause and Prevention*, 100; Aiken, 206; Drake, 100.

39. Barton, *Cause and Prevention*, 100.

40. Dessens, 1, 23–26.

41. Freiberg, 293; Le Gardeur, "New Orleans Theater," 87.

42. Dessens, 24; Campanella, *Geographies of New Orleans*, 9.

43. Dessens, 79–80, 204; Sitterson, *Sugar Country*, 8, 118–20; Stubbs, 650.

44. Sitterson, *Sugar Country*, 24.

45. Notable outbreaks took place in 1799, 1800, 1804, 1809, and 1811. See Patterson, 857; Carpenter, 17.

46. Sitterson, *Sugar Country*, 28. Cotton plantations also developed alongside sugar plantations in the early nineteenth century owing to technological improvements, most significantly the cotton gin.

47. Aiken, 210; Campanella, *Geographies of New Orleans*, 9.

48. Sitterson, *Sugar Country*, 120.

49. Ibid.; *Green Fields*, 31.

50. Kelman, *River and Its City*, 50.

51. Ibid., 54.

52. Tomich, 345.

53. Louisianans measured sugar in hogsheads, which were wooden barrels that held one thousand to twelve hundred pounds of sugar. The barrels had holes at the bottom, which allowed planters to drain molasses from the crystalized sugar. Silliman, 122; Follett, 12.

54. Mintz, 6.

55. Woloson, 34, 88, 102, 115.

56. See Barton's description of the levée in *Report of the Sanitary Commission*, 390; see also Trask, *Fearful Ravages*, 7.

57. Hilliard, 258.

58. Otto, 120–21.

59. Hilliard, 263.

60. Silliman, 15.

61. Follett, 10–12, 39–40, quotation on 85. Follett quotes an overseer on John Burnside's sugar plantation in Ascension Parish.

62. Changing perceptions of immunity among local and visiting observers, including medical professionals, are discussed in detail in chapter 3.

63. Barton, *Cause and Prevention*, 101–3. The New Basin Canal was also known as the Orleans Bank Canal or Bank Canal.

64. Fenner, "Reports from Louisiana: Article I," 18.

65. Kelman, *River and Its City*, 60–61.

66. A. Oakey Hall, 27.

67. Christophers, 54–55.

68. These lands were generally low, with the exception of some elevated lands along the bayous: notably, the ridge along Bayou St. John (known as Bayou Road) and the Metairie Ridge (or Metairie Road) along Bayou Gentilly.

69. Gillett, 93.

70. Christophers, 54.

71. Boyce, *Yellow Fever Prophylaxis*, 11.

72. Reed, 467–72.

73. Slaves often served as the primary laborers in railroad construction. Yanochik, Thornton, and Ewing, 727; Reed, 467–77; Black; Colton, Norton, and Persac. See also Peirce F. Lewis.

74. *Report of the Sanitary Commission*, 318, 396.

75. Ibid., 318.

76. Ibid., 396.

77. Aiken, 210; Campanella, "Ethnic Geography of New Orleans," 706; and *Geographies of New Orleans*, 13.

78. Sarbough, 45.

79. Spletstoser, 38, 356; Conway, Appendix E.

80. Campanella, "Ethnic Geography of New Orleans," 706–7; Conway, 221–22.

81. Journal of Benjamin Henry Latrobe, March 8, 1819, quoted in Huber, 7.

82. Huber, 3–4.

83. The St. Louis Cemetery II is presently located on Claiborne Avenue, between St. Louis and Iberville Streets. See Huber, 10.

84. Ibid., 6–7. The St. Louis I Cemetery is now located between Basin, Conti, Treme, and St. Louis Streets.

85. Contemporary sources commonly referred to the Girod Street Cemetery as the "Protestant Cemetery" and the Cypress Grove Cemetery as the "Firemen's Cemetery." Fenner, "Reports from Louisiana: Article I," 25; Huber, 18, 27.

86. Huber, 33.

87. Christophers, 57.

88. McDowell, 12.

89. Fenner, "Reports from Louisiana: Article I," 23. For photographs of cemetery architecture with crevices that encouraged the breeding of mosquitoes, see Christovich, 42–43, 75–76, 96, 105 and 55, 91, 110, 120.

CHAPTER THREE

1. Stepan, *Picturing Tropical Nature*, 153; Valenčius, 125.

2. Andrew Anderson, 147.

3. Ibid., 139–46; Stowe, *Doctoring the South*, 259, 274; Valenčius, 79–81. The use of various names for fevers accompanied by black bile or internal hemorrhaging was often related to the perceived race or nativity of the patient.

4. Colten, *Southern Waters*, 92–93.

5. Fenner, "Reports from Louisiana: Article I," 23.

6. Barton, "Report upon the Meteorology," 135–37.

7. *Report of the Sanitary Commission*, 389–90, 404–5.

8. Ibid., 429–30.

9. Fenner, "Reports from Louisiana: Article I," 17–18.

10. Nott, "Examination into the Health," 15.

11. Andrew Anderson, 139–48.

12. A. Oakey Hall, 56–57.

13. *Report of the Sanitary Commission*, 40.

14. Ibid., 38–40, 51.

15. Ibid., 532.

16. Howard, 1; Carpenter and LaCasse, 38, 138.

17. *Report of the Sanitary Commission*, 532.

18. Nott, "Yellow Fever Contrasted," 565, 600; and "Cause of Yellow Fever," 563.

19. Dauer and Carrera, 586.

20. "Beauperthuy on Mosquito-Born Diseases"; Boyce, *Mosquito or Man?*, 23–26; Dauer and Carrera, 585–86.

21. Fenner, *History of the Epidemic*, 4.

22. See Augustin, 781, 844–902, 937–54, 1001.

23. Patterson, 858; Aiken, 210; Touatre, 143–44. According to Touatre, the population after the epidemic was less than fifty thousand and the mortality rate was 85 percent.

24. Colten, *Southern Waters*, 94.

25. *Report of the Sanitary Commission*, 26–27. The category of "social condition" referred to "personal and social habits" and included temperance and crowded housing units.

26. *Report of the Sanitary Commission*, 26–27.

27. See reports published in the *Report of the Sanitary Commission*, 35–36.

28. Galbraith and Barrett, 756.

29. Most historians who maintain the view that Africans and people of African descent were immune or less susceptible to yellow fever cite Kenneth Kiple's extensive work on race and disease in the Caribbean. Kiple's research has had significant historiographical consequences. Some of his oft-cited works include Kiple and King, 45–47; Kiple and Kiple, "Black Yellow Fever Immunities"; and Kiple, *African Exchange*, 7–34. Prominent scholars of the US South who support views of black immunity and/or resistance include Margaret Humphreys, Todd Savitt, and Jo Ann Carrigan. See Humphreys, *Yellow Fever*, 7; Savitt, *Medicine and Slavery*, 241; Carrigan, *Saffron Scourge*, 253; see also Apel, 23, 158; Patterson, 861–62; Coelho and McGuire, 94. For a comprehensive account of historiographical debates on the question of the nonexistence of inheritable immunity to yellow fever, see Espinosa, "Question of Racial Immunity." See also McCandless, 133–47; Hogarth, 23.

30. O'Malley, "Beyond the Middle Passage," 134–36.

31. Curtin, *Atlantic Slave Trade*, 282–83.

32. Placide, 147; Hearn, *Two Years*, 321–22.

33. Anecdotal data from Atlantic slave ships describes fevers and deaths among slaves, who were thrown overboard. Rediker, 171–72; Bankole, 14.

34. Dunn, 303.

35. Ibid., 313.

36. Ibid., 303.

37. Oldmixon, 113.

38. Schwartz, 188; Boxer, 152–54. Note that neither author provides detailed accounts of the epidemic. Schwartz bases his claim on the closing of sugar mills during the epidemic, combined with general reports of high death rates.

39. Curtin, *Rise and Fall*, 80.

40. Grainger, 11.

41. Walker, 261–62. Walker references Josiah Nott.

42. Montejo, 18–21, quotations on 41–42.

43. Andrew Anderson, 148–49.

44. The term "Creole" has a complicated and contested history; the most accurate and inclusive interpretation defines a "Creole" as any person native to the Gulf Coast, the Caribbean, or any colonial territory, who identified as such.

Refer to the introduction for a detailed explanation of the multiple meanings of "Creole" in different historical and geographical contexts.

45. Din, 17.

46. Dessens, 1.

47. Campanella, *Geographies of New Orleans,* 9.

48. Domínguez, 113.

49. Johnson, *Soul by Soul,* 5–7.

50. Spletstoser, 262; Carrigan, "Yellow Fever," 59.

51. A. Oakey Hall, 10–11.

52. P. H. Lewis, 32.

53. Dowler, "Review," 67.

54. Barton, "Report upon the Meteorology," 129–31.

55. Fenner, "Reports from Louisiana: Article I," 33–34.

56. Gehman.

57. Alexander, 1:167.

58. Mackay, 304–5.

59. James Jones, 513.

60. A. P. Jones, 182.

61. Campanella, *Geographies of New Orleans,* 10–12.

62. Campanella, "Ethnic Geography of New Orleans," 706–7; See also Hoff and Smith.

63. Pierson, 628.

64. J. R. McNeill, *Mosquito Empires,* 35; Carrigan, *Saffron Scourge,* 256–57.

65. *Report of the Sanitary Commission,* 208; Barton, *Cause and Prevention,* 32.

66. Bartlett, 509.

67. Espinosa, "Question of Racial Immunity," 442.

68. Augustin, 150–51; Rubert Boyce, *Yellow Fever and Its Prevention,* 65.

69. Moch, 126–27.

70. Fussell, 847; Spletstoser, 38, 356; Campanella, *Geographies of New Orleans,* 12–13.

71. *Report of the Sanitary Commission,* 248; Patterson, 858; Pritchett and Tunali, 518.

72. *Report of the Sanitary Commission,* 248.

73. Kelman, "New Orleans's Phantom," 4–5.

74. Ibid., 10–11.

75. Carrigan, "Yellow Fever," 63.

76. Ibid., 60–61.

77. Ibid., 63.

78. Carrigan, *Saffron Scourge,* 236, 256.

79. Savitt, *Race and Medicine,* 55–57. Note that usage of the term "black" became popular among people of African descent during the American Civil Rights

Movement in the 1960s. Records from the late nineteenth century through this period most often used the term "negro," while mid-nineteenth century records usually used the term "colored." See Tom W. Smith, 497.

80. Fenner, *History of the Epidemic*, 56.

81. Ibid., 51.

82. Shannon, ix–xxiii; Lind (1811); James Johnson, 185, 361; Cartwright, "Slavery in the Light," 718–22; McCandless, 133–47.

83. Fredrickson, 56–57; Hannaford, 188; Crais and Scully, 2.

84. Stepan, *Idea of Race in Science*, xvii–xviii.

85. Crais and Scully, 2–3.

86. Cartwright, "Slavery in the Light." Note that most of the scholarship on Cartwright erroneously claims that he was the first (and perhaps only) "Professor of Diseases of the Negro" at the University of Louisiana. Willoughby; Marshall, 9.

87. Cartwright, "Diseases and Physical Peculiarities," 422, 425.

88. Cartwright, "Ethnology of the Negro," 150.

89. Nott and Gliddon, *Indigenous Races of the Earth*, 362–63, 364–67.

90. Influential publications include Nott and Gliddon's *Types of Mankind*, which was published in ten editions between 1854 and 1871; and *Indigenous Races of the Earth* (1857), both published in the United States and Britain; Nott, *Two Lectures*; and *Essay on the Natural History*. See also Stepan, *Picturing Tropical Nature*, 257.

91. Nott, *Two Lectures*, 29–32; Nott, "Mulatto a Hybrid," 4.

92. "Testimony of Dr. J.C. Nott," in *Report of the Sanitary Commission*, 97; Nott and Gliddon, *Indigenous Races of the Earth*, 367.

93. Stepan, *Picturing Tropical Nature*, 93–95.

94. Nott and Gliddon, *Types of Mankind*, xxiv.

95. Wallis, 40; Molly Rogers, 18; Stepan, *Picturing Tropical Nature*, 98–99.

96. Stepan, *Picturing Tropical Nature*, 92, 99.

97. Harrison, "Tender Frame of Man," 68–70.

CHAPTER FOUR

1. Steiner, *Disease in the Civil War*, 10–11; McPherson, 487–88; Andrew McIlwaine Bell, 1–2.

2. Andrew McIlwaine Bell, 105; J. R. McNeill, *Mosquito Empires*.

3. Trask, *Fearful Ravages*, 61.

4. Gillson; Carrigan, *Saffron Scourge*, 84; Trask, *Fearful Ravages*, 61.

5. Carrigan, *Saffron Scourge*, 84.

6. See chapter 3 for an analysis of creolism, race, and perceptions of immunity to yellow fever.

7. Ashkenazi, 350.

8. Humphreys, *Intensely Human,* 105.

9. Charles Boothby to Lizzie Boothby, April 20, 1863, Charles Boothby Papers, box 1, folder 7.

10. Charles Lee Lewis, 162–63; Farragut, *Life of Farragut,* 8.

11. Andrew McIlwaine Bell, 84.

12. Trask, *Fearful Ravages,* 64.

13. Charles Boothby to Lizzie Boothby, April 20, 1863, Charles Boothby Papers, box 1, folder 7; see also Luther M. Fairbanks Letters.

14. Andrew McIlwaine Bell, 27.

15. Ashkenazi, 370.

16. Touatre, 148; Carrigan, *Saffron Scourge,* 97.

17. Fenner, "Remarks on the Sanitary Condition," 42–43; Touatre, 148; Joseph Jones, 699; Dromgoole, 121.

18. Tomes, 28–33; C. B. White, 9–14.

19. Tomes, 28–33.

20. Milner, 35–36.

21. Fenner, "Remarks on the Sanitary Condition," 42.

22. Milner, 4.

23. Ibid., 33–36.

24. C. B. White, 9–10; Kovalenko et al.

25. Carrigan, *Saffron Scourge,* 100; John H. Ellis, 38.

26. Trask, *Fearful Ravages,* 65–66.

27. Brown, 2.

28. Carrigan, *Saffron Scourge,* 100; John H. Ellis, 38; see also Lister.

29. C. B. White, 9–10; Aiken, 212.

30. Matas, 12.

31. C. B. White, 7, 14.

32. Herrick, 645.

33. Obadale-Starks, 3, 29.

34. Patterson, 858.

35. Heitmann, 49.

36. Ibid., 9, 56–57.

37. Sitterson, *Sugar Country,* 29; Bouchereau, *Statement, 1872–1874,* v.; and *Statement, 1882–1883,* xliv.

38. Sitterson, *Sugar Country,* 231.

39. Champomier, 44; Bouchereau, *Statement, 1872–1874,* v; and *Statement, 1882–1883,* xliv; Sitterson, *Sugar Country,* 29.

40. Heitmann, 51, 56–58.

41. Woloson, 31.

42. Ibid., 31; Vogt, 58. It appears that these statistics account only for refined sugar made by European companies and do not include sugar made by Asian producers.

43. Woloson, 31.

44. Heitmann, 56.

45. *Sugar in Hawaii*, 21–22; Woloson, 31.

46. Campanella, "Ethnic Geography of New Orleans," 707; Fussell, 847–48.

47. Herrick, 646.

48. Dromgoole, 121; Capers, 493; John H. Ellis, 41; Bloom, 91–92; Patterson, 858. In Memphis, more than five thousand of the remaining people were relocated to refugee camps during the two weeks following the outbreak.

49. *Conclusions of the Board*, 31–35, 38; Dromgoole, 121; Bloom, 91, 141; Patterson, 858; Carrigan, *Saffron Scourge*, 112, 127.

50. *Annual Report of National Board of Health*, 69–78; John H. Ellis, 38.

51. John H. Ellis, 37–38.

52. Ibid., 38, 184; see also Espinosa, *Epidemic Invasions*, 14.

53. Patton, 121, quoted in John H. Ellis, 38.

54. O'Neill, 34. For this reason, some feared planting wet crops such as rice. Morris, 171–73.

55. Diary of Amanda Dougherty Worthington of Washington County, Mississippi (Panther Burn Plantation, on the Yazoo-Mississippi Delta), quoted in Saikku, 102. See also Morris, 172.

56. Saikku, 105; Morris, 171–73; Humphreys, *Malaria*, 52. Throughout the colonial period, and for most of the nineteenth century, local sources recorded the presence of various types of fevers, but not yellow fever. For example, in Memphis, despite the acknowledged presence of malaria in the country and awareness of yellow fever epidemics in other cities, no cases of yellow fever were reported until 1855. See also letters to J. D. Plunkett, 1879, Tennessee Department of Public Health Records, Tennessee State Library and Archives, Record Group 1:14.

57. Reports of sporadic cases in Memphis appear in 1828, 1853, 1855, and 1866, and more than 200 deaths were reported in 1867. The only large epidemic prior to 1878 was in 1872, with 10,000 cases and 2,000 deaths reported. Augustin, 1004.

58. See Davis in Colten, *Transforming New Orleans*, 98.

59. Morris, 142, 152–53; American expansion had changed views of the importance of the Mississippi River, which emerged as a central thoroughfare that connected the western plains to New Orleans.

60. "Mississippi Jetties," 46. See also Kelman, *River and Its City*, 127–30. Sandbars constituted a major problem in 1869 and 1873, blocking access to New Orleans from the Caribbean.

61. For an explanation of problems with river passes, see Kelman, *River and Its City*, 127–28.

62. Ibid., 130.

63. Congress approved Eads's plan after extensive debates about whether to build a canal or use jetties to open the mouth. See Morris, 154–59; Kelman, *River and Its City*, 130. See also Cowden.

64. Corthell, 235–36.

65. Ibid., 235; appendix, 24; "Mississippi Jetties," 57.

66. Corthell believed that the epidemic had begun in New Orleans and then spread to the jetty workers. He wrote that the epidemic began among workers in early August, after they had sent a vessel to New Orleans. Corthell, 186–87.

67. A. P. Jones, 208–9; Bloom, 59.

68. During Reconstruction, federal railroad land grants enabled the construction of major railroad construction projects in the Mississippi Valley. Kelman, *River and Its City*, 120–22, 124; Huffard, 86.

69. Capers, 484.

70. Kelman, *River and Its City*, 123.

71. Ibid., 120.

72. Huffard, 85–87.

73. Poor (1872), xxxii; and Poor (1889), vi; Kelman, *River and Its City*, 122. Kelman states that at the start of the war, there were fewer than 300 miles of track in Louisiana, while Poor states that there were 335 miles of track in 1860. Track in Louisiana doubled again in five years, by 1885.

74. Huffard, 87.

75. Ibid., 85, 87. Despite concerns about spreading the contagion, river quarantines were not strictly enforced.

76. Power, 165.

77. Dell Orto, 643.

78. The combined incubation and infective period of yellow fever is probably about ten days. See Manson, *Relation of the Panama Canal*, 10–11.

79. Power, 136, 174–75; Keating, 134. See also Huffard, 88; Bloom, 92.

80. Louisiana State Medical Society, 172; Ryan, 244–54; Bond and Sherman, 45–49; Quinn, 139.

81. J. R. McNeill, *Mosquito Empires*, 59.

82. Diaz and McCabe, 21–27.

83. Spinzig's motive for proving that yellow fever is caused by meteorological change was to avoid federal quarantine and sanitation interventions. Spinzig, *Epidemic Diseases*, 190–98.

CHAPTER FIVE

1. Ngalamulume, 191.

2. Scott, "Defining the Boundaries," 74.

3. Logsdon and Bell, 243.

4. Domínguez, 142; Cable, *Grandissimes;* and *Old Creole Days.*

5. Scott, "Fault Lines, Color Lines," 70.

6. Ryan.

7. Foner, 437.

8. Scott, "Fault Lines, Color Lines," 71.

9. Chaillé, *Intimidation*, 7, 35.

10. Mahala P. H. Roach Diary, vol. 22, August 24, 1878, Roach and Eggleston Family Papers.

11. Power, 201.

12. Blum, 147–48.

13. New Orleans Citizens, 10; *Report of Central Relief Committee*, 13.

14. New Orleans Citizens, 1.

15. Ibid., 10, 14.

16. Ibid., 21; *Report of the Central Relief Committee*,

17. Ibid.

18. Ibid., 27; Bloom, 91, 141; Dromgoole, 121; Patterson, 858.

19. Dromgoole, 89.

20. Power, 206.

21. Mary Gay to her mother, October 21, 1867, Edward J. Gay and Family Papers, Mss. 1295.

22. Howard A. White, 90.

23. Holcombe, *Report on the Yellow Fever*, 4.

24. Ryan, 244–54; Bond and Sherman, 45–49; Quinn, 139.

25. Quinn, 139; Capers, 493.

26. Dromgoole, 62–63.

27. Ibid., 123, 62–63.

28. Ibid., 63–64.

29. Ibid., 62–63.

30. Keating, 111.

31. Dromgoole, 52, 69.

32. Ibid., 71–72.

33. Keating, 113–14.

34. Keith, 153.

35. *Conclusions of the Board*, 38–39; Keating, 135.

36. Dromgoole, 108; *Conclusions of the Board*.

37. Dromgoole, 123.

38. *Conclusions of the Board*, Provisional Table; Power, 181; Dromgoole, 125.

39. Dromgoole, 116.

40. Ibid.

41. *Conclusions of the Board*, 37–38. Most of the following data from the Federal Board of Experts' report can be found in the provisional table at the end of the document.

42. Chaillé, *Life and Death*; and *Intimidation*.

43. Dromgoole, 124.

44. *Conclusions of the Board*, 10.

45. Izett Anderson, 18–21. Anderson also believed that dogs, cats, birds, horses, and other domestic animals contracted yellow fever in Gibraltar.

46. Hearn, *Two Years*, 321–22; Starr, xii–xiii.

47. Finlay, *Obras Completas* 2:165–69, 172–73; see also Stepan, "Interplay," 400.

48. See chapter 3; Montejo, 18–21, 41–42.

49. Schmidt, 211–12.

50. Quoted in Dromgoole, 59; *New York Times*, February 17, 1886, 5.

51. Schmidt, 23–24.

52. Tomes, 32–33.

53. Ibid., 28.

54. Dowell, 13.

55. Dromgoole, 46.

56. Louis Manigault to Joseph Jones, September 1867, box 3, folder 1, Joseph Jones Papers.

57. A. P. Jones, 711–13.

58. See chapter 4. Power, 136, 174–75; Keating, 134; see also Huffard, 88; Bloom, 92.

59. Keating, 134; Power, 136.

60. Tennessee Department of Public Health Records, Record Group 1:14.

61. Blum; Humphreys, *Yellow Fever;* John H. Ellis, *Yellow Fever.*

62. *Memphis Daily Avalanche*, March 11, 1879, quoted in Humphreys, *Yellow Fever*, 63–64.

63. Auxiliary Sanitary Association, 8; John H. Ellis, 86.

64. "Editorial," 625.

65. *Conclusions of the Board*, 27.

66. *Annual Report of National Board of Health*, 13.

67. Ibid., 33.

CHAPTER SIX

1. In 1933, under the leadership of Samuel Zemurray, the United Fruit Company moved its headquarters to New Orleans. See Colby, 181–84.

2. Trask, *Fearful Ravages*, 105; Humphreys, *Yellow Fever*, 150–51; Pierce and Writer, 165–72; Dickerson, 167–75; Spielman and D'Antonio, 99–103; Molly Caldwell Crosby, 191–92. See also Wilson; and Ralph Nading Hill.

3. Entomologists have since reclassified this mosquito numerous times. In 1901 medical authorities in the United States renamed the species *Stegomyia fasciata (S. fasciata)*. Until the 1950s, medical researchers classified the mosquito now known as *A. aegypti* as the *S. fasciata* or *S. calopus* (before 1930). Finlay, "Mosquito Hypothetically Considered"; and "Yellow Fever: Its Transmission," 395–409; Gorgas, 16–17.

4. Numerous major medical schools were established in Philadelphia, including Jefferson Medical College (1824), the Pennsylvania College Medical Department (1839), the Philadelphia College of Medicine (1847), Franklin Medical

College (1847), Hahnemann Medical College (1848), and the Medical College of Pennsylvania (1850). Kilbride, 701–4; O'Hara, 16.

5. Kilbride, 701–4.

6. Finlay, *Obras Completas,* 1:106–7, 120–21, 186; and "Yellow Fever and Atmospheric Alkalinity"; See also *Annual Report of National Board of Health,* 162; *Appletons' Annual Cyclopædia,* 471; Stepan, "Interplay," 399–403.

7. Stepan, "Interplay," 403; Finlay, Finlay, and Kahn, 58–59.

8. Stepan, "Interplay," 399–403.

9. Finlay, *Obras Completas,* 1:197.

10. Sprague, 171–74.

11. Martha Sternberg, 112; *Annual Report of Supervising Surgeon-General,* 213; *New York Times,* June 28, 1885.

12. Sternberg, "Microscopical Investigations," 382–83; Gorgas, 7–8; Sprague, 172–73; Touatre, 153–54.

13. Joseph Goldberger to Mary Farrar Goldberger, 1906, folder 6, Joseph Goldberger Papers. Goldberger is most famous for his research on pellagra in the South.

14. Gorgas, 14–17.

15. Stepan, "Interplay," 397, 401.

16. See Espinosa, *Epidemic Invasions,* 55–63.

17. Robert T. Hill, 33; Navarro, 9; Espinosa, *Epidemic Invasions,* 17–18; Cirillo, 6.

18. Cirillo, 1.

19. Stepan, "Interplay," 409.

20. Of all of the board members, only Agramonte had acquired immunity to yellow fever. Wilson, 102–3.

21. Gorgas, 7–8.

22. Ibid., 5, 6.

23. James Carroll died in 1907 of myocarditis, which his physicians attributed to the severe attack of yellow fever that he had contracted in 1900. Several newspapers asserted that Walter Reed also died as a result of his yellow fever experiments, but in fact he died in 1902 from appendicitis. See Martha Sternberg, 277.

24. *Annual Reports of War Department,* 726–27; McCarthy, "Century of Yellow Fever Research," 1772.

25. Cirillo, 118.

26. In 1912 the US Public Health and Marine Hospital Service was renamed the Public Health Service.

27. Boyce, *Mosquito or Man?,* 157.

28. Heitmann, 55–56; *Sugar in Hawaii,* 21–22; Merleaux, 26–28; Tucker, 1–3.

29. Boyce, *Yellow Fever Prophylaxis,* 6–7.

30. Ibid.; folder 1, Joseph Goldberger Papers.

31. Walter Wyman to Joseph Goldberger, March 22, 1904, folder 3, Goldberger Papers.

32. Stepan, *Beginnings of Brazilian Science,* 88–89.

33. Boyce, *Mosquito or Man,* 188.

34. Stepan, *Beginnings of Brazilian Science,* 88–89.

35. Ibid., 91; Boyce, *Mosquito or Man,* 188.

36. Gorgas, 138; Bunau-Varilla, 542.

37. Manson, *Relation of the Panama Canal,* 5; Haynes, 2.

38. Manson, *Relation of the Panama Canal,* 10–11.

39. Gorgas, 139.

40. Porch and Muller, 3–4.

41. Ibid., 8, 11.

42. Boyce, *Mosquito or Man,* 185.

43. Sutter, 725, 736, 740–41, quotations on 725 and 736.

44. Ibid., 725, 735.

45. Gorgas, 289.

46. Boyce, *Yellow Fever Prophylaxis,* 6–7; folder 1, Goldberger Papers.

47. A. H. Glenman (Acting Surgeon General) to Joseph Goldberger, July 26, 1905, folder 4, Goldberger Papers.

48. Boyce, *Yellow Fever Prophylaxis,* 16.

49. Ibid., 18–19.

50. Ibid., 50–60.

51. Ibid., 38. "Swamp" mosquitoes were usually anophelenes that carried malaria, which remained endemic in Louisiana until the 1950s.

52. Ibid., 46–48.

53. Ibid., 40, 53.

54. Boyce, *Mosquito or Man,* 178–80.

55. Ibid., 192–93; and *Health Progress and Administration,* 162.

56. Boyce, *Health Progress and Administration,* 49.

57. Boyce, *Mosquito or Man,* 192–95; and "Colonization of Africa," 395.

58. Colby, 79–86.

59. The University of Louisiana was founded as a medical college by several doctors in New Orleans in 1834. The Medical College of Louisiana became the Medical Department of the newly established University of Louisiana in 1847. The public University of Louisiana was incorporated as a private institution in 1884, after a donation of more than $1 million from Paul Tulane. *Bulletin of Tulane University* (1912), 12.

60. Soluri, 41–43; see also Cohen. Zemurray later served as director of the United Fruit Company in the 1930s.

61. *Bulletin of Tulane University* (1912), 81.

62. United Fruit Company, *Annual Report, 1912,* 8, 53–55.

63. United Fruit Company, *Annual Report, 1913,* 28–29.

64. United Fruit Company, *Annual Report, 1915,* 49, 80.

65. Adams, 268.

66. Bass, 179.

67. Colby, 37–38, 45, 71–72, 124–25; Tucker, 54.

68. Espinosa, *Epidemic Invasions,* 7–9; Stepan, *Eradication,* 41–56; Palmer, 102.

69. Warwick Anderson, *Colonial Pathologies,* 215–16; Arnold, *Warm Climates and Western Medicine;* and *Colonizing the Body.*

70. Arnold, *Warm Climates and Western Medicine,* 5.

71. Haynes, 176.

72. Ibid., 3.

73. Arnold, *Warm Climates and Western Medicine,* 4.

74. Manson, *Tropical Disease,* ix–xii.

75. Arnold, *Warm Climates and Western Medicine,* 4.

76. Ibid., 6.

77. Ibid.; Duffy, *Rudolph Matas History of Medicine,* 12.

78. Duffy, *Rudolph Matas History of Medicine,* 346–47.

79. Valenčius, 231.

80. Arnold, *Warm Climates and Western Medicine,* 6.

81. Duffy, *Rudolph Matas History of Medicine,* 29, 37–38.

82. Valenčius, 189.

83. Ibid., 256.

84. Ibid., 232.

85. O'Leary, 116.

86. Pierce and Writer, 93–95.

EPILOGUE

1. Ralph Nading Hill, 21; Strode, 37; Fortier, 82; Hanson, 139; Monath, "Yellow Fever: Victor, Victoria?," 1.

2. Robertson et al. James L. A. Webb has shown a similar process of unintended outcomes of malaria control policies in tropical West Africa. See Webb, *Long Struggle against Malaria,* 114–32.

3. Barrett and Higgs, 212.

4. World Health Organization, *Geographical Distribution of Arthropod-Borne Diseases and Their Principal Vectors* (Geneva: World Health Organization, 1989), 47–50.

5. Bryan, Moss, and Kahn, 287; Tomori, 400.

6. Galbraith and Barrett, 764–65.

7. Bryan, Moss, and Kahn, 287–89; Galbraith and Barrett, 764–65.

8. Soper et al., 555.

9. Ellis and Barrett, 332.

10. Barrett and Higgs, 211.

11. Descriptions of dead monkeys during the earliest recorded yellow fever outbreaks among British colonists in Bolama suggest that yellow fever might not have been endemic in parts of West Africa in the eighteenth century. See Billy G. Smith, 2, 69.

12. Coleman, 11.

13. Strode, 1–38; Monath, "Yellow Fever: Victor, Victoria?," 1.

14. Recent (2016) reports from the World Health Organization and the Centers for Disease Control and Prevention maintain that yellow fever is a risk throughout sub-Saharan Africa. World Health Organization, "Meeting of the Emergency Committee."

15. Monath, "Yellow Fever: Victor, Victoria?," 5–8.

16. Ibid., 11–12.

17. Ibid., 24–25.

18. Ibid., 1.

19. Ellis and Barrett, 332; Tomori, 391.

20. Current data comes from a modeling study that the World Health Organization conducted in 2013, using African data sources. World Health Organization, "Yellow Fever." See also Ellis and Barrett, 332; Tomori, 391.

21. Barrett and Higgs, 222; Tomori; see also United Nations, *World Urbanization Prospects*, 16, 19.

22. Barrett and Higgs, 209; Monath, "Yellow Fever: An Update," 12.

23. Tomori, 391.

24. Bryan, Moss, and Kahn, 289; Tomori, 391; Ellis and Barrett, 331.

25. Galbraith and Barrett, 758–59.

26. Monath, "Yellow Fever: An Update," 12; Galbraith and Barrett, 758–59.

27. World Health Organization, "Meeting of the Emergency Committee"; and "Yellow Fever Situation Report."

28. Ellis and Barrett, 339.

29. Ibid., 331, 341; Heather Bell, 163–64.

30. World Health Organization, "Yellow Fever."

31. Nepstad, Stickler, and Almeida, 1595–97;. Eden, McGregor, and Vieira, 283; Buschbacher, 22.

32. Coleman, 11.

33. Tomori, 391.

34. Monath, "Yellow Fever: An Update," 19; Centers for Disease Control and Prevention; Kraemer et al., 5.

35. Galbraith and Barrett, 759.

36. Kraemer et al., 2–5.

37. Monath, "Yellow Fever: Victor, Victoria?," 4; Centers for Disease Control and Prevention.

38. J. R. McNeill, *Mosquito Empires*, 7.

39. James L. A. Webb has shown how ecological changes, combined with unanticipated consequences of malaria control programs, contributed to the re-

surgence of malaria in tropical West Africa in the twentieth century. Large-scale damming and hydroelectric projects transformed local ecologies and resulted in an increase in the transmission of malaria. The sporadic use of antimalarials and insecticides resulted in the development of resistance among malaria parasites and *Anopheles* mosquitoes. Gaps in malaria control efforts caused the loss of acquired immunities among local populations, resulting in higher mortality and morbidity rates among African adults. See Webb, *Long Struggle against Malaria,* 114–32.

40. Thanispong, Sathantriphop, and Chareonviriyaphap, 351, 354; Rajatileka et al., 54; Tikar et al.; Che-Mendoza, Penilla, and Rodríguez, 1386, 1391; Montella et al., 467; Lima et al., 331; Ponlawot, Scott, and Harrington, 823.

41. Carson, 225; Lear, 356–57; Dunlap, 202.

42. Landau-Ossondo et al., 391; Beard, 78, 82.

43. Coleman, 11; Monath, "Yellow Fever: Victor Victoria?," 1, 11, 15; Barrett and Higgs, 210; Massad et al., 3908.

44. Bryan, Moss, and Kahn, 289.

45. Massad et al., 3909; Barnett, Wilder-Smith, and Wilson, 582.

46. Monath, "Yellow Fever: An Update," 17.

47. Staples and Monath, 962.

Bibliography

This listing contains both sources cited in the notes and other valuable references.

MANUSCRIPT SOURCES

Louisiana and Lower Mississippi Valley Collection, Louisiana State University, Baton Rouge
Charles Boothby Papers
Warren D. Brickell Papers
Robert O. Butler Papers
Samuel Cartwright Papers
Charity Hospital Papers
Luther M. Fairbanks Letters
Edward J. Gay and Family Papers
Fisher (Alice Risley) Family Papers
Mary Elizabeth Carter Rives Papers
John B. Vinet Papers.

Historic New Orleans Collection, www.hnoc.org/
Antebellum Letter Collection
Butler Family Papers
Muggah Family Papers

Southern Historical Collection, University of North Carolina, Chapel Hill
Joseph Goldberger Papers
William H. Holcombe Papers
Roach and Eggleston Family Papers

Louisiana Research Collection, Tulane University, New Orleans
Journal of Magnolia Plantation

David M. Rubenstein Rare Book and Manuscript Library, Duke University, Durham, NC
Joseph Jones Papers.

Tennessee State Library and Archives. Nashville
Department of Public Health Records

PUBLISHED DOCUMENTS

Adams, Frederick Upham. *Conquest of the Tropics: The Story of the Creative Enterprises Conducted by the United Fruit Company.* Garden City, NY: Doubleday, Page, 1914.

Agramonte, Aristides. "The Inside History of a Great Medical Discovery." *Scientific Monthly* 1, no. 3 (December 1915): 209–37.

Aiken, Gayle. "The Medical History of New Orleans." In *Standard History of New Orleans, Louisiana,* edited by Henry Rightor, 203–25. Chicago: Lewis, 1900.

Alexander, James Edward. *Transatlantic Sketches, Comprising Visits to the Most Interesting Scenes in North and South America, and the West Indies, with Notes on Negro Slavery and Canadian Emigration.* 2 vols. London: R. Bentley, 1833.

Anderson, Andrew. *Ten Lectures Introductory to the Study of Fever.* London: J. Churchill, 1861.

Anderson, Benedict. *Imagined Communities: Reflections on the Origin and Spread of Nationalism.* London: Verso, 1983.

Anderson, Izett. *Yellow Fever in the West Indies.* London: H. K. Lewis, 1898.

Anderson, Warwick. *Colonial Pathologies: American Tropical Medicine, Race, and Hygiene in the Philippines.* Durham, NC: Duke University Press, 2006.

———. *The Cultivation of Whiteness: Science, Health, and Racial Destiny in Australia.* Durham, NC: Duke University Press, 2006.

———. "Immunities of Empire: Race, Disease, and the New Tropical Medicine, 1900–1920." *Bulletin of the History of Medicine* 70, no. 1 (1996): 94–118.

Annual Report of Supervising Surgeon-General of the Marine-Hospital Service of the United States for the Fiscal Year 1889. Washington, DC: Government Printing Office, 1889.

Annual Report of the National Board of Health. Washington, DC: Government Printing Office, 1879–85.

Annual Reports of the War Department for the Fiscal Year Ended June 30, 1901;

Reports of Chiefs of Bureaus. Washington, DC: Government Printing Office, 1901.

Apel, Thomas A. *Feverish Bodies, Enlightened Minds: Science and the Yellow Fever Controversy in the Early American Republic.* Stanford, CA: Stanford University Press, 2016.

Appletons' Annual Cyclopædia and Register of Important Events of the Year 1879: Embracing Political, Civil, Military, and Social Affairs; Public Documents; Biography, Statistics, Commerce, Finance, Literature, Science, Agriculture, and Mechanical Industry. New York: D. Appleton, 1886.

Arnold, David. *Colonizing the Body: State Medicine and Epidemic Disease in Nineteenth-Century India.* Berkeley: University of California Press, 1993.

———, ed. *Imperial Medicine and Indigenous Societies.* Manchester, UK: Manchester University Press, 1989.

———. *The New Cambridge History of India: Science, Technology, and Medicine in Colonial India.* Cambridge: Cambridge University Press, 1987.

———. *The Problem of Nature: Environment, Culture, and European Expansion.* Oxford: Blackwell, 1996.

———, ed. *Warm Climates and Western Medicine: The Emergence of Tropical Medicine, 1500–1900.* Amsterdam: Editions Rodopi B.V., 1996.

Arthur, Stanley C., and George Campbell Huchet de Kernion, eds. *Old Families of Louisiana.* New Orleans: Harmanson, 1931.

Ashkenazi, Elliot, ed. *The Civil War Diary of Clara Solomon: Growing Up in New Orleans, 1861–1862.* Baton Rouge: Louisiana State University Press, 1995.

Augustin, George. *History of Yellow Fever.* New Orleans: Searcy & Pfaff, 1909.

Auxiliary Sanitary Association of New Orleans. *An Address from the Auxiliary Sanitary Association of New Orleans to the Other Cities and Towns in the Mississippi Valley.* New Orleans: L. Graham Book Printer, 1879.

Bankole, Katherine. *Slavery and Medicine: Enslavement and Medical Practices in Antebellum Louisiana.* New York: Garland, 1998.

Barnett, Elizabeth D. "Yellow Fever." In *International Encyclopedia of Public Health,* edited by Kris Heggenhougen and Stella Quah, 657–64. Amsterdam: Elsevier, 2008.

Barnett, Elizabeth D., Annelies Wilder-Smith, and Mary E. Wilson. "Yellow Fever Vaccines and International Travelers." *Expert Reviews of Vaccines* 7, no. 5 (2008): 579–87.

Barrett, Alan D. T., and Stephen Higgs. "Yellow Fever: A Disease That Has Yet to Be Conquered." *Annual Review of Entomology* 52 (2007): 209–29.

Barrett, Alan D. T., and Thomas P. Monath. "Epidemiology and Ecology of Yellow Fever Virus." *Advanced Virus Research* 61 (2003): 291–315.

Bartlett, Elisha. *The History, Diagnosis, and Treatment of the Fevers of the United States*. Philadelphia: Blanchard and Lea, 1856.

Barton, E. H. *The Cause and Prevention of Yellow Fever at New Orleans and Other Cities in America and a Supplement*. New York: H. Bailliere, 1857.

———. "Report upon the Meteorology, Vital Statistics and Hygiene of the State of Louisiana." *Southern Medical Reports* 2 (1850): 107–47.

Bashford, A. "The History of Public Health during Colonialism." In *International Encyclopedia of Public Health*, edited by Kris Heggenhougen and Stella Quah. Amsterdam: Elsevier, 2008.

Bass, C. C. "Cultivation of Malarial Plasmodia in Vitro." *Transactions of the American Society of Tropical Medicine* 8 (1913): 567–79.

Beard, John. "DDT and Human Health." *Science of the Total Environment* 355 (2006): 78–89.

"Beauperthuy on Mosquito-Born Diseases." *Science* 28, no. 708 (July 1908): 114.

Becnel, Thomas A. *The Barrow Family and the Barataria and Lafourche Canal: The Transportation Revolution in Louisiana, 1829–1925*. Baton Rouge: Louisiana State University Press, 1989.

Begnaud, Allen. "The Louisiana Sugar Cane Industry: An Overview." In *Green Fields: Two Hundred Years of Louisiana Sugar*, 29–50. Lafayette: Center for Louisiana Studies, 1980.

Belknap, William W. "Letter from the Secretary of War, Communicating Additional Information regarding a Quarantine System for the Southern and Gulf Coasts," December 19, 1872. In *Senate Executive Documents for the Third Session of the Forty-Second Congress of the United States of America*, document 9. Washington, DC: Government Printing Office, 1873.

Bell, Andrew McIlwaine. *Mosquito Soldiers: Malaria, Yellow Fever, and the Course of the American Civil War*. Baton Rouge: Louisiana State University Press, 2010.

Bell, Heather. *Frontiers of Medicine in the Anglo-Egyptian Sudan, 1899–1940*. Oxford University Press, 1999.

Benjumeda y Fernandez, D. José. *Memoria sobre la fiebre amarilla observada en la ciudad de la Habana*. Cadiz: Imprenta de la Revista Médica, 1870.

Bérenger-Féraud, Laurent Jean Baptiste. *Traité théorique & clinique de la fièvre jaune*. Paris: Octave Doin, 1890.

Black, Robert C., III. *Railroads of the Confederacy*. Chapel Hill: University of North Carolina Press, 1952.

Blackwell, Elizabeth. *Pioneer Work in Opening the Medical Profession to Women*. Edited by Amy Sue Bix. Amherst, NY: Humanity Books, 2005.

Blane, Gilbert. *Select Dissertations on Several Subjects of Medical Science*. London: T. and G. Underwood, 1822.

Blassingame, John W. *Black New Orleans, 1860–1880.* Chicago: University of Chicago Press, 1973.

Bloodgood, Delavan. *An Account of the Yellow Fever Which Appeared in December, 1866, and Prevailed on Board the United States Ship Jamestown, Store and Hospital Ship at Panama.* Washington, DC: Government Printing Office, 1873.

Bloom, Khaled. *The Mississippi Valley's Great Yellow Fever Epidemic of 1878.* Baton Rouge: Louisiana State University Press, 1993.

Blum, Edward J. *Reforging the White Republic: Race, Religion, and American Nationalism, 1865–1898.* Baton Rouge: Louisiana State University Press, 2005.

Bond, Beverly, and Janann Sherman. *Memphis in Black and White.* Charleston, SC: Arcadia, 2003.

Bosma, Ulbe. *The Sugar Plantation in India and Indonesia: Industrial Production, 1770–2010.* Cambridge: Cambridge University Press, 2013.

Bouchereau, Alcée. *Statement of the Sugar and Rice Crops Made in Louisiana, 1872–1874.* New Orleans: Pelican Book and Job, 1873–75.

———. *Statement of the Sugar and Rice Crops Made in Louisiana, 1882–1883.* New Orleans: L. Graham 1883.

Bourdelais, Patrice. *Epidemics Laid Low: A History of What Happened in Rich Countries.* Translated by Bart K. Holland. Baltimore: Johns Hopkins University Press, 2006. First publication 2003.

Boyce, Rubert. "The Colonization of Africa." *Journal of the Royal African Society* 10, no. 40 (July 1911): 392–97.

———. *Health Progress and Administration in the West Indies.* New York: E. P. Dutton, 1910.

———. "The History of Yellow Fever in West Africa." *British Medical Journal* 1, no. 2613 (January 1911): 181–85.

———. "The History of Yellow Fever in West Africa (Continued)." *British Medical Journal* 1, no. 2614 (February 1911): 249–50.

———. "The History of Yellow Fever in West Africa (Concluded)." *British Medical Journal* 1, no. 2615 (February 1911): 301–6.

———. *Mosquito or Man? The Conquest of the Tropical World.* London: John Murray, 1910.

———. *Yellow Fever and Its Prevention: A Manual for Medical Students and Practitioners.* New York: E. P. Dutton, 1911.

———. *Yellow Fever Prophylaxis in New Orleans, 1905.* London: Williams & Norgate, 1906.

Boxer, C. R. *The Portuguese Seaborne Empire, 1415–1825.* New York: Alfred A. Knopf, 1969.

Brasseaux, Carl A. *French, Cajun, Creole, Houma: A Primer on Francophone Louisiana*. Baton Rouge: Louisiana State University Press, 2005.

———. "The Image of Louisiana and the Failure of Voluntary French Emigration, 1683-1731." In *The Louisiana Purchase Bicentennial Series in Louisiana History*, vol. 1, *The French Experience in Louisiana*. Lafayette: Center for Louisiana Studies, 1995.

———, ed. *The Louisiana Purchase Bicentennial Series in Louisiana History: Vol. 10, A Refuge for All Ages: Immigration in Louisiana History*. Lafayette: Center for Louisiana Studies, 1996.

Brasseaux, Carl A., Keith P. Fontenot, and Claude F. Oubre. *Creoles of Color in the Bayou Country*. Jackson: University of Mississippi Press, 1994.

Breeden, James O. *Joseph Jones, M.D.: Scientist of the Old South*. Louisville: University Press of Kentucky, 1975.

Brickell, Warren D. "Biographical Sketch of Erasmus Darwin Fenner." *Southern Journal of the Medical Sciences* 39 (November 1866): 402-23.

Bronner, Simon J. "'Gombo' Folkloreistics: Lafcadio Hearn's Creolization and Hybridization in the Formative Period of Folklore Studies." *Journal of Folklore Research* 42, no. 2 (May–August 2005): 141-84.

Brown, Harvey E. "Letter from the Secretary of War, Communicating Additional Information regarding a Quarantine System for the Southern and Gulf Coasts," December 19, 1872. In *Senate Executive Documents for the Third Session of the Forty-Second Congress of the United States of America*. Washington, DC: Government Printing Office, 1873.

Bryan, Charles S. *A Most Satisfactory Man: The Story of Theodore Brevard Hayne, Last Martyr of Yellow Fever*. Spartanburg, SC: Reprint, 1996.

Bryan, Charles S., Sandra W. Moss, and Richard J. Kahn. "Yellow Fever in the Americas." *Infectious Disease Clinics of North America* 18 (2004): 668-73.

Bryant, Juliet E., Edward C. Holmes, and Alan D. T. Barrett. "Out of Africa: A Molecular Perspective on the Introduction of Yellow Fever into the Americas." *PLoS Pathogens* 3, no. 5 (May 2007): 668-73.

Bulletin of Tulane University of Louisiana 13, no. 7 (July 1912).

Bulletin of Tulane University of Louisiana 15, no. 10 (August 1914).

Bunau-Varilla, Philippe. *Panama: The Creation, Destruction, and Resurrection*. New York: McBride, Nast, 1914.

Buschbacher, Robert J. "Tropical Deforestation and Pasture Development." *BioScience* 36, no. 1 (1986): 22-28.

Cable, George Washington. *The Creoles of Louisiana*. New York: Charles Scribner's, 1884.

———. *The Grandissimes: A Story of Creole Life*. New York: Charles Scribner's, 1880.

———. *Old Creole Days.* New York: Charles Scribner's, 1900.

Cameron, John F. "Camps; Depopulation of Memphis; Epidemics of 1878 and 1879." In *Public Health Reports and Papers,* 5:152–63. Boston: Houghton, Mifflin, 1880.

Campanella, Richard. "An Ethnic Geography of New Orleans." *Journal of American History* 94, no. 3 (2007): 704–15.

———. *Geographies of New Orleans: Urban Fabrics before the Storm.* Lafayette: Center for Louisiana Studies at the University of Southwestern Louisiana, 2006.

Capers, Gerald M. "Yellow Fever in Memphis in the 1870's." *Mississippi Valley Historical Review* 24, no. 4 (March 1938): 483–502.

Carpenter, Stanley J., and Walter J. LaCasse. *Mosquitoes of North America (North of Mexico).* Berkeley: University of California Press, 1955.

Carpenter, W. M. *Sketches from the History of Yellow Fever; Showing Its Origin Together with Facts and Circumstances Disproving Its Domestic Origin and Demonstrating Its Transmissibility.* New Orleans: J. B. Steel, 1844.

Carrigan, Jo Ann. *The Saffron Scourge: A History of Yellow Fever in Louisiana, 1796–1905.* Lafayette: Center for Louisiana Studies, 1994.

———. "Yellow Fever: Scourge of the South." In *Disease and Distinctiveness in the American South,* edited by Todd L. Savitt and James Harvey Young. Knoxville: University of Tennessee Press, 1988.

Carroll, James. *Lessons to Be Learned from the Present Outbreak of Yellow Fever in Louisiana.* Washington, DC: Government Printing Office, 1911.

Carson, Rachel. *Silent Spring.* New York: Houghton Mifflin, 1962.

Carter, Henry Rose. *Yellow Fever: Its Nature, Diagnosis, Treatment, and Prophylaxis, and Quarantine Regulations Relating Thereto, by the Officers of the U.S. Marine Hospital Service.* Washington, DC: Government Printing Office, 1898.

———. *The Methods of Conveyance of Yellow Fever Infection.* Washington, DC: Government Printing Office, 1902.

———. *Shipment of Merchandise from a Town Infected with Yellow Fever.* Washington, DC: Government Printing Office, 1899.

———. *Yellow Fever: An Epidemiological and Historical Study of Its Place of Origin.* Edited by Laura Armistead Carter and Wade Hampton Frost. Baltimore: Williams & Wilkins, 1931.

Cartwright, Samuel A. "The Diseases and Physical Peculiarities of the Negro Race." *Southern Medical Reports* (1850): 421–29.

———. "Ethnology of the Negro of Prognathous Race: A Lecture Delivered Nov. 30, 1857, before the New Orleans Academy of Sciences." *New Orleans Medical and Surgical Journal* (March 1858): 149–63.

———. "Report on the Diseases and Physical Peculiarities of the Negro Race." *New Orleans Medical and Surgical Journal* (May 1851): 691–715.

———. "Slavery in the Light of Ethnology." In *Cotton Is King, and Proslavery Arguments,* edited by E. N. Elliott, 691–728. Augusta, GA: Pritchard, Abbott & Loomis, 1860.

Cassedy, James H. *Medicine in America: A Short History.* Baltimore: Johns Hopkins University Press, 1991.

Centers for Disease Control and Prevention (CDC). "Areas with Risk of Yellow Fever Virus Transmission in Africa." https://www.cdc.gov/yellowfever/maps/africa.html.

———. "Estimated Range of Aedes albopictus and Aedes aegypti in the United States, 2016." www.cdc.gov/zika/pdfs/zika-mosquito-maps.pdf.

Cercle des Philadelphes. *Recherches, mémoires et observations sur les maladies épizootiques de Saint-Domingue.* Cap-François, Saint-Domingue: De l'Imprimerie Royale, 1788.

Chaillé, Stanford E. *The Importance of Introducing the Study of Hygiene into the Public and Other Schools.* New Orleans: L. Graham, 1882.

———. *Intimidation and the Number of White and Colored Voters in Louisiana in 1876, as Shown by Statistical Data Derived from Republican Official Reports.* New Orleans: Picayune Office Job Print, 1877.

———. *Life and Death in New Orleans from 1787 to 1869, and More Especially during the Five Years, 1856 to 1860.* New Orleans: "Bronze Pen" Steam Book and Job, 1869.

———. "The Yellow Fever, Sanitary Condition, and Vital Statistics of New Orleans during Its Military Occupation, the Four Years 1862–5." *New Orleans Medical and Surgical Journal* (July 1870): 563–98.

Champomier, P. A. *Statement of the Sugar Crop of Louisiana.* New Orleans: Cook, Young, 1844–62.

Chastel, C. "Yellow Fever, Historical." In *International Encyclopedia of Public Health,* edited by Kris Heggenhougen and Stella Quah, 665–75. Amsterdam: Elsevier, 2008.

Che-Mendoza, Azael, R. Patricia Penilla, and D. Américo Rodríguez. "Insecticide Resistance and Glutathione S-Transferases in Mosquitoes: A Review." *African Journal of Biotechnology* 8, no. 8 (2009): 1386–97.

Chernin, Eli. "Josiah Clark Nott, Insects, and Yellow Fever." *Bulletin of the New York Academy of Medicine* 59, no. 9 (1993): 790–802.

Christophers, S. R. *Aedes Aegypti (L.) the Yellow Fever Mosquito: Its Life History, Bionomics and Structure.* Cambridge: Cambridge University Press, 1960.

Christovich, Mary-Louise, ed. *New Orleans Architecture: Vol. 3, The Cemeteries.* Gretna, LA: Pelican, 1974.

Cirillo, Vincent J. *Bullets and Bacilli: The Spanish-American War and Military.* New Brunswick, NJ: Rutgers University Press, 2004.

Coelho, Philip R. P., and Robert A. McGuire. "African and European Bound Labor in the British New World: The Biological Consequences of Economic Choices." *Journal of Economic History* 57, no. 1 (1997): 83–115.

Cohen, Rich. *The Fish That Ate the Whale: The Life and Times of America's Banana King.* New York: Farrar, Straus and Giroux, 2012.

Colby, Jason M. *The Business of Empire: United Fruit, Race, and U.S. Expansion in Central America.* Ithaca, NY: Cornell University Press, 2011.

Coleman, William. *Yellow Fever in the North: The Methods of Early Epidemiology.* Madison: University of Wisconsin Press, 1987.

Colten, Craig E. *Perilous Place, Powerful Storms: Hurricane Protection in Coastal Louisiana.* University Press of Mississippi, 2009.

———. *Southern Waters: The Limits to Abundance.* Baton Rouge: Louisiana State University Press, 2014.

———. *Transforming New Orleans and Its Environs: Centuries of Change.* Pittsburgh: University of Pittsburgh Press, 2001.

———. *An Unnatural Metropolis: Wresting New Orleans from Nature.* Baton Rouge: Louisiana State University Press, 2005.

Colton, J. H., B. M. Norton, and A. Persac. *Norman's Chart of the Lower Mississippi River.* New Orleans: B. M. Norman, 1858.

Conclusions of the Board of Experts Authorized by Congress to Investigate the Yellow Fever Epidemic of 1878; Being in Reply to Questions of the Committees of the Senate and House of Representatives of the United States, upon the Subject of Epidemic Diseases. Washington, DC: Judd & Detweiler, 1879.

Conrad, Glenn R., and Ray F. Lucas. *White Gold: A Brief History of the Louisiana Sugar Industry, 1795–1995.* Lafayette: Center for Louisiana Studies, 1995.

Conway, A. A. "New Orleans as a Port of Immigration, 1820–1860." MA thesis, University of London, 1949.

Cooper, Donald B. "Brazil's Long Fight against Epidemic Disease, 1849–1917, with Special Emphasis on Yellow Fever." *Bulletin of the New York Academy of Medicine* 51, no. 5 (1975): 672–96.

Cooper, Donald B., and Kenneth F. Kiple. "Yellow Fever." In *The Cambridge World History of Disease,* edited by Kenneth F. Kiple, 1100–1108. Cambridge: Cambridge University Press, 1993.

Cooper, Frederick, and Randall M. Packard, eds. *International Development and the Social Sciences: Essays on the History and Politics of Knowledge.* Berkeley: University of California Press, 1997.

Corthell, Elmer Lawrence. *A History of the Jetties at the Mouth of the Mississippi River.* New York: J. L. Wiley, 1881.

Cowden, John. *The Barataria Ship Canal and Its Importance to the Valley of the Mississippi.* Memphis: Tracy, 1877.

Crais, Clifton, and Pamela Scully. *Sara Baartman and the Hottentot Venus: A Ghost Story and Biography.* Princeton, NJ: Princeton University Press, 2009.

Crosby, Alfred. *The Columbian Exchange: Biological and Cultural Consequences of 1492.* Westport, CT: Praeger, 2003.

———. *Ecological Imperialism: The Biological Expansion of Europe, 900–1900.* Cambridge: Cambridge University Press, 1986.

Crosby, Molly Caldwell. *The American Plague: The Untold Story of Yellow Fever, the Epidemic That Shaped Our History.* New York: Berkley Books, 2006.

Cueto, Marcos, ed. *Missionaries of Science: The Rockefeller Foundation and Latin America.* Bloomington: Indiana University Press, 1994.

Curtin, Philip D. *The Atlantic Slave Trade: A Census.* Madison: University of Wisconsin Press, 1969.

———. *Death by Migration: Europe's Encounter with the Tropical World in the Nineteenth Century.* Cambridge: Cambridge University Press, 1989.

———. *Disease and Imperialism before the Nineteenth Century.* Minneapolis: Associates of the James Bell Ford Library, University of Minnesota, 1990.

———. "Disease Exchange across the Atlantic," *History and Philosophy of the Life Sciences* 15, no. 3 (1993): 329–56.

———. "The End of the 'White Man's Grave'? Nineteenth-Century Mortality in West Africa." *Journal of Interdisciplinary History* 21, no. 1 (1990): 63–88.

———. "Epidemiology and the Slave Trade." *Political Science Quarterly* 83, no. 2 (1968): 190–216.

———. *The Rise and Fall of the Plantation Complex.* Cambridge: Cambridge University Press, 1990.

———. *The Tropical Atlantic in the Age of the Slave Trade.* Washington, DC: American Historical Association, 1991.

———. "'The White Man's Grave': Image and Reality, 1780–1850." *Journal of British Studies* 1, no. 1 (1961): 94–110.

Curtin, Philip D., Steven Feierman, Leonard Thompson, and Jan Vansina. *African History: From Earliest Times to Independence.* New York: Longman Group, 1978.

Curtis, Andrew, Jacqueline W. Mills, and Jason K. Blackburn. "A Spatial Variant of the Basic Reproduction Number for the New Orleans Yellow Fever Epidemic of 1878." *Professional Geographer* 59, no. 4 (2007): 492–502.

Curtis, James L. *Blacks, Medical Schools, and Society.* Ann Arbor: University of Michigan Press, 1971.

Dauer, C. C., and G. M. Carrera. "Carlos Finlay's Contribution to the Epidemiology of Yellow Fever." *Yale Journal of Biology and Medicine* (1937): 585–88.

Dean, Warren. *With Broadax and Firebrand: The Destruction of the Brazilian Atlantic Forest.* Berkeley: University of California Press, 1995.

Delaporte, François. *The History of Yellow Fever: An Essay on the Birth of Tropical Medicine.* Translated by Arthur Goldhammer. Cambridge: MIT Press, 1991.

Deléry, Charles. *Mémoire sur l'épidémie de fièvre jaune: Qui a regné à la Nouvelle-Orléans et dans les campagnes pendant l'année 1867.* New Orleans: L. Marchand, 1867.

———. *Precis historique de la fièvre jaune.* New Orleans: Imprimerie Franco-Americaine, 1859.

Dell Orto, John. "Yellow Fever." *New Orleans Medical and Surgical Journal* (February 1879): 638–47.

de Meillon, Botha, Anthony Sebastian, and Z. H. Khan. "Cane-Sugar Feeding in *Culex pipiens fatigans.*" *Bulletin of the World Health Organization* 36, no. 1 (1967), 53–65.

Dessens, Nathalie. *Creole City: A Chronicle of Early American New Orleans.* Gainesville: University Press of Florida, 2015.

———. *From Saint-Domingue to New Orleans: Migration and Influence.* Gainesville: University Press of Florida, 2007.

Diaz, Henry F., and Gregory J. McCabe. "A Possible Connection between the 1878 Yellow Fever Epidemic in the Southern United States and the 1877–1878 El Niño Episode." *Bulletin of the American Meteorological Society* 80, no. 1 (1999): 21–27.

Dickerson, James L. *Yellow Fever: A Deadly Disease Poised to Kill Again.* Amherst, NY: Prometheus Books, 2006.

Din, Gilbert C. *The Canary Islanders of Louisiana.* Baton Rouge: Louisiana State University Press, 1988.

Domínguez, Virginia R. *White by Definition: Social Classification in Creole Louisiana.* New Brunswick, NJ: Rutgers University Press, 1986.

Dormon, James H. *Creoles of Color in the Gulf South.* Knoxville: University of Tennessee Press, 1996.

Dowell, Greensville. *Yellow Fever and Malarial Diseases: Embracing a History of the Epidemics of Yellow Fever in Texas: New Views on Its Diagnosis, Treatment, Propagation and Control.* Philadelphia: Medical Publication, 1876.

Dowler, Bennet. "Researches upon the Necropolis of New Orleans." *New Orleans Medical and Surgical Journal* (November 1850): 275–300.

———. "Review." *New Orleans Medical and Surgical Journal* (November 1850): 54–67.

Dowler, M. Morton. *On the Reputed Causes of Yellow Fever and the So Called Sanitary Measures of the Day*. New Orleans: Picayune Print, 1854.

Downs, Jim. *Sick from Freedom: African-American Illness and Suffering during the Civil War and Reconstruction*. Oxford: Oxford University Press, 2012.

Drake, Daniel. *A Systematic Treatise, Historical, Etiological and Practical, on the Principal Diseases of the Interior Valley of North America: As They Appear in the Caucasian, African, Indian and Esquimaux Varieties of Its Population*. Cincinnati: Winthrop B. Smith, 1850.

Dromgoole, J. P. *Yellow Fever: Heroes, Honors, and Horrors of 1878*. Louisville: John P. Morton, 1879.

Dubois, Laurent, and John D. Garrigus. *Slave Revolution in the Caribbean, 1789–1804: A Brief History with Documents*. New York: Palgrave Macmillan, 2006.

Duffy, John. "French Influence on the Development of Medicine in Louisiana." *Biomedicine & Pharmacotherapy* 44, no. 3 (1990): 147–52.

———, ed. *The Rudolph Matas History of Medicine in Louisiana*. 2 vols. Baton Rouge: Louisiana State University Press, 1958.

———. *Sword of Pestilence: The New Orleans Yellow Fever Epidemic of 1853*. Baton Rouge: Louisiana State University Press, 1966.

Dunlap, Thomas R. *DDT: Scientists, Citizens, and Public Policy*. Princeton, NJ: Princeton University Press, 1981.

Dunn, Richard. *Sugar and Slaves: The Rise of the Planter Class in the English West Indies, 1624–1713*. Chapel Hill: University of North Carolina Press, 1972.

Dutroulau, A. F. *Traité des maladies des Européens dans les pays chauds (régions tropicales): Climatologie, maladies endémiques*. Paris: J. B. Baillière, 1868.

Echenberg, Myron. "'For Their Own Good': The Pasteur Institute of Dakar and the Quest for an Anti-Yellow Fever Vaccine in French Colonial Africa, 1924–1960." In *Les conquêtes de la médecine moderne en Afrique*, edited by Jean-Paul Bado, 53–69. Paris: Editions Karthala, 2006.

Eden, Michael J., Duncan F. M. McGregor, and Nelson A. Q. Vieira. "Pasture Development on Cleared Forest Land in Northern Amazonia." *Geographical Journal* 146, no. 3 (1990): 283–96.

"Editorial: Yellow Fever Board of Experts." *Atlanta Medical and Surgical Journal* 16, no. 10 (January 1879): 624–25.

Eisenberg, Peter L. *The Sugar Industry in Pernambuco: Modernization without Change, 1840–1910*. Berkeley: University of California Press, 1974.

Eliason, D. A. "Feeding Adult Mosquitoes on Solid Sugars." *Nature* 4903 (1963): 289.

Elliott, E. N., ed. *Cotton Is King, and Proslavery Arguments.* Augusta, GA: Pritchard, Abbott & Loomis, 1860.

Ellis, Brett R., and Alan D. T. Barrett. "The Enigma of Yellow Fever in East Africa." *Reviews in Medical Virology* 18 (2008): 331–46.

Ellis, John H. *Yellow Fever and Public Health in the New South.* Lexington: University Press of Kentucky, 1992.

Espinosa, Mariola. *Epidemic Invasions: Yellow Fever and the Limits of Cuban Independence, 1878–1930.* Chicago: University of Chicago Press, 2009.

———. "The Question of Racial Immunity to Yellow Fever in History and Historiography." *Social Science History* 38, nos. 3–4 (Fall–Winter 2014): 437–53.

Faget, J. C. *Etude medicale de quelques questions importantes pour la Louisiane, et expose succinct d'une endémie paludéenne, de forme catarrhale, qui a sévi a la Nouvelle-Orléans, particulièrement sur les enfants, pendant l'épidémie de fièvre jaune de 1858.* New Orleans: Imprimerie Franco-Américaine, 1859.

Farley, John. *To Cast Out Disease: A History of the International Division of the Rockefeller Foundation (1913–1951).* Oxford: Oxford University Press, 2004.

Farragut, Loyall. *The Life of David Glasgow Farragut: First Admiral of the United States Navy, Embodying His Journal and Letters.* Berlin: Nabu Press, 2010. Original publication 1879.

———. *Monographie sur le type et la spécificité de la fièvre jaune établis avec l'aide de la montre et du thermometer.* New Orleans: Am. Lutton, 1875.

———. *The Type and Specificity of Yellow Fever Established with the Aid of the Watch and Thermometer.* New Orleans: Am. Lutton, 1875.

Faust, Drew Gilpin, ed. *The Ideology of Slavery: Proslavery Thought in the Antebellum South, 1830–1860.* Baton Rouge: Louisiana State University Press, 1981.

Fee, Elizabeth. "Public Health and the State: The United States." In *The History of Public Health and the Modern State*, edited by Dorothy Porter. New York: Rodopi, 1994.

Fenner, E. D. *History of the Epidemic Yellow Fever at New Orleans, La. in 1853.* New York: Clayton, 1854.

———. "Remarks on the Sanitary Condition of the City of New Orleans, during the Period of Federal Military Occupation, from May 1862 to March 1866." *Southern Journal of the Medical Sciences* 1 (May 1866): 22–43.

———. "Reports from Louisiana: Article I." *Southern Medical Reports* 1 (1849): 17–55.

———. "Reports from Louisiana: Article III. Special Report on the Fevers of New Orleans in the Year 1850." *Southern Medical Reports* 2 (1850): 79 99.

Fett, Sharla M. "Body and Soul: African American Healing in Southern Antebellum Communities, 1800–1860." PhD diss., Rutgers, the State University of New Jersey, 1995.

———. *Working Cures: Healing, Health, and Power on Southern Slave Plantations.* Chapel Hill: University of North Carolina Press, 2002.

Finlay, Carlos. "Inoculations for Yellow Fever by Means of Contaminated Mosquitoes." *American Journal of the Medical Sciences* 102 (1891): 264–68.

———. "The Mosquito Hypothetically Considered as the Agent of Transmission of Yellow Fever." *New Orleans Medical and Surgical Journal* (February 1882): 601–16.

———. *Obras Completas.* 5 vols. Havana: Academia de Ciencias de Cuba, Muséo Histórico, de las Ciencias Médicas 'Carlos J. Finlay,' 1965–71.

———. "Reports from Sanitary Officers in Habana, Cuba [1901–2]." In *Yellow Fever: A Compilation of Various Publications: Results from the Work of Maj. Walter Reed, Medical Corps, United States Army, and the Yellow Fever Commission,* 221–38. Washington, DC: Government Printing Office, 1911.

———. "Yellow Fever: Its Transmission by Means of the Culex Mosquito." *American Journal of the Medical Sciences* 92 (1886): 392–409.

———. "Yellow Fever and Atmospheric Alkalinity." *British Medical Journal* 2 (1880): 492.

Finlay, Carlos Eduardo, Carlos Juan Finlay, and Morton Charles Kahn. *Carlos Finlay and Yellow Fever.* Oxford: Institute of Tropical Medicine of the University of Havana by Oxford University Press, 1940.

Follett, Richard. *The Sugar Masters: Planters and Slaves in Louisiana's Cane World, 1820–1860.* Baton Rouge: Louisiana State University Press, 2005.

Foner, Eric. *Reconstruction: America's Unfinished Revolution, 1863–1877.* New York: Harper Collins, 1988.

Fong, Y. L., F. C. Cadigan, and G. R. Coatney. "A Presumptive Case of Naturally Occurring Plasmodium Knowlesi Malaria in Man in Malaysia." *Transactions of the Royal Society of Tropical Medicine and Hygiene* 65, no. 6 (1971): 839–40.

Forstall, E. J. "Louisiana Sugar." *DeBow's Review* 1, no. 1 (January 1846): 53–56.

Fortier, James Joseph Alcée. *The Spanish-American War of 1898.* New Orleans: Press of T. J. Moran's Sons, 1939.

Fraginals, Manuel Moreno. *The Sugarmill (El Ingenio): The Socioeconomic Complex of Sugar in Cuba, 1760–1860.* Translated by Cedric Belfrage. New York: Monthly Review Press, 1976.

Fredrickson, George. *Racism: A Short History.* Princeton, NJ: Princeton University Press, 2002.

Freiberg, Edna B. *Bayou St. John in Colonial Louisiana, 1699–1803*. New Orleans: Harve Press, 1980.

Friedrichs, E. D., ed. *Mayors of New Orleans, 1803–1936*. New Orleans: Work Projects Administration, City Hall Archives, 1940.

Funes Monzote, Reinaldo. *From Rainforest to Cane Field in Cuba: An Environmental History since 1492*. Translated by Alex Martin. Chapel Hill: University of North Carolina Press, 2008.

Fussell, Elizabeth. "Constructing New Orleans, Constructing Race: A Population History of New Orleans." *Journal of American History* 94, no. 3 (December 2007): 846–55.

Galbraith, Sareen E., and Alan D. T. Barrett. "Yellow Fever." In *Vaccines for Biodefense and Emerging and Neglected Diseases*, edited by Alan D. T. Barrett and Lawrence Stanberry, 753–85. Amsterdam: Elsevier, 2009.

Galloway, J. H. "The Mediterranean Sugar Industry." *Geographical Review* 67, no. 2 (1977): 177–94.

———. "Sugar." In *The Cambridge World History of Food*, edited by Kenneth F. Kiple and Kriemhild Coneè Ornelas, 437–49. Cambridge: Cambridge University Press, 2000.

———. *The Sugar Cane Industry: An Historical Geography from Its Origins to 1914*. Cambridge: Cambridge University Press, 1989.

———. "Tradition and Innovation in the American Sugar Industry, c. 1500–1800: An Explanation." *Annals of the Association of American Geographers* 75, no. 3 (1985): 334–51.

Gamble, Vanessa Northington. *Germs Have No Color Lines: Blacks and American Medicine, 1900–1945*. New York: Garland, 1989.

Garcia, Alejandro, and Oscar Zanetti. *Sugar and Railroads: A Cuban History, 1837–1959*. Chapel Hill: University of North Carolina Press, 1998.

Garrett, Laurie. *The Coming Plague: Newly Emerging Diseases in a World out of Balance*. New York: Penguin Books, 1994.

Geggus, David. "Yellow Fever in the 1790s: The British Army in Occupied Saint Domingue." *Medical History* 23 (1979): 38–58.

Gehman, Mary. *Women and New Orleans*. New Orleans: Margaret Media, 1988.

Geographical Distribution of Arthropod-Borne Diseases and Their Principal Vectors. Geneva: World Health Organization, 1989.

Gillett, J. D. *The Mosquito: Its Life, Activities, and Impact on Human Affairs*. New York: Doubleday, 1972.

Gillson, Gordon. "The Louisiana State Board of Heath: The Formative Years." PhD diss., Louisiana State University, 1960.

Goodyear, James D. "The Sugar Connection: A New Perspective on the History of Yellow Fever." *Bulletin of the History of Medicine* 52 (1978): 5–21.

Gorgas, William Crawford. *Sanitation in Panama*. New York: D. Appleton, 1918.

Goucher, Candace. *Congotay! Congotay! A Global History of Caribbean Food*. London: M. E. Sharpe, 2014.

Grainger, James. *An Essay on the More Common West-India Diseases and the Remedies Which That Country Itself Produces: To Which Are Added, Some Hints on the Management &c. of Negroes*. Edinburgh, Scotland: Mundell, 1802.

Green Fields: Two Hundred Years of Louisiana Sugar. Lafayette: Center for Louisiana Studies, 1980.

Gregory, Frederick. "The Impact of the Darwinian Revolution on Protestant Theology in the Nineteenth Century." In *God and Nature: Historical Essays on the Encounter between Christianity and Science*, edited by David C. Lindberg and Ronald L. Numbers. Berkeley: University of California Press, 1986.

Guerra, Francisco. "Aleixo De Abreu (1568–1630), Author of the Earliest Book on Tropical Medicine Describing Amoebiasis, Malaria, Typhoid Fever, Scurvy, Yellow Fever, Dracontiasis, and Tungiasis in 1623." *Journal of Tropical Medicine and Hygiene* 71 (1968): 51–69.

———. "The Influence of Disease on Race, Logistics, and Colonization in the Antilles." *American Journal of Tropical Medicine and Hygiene* 69 (1966): 21–35.

Hahn, Marilyn Davis. *Old St. Stephen's Land Office Records and American State Papers for Public Lands:* Vol. 1, *1768–1888*. Easley, SC: Southern Historical Press, 1983.

Hall, A. Oakey. *The Manhattaner in New Orleans; or, Phases of "Crescent City" Life*. New York: J. S. Bedfield, 1851.

Hall, Gwendolyn Midlo. *Africans in Colonial Louisiana: The Development of Afro-Creole Culture in the Eighteenth-Century*. Baton Rouge: Louisiana State University Press, 1992.

Hammond, William A. *Military Medical and Surgical Essays Prepared for the United States Sanitary Commission*. Philadelphia: J. B. Lippincott, 1864.

Hanger, Kimberly S. *Bounded Lives, Bounded Places: Free Black Society in Colonial New Orleans, 1769–1803*. Durham, NC: Duke University Press, 1997.

Hannaford, Ivan. *Race: The History of an Idea in the West*. Baltimore: Johns Hopkins University Press, 1996.

Hanson, Henry. *The Pied Piper of Peru*. Jacksonville, FL: Convention Press, 1961.

Hargis, Robert B. S. *The Ship Origin of Yellow Fever with Comments on the Preliminary Report of the Havana Yellow Fever Commission*. Pensacola, FL: Gazette Book and Job, 1880.

――. *Yellow Fever: Its Ship Origin and Prevention*. Philadelphia: D. G. Brinton, 1880.

Harris, Seale. *Woman's Surgeon: The Life Story of J. Marion Sims*. New York: Macmillan, 1950.

Harrison, Mark. *Climates and Constitutions: Health, Race, Environment and British Imperialism in India, 1600–1850*. Oxford: Oxford University Press, 1999.

――. *Medicine in the Age of Commerce and Empire: Britain and Its Tropical Colonies, 1660–1830*. Oxford: Oxford University Press, 2010.

――. "The Tender Frame of Man": Disease, Climate, and Racial Difference in India and the West Indies, 1760–1860." *Bulletin of the History of Medicine* 70, no. 1 (1996): 68–93.

Harrison-Chirimuuta, Rosalind J. "AIDS from Africa: Western Science or Racist Mythology?" In *Western Medicine as Contested Knowledge*, edited by Andrew Cunningham and Bridie Andrews, 46–68. Manchester, UK: Manchester University Press, 1997.

Haynes, Douglas. *Imperial Medicine: Patrick Manson and the Conquest of Tropical Disease*. Philadelphia: University of Pennsylvania Press, 2001.

Hays, J. N. *Epidemics and Pandemics: Their Impacts on Human History*. Santa Barbara: ABC CLIO, 2005.

Headrick, Daniel. *The Tools of Empire: Technology and European Imperialism in the Nineteenth Century*. Oxford: Oxford University Press, 1981.

Heagerty, J. J. "Mal de Siam." *Canadian Medical Association Journal* 15, no. 12 (1925): 1243–45.

Hearn, Lafcadio. "――!――!! Mosquitoes!!!" *New Orleans Daily City Item*, July 28, 1880.

――. *Leaves from the Diary of an Impressionist: Early Writings by Lafcadio Hearn*. Boston: Houghton Mifflin, 1911.

――. *Two Years in the French West Indies*. New York: Harper, 1889.

Heggenhougen, Kris, and Stella Quah, eds. *International Encyclopedia of Public Health*. Amsterdam: Elsevier, 2008.

Heitmann, John Alfred. *The Modernization of the Louisiana Sugar Industry, 1830–1910*. Baton Rouge: Louisiana State University Press, 1987.

Herrick, S. S. "Review of Yellow Fever in New Orleans, 1869–1874." *New Orleans Medical and Surgical Journal* (March 1875): 649–52.

Higman, B. W. "The Sugar Revolution." *Economic History Review* 53, no. 2 (2000): 213–36.

Hill, David R. "Mapping the Rise of Yellow Fever Infection." *Current Infectious Disease Reports* 14, no. 3 (June 2012): 246–55.

Hill, Ralph Nading. *The Doctors Who Conquered Yellow Fever.* New York: Random House, 1957.

Hill, Robert T. *Cuba and Porto Rico with the Other Islands of the West Indies: Their Topography, Climate, Flora, Products, Industries, Cities, People, Political Conditions, Etc.* New York: Century, 1899.

Hilliard, Sam B. "Site Characteristics and Spatial Stability of the Louisiana Sugarcane Industry." *Agricultural History* 53, no. 1 (1979): 254–69.

Hirsch, Arnold R., and Joseph Logsdon, eds. *Creole New Orleans: Race and Americanization.* Baton Rouge: Louisiana State University Press, 1992.

Hirsch, August. *Handbook of Geographical and Historical Pathology,* vol. 3, *Diseases of Organs and Parts.* Translated by Charles Creighton. London: New Sydenham Society, 1886.

Historical Sketch Book and Guide to New Orleans and Environs, with Map. Edited by New Orleans Press. New York: W. H. Coleman, 1885.

Hoff, Brent, and Carter Smith III. *Mapping Epidemics: A Historical Atlas of Disease.* London: Franklin Watts, 2000.

Hogarth, Rana. "Comparing Anatomies, Constructing Races: Medicine and Slavery in the Atlantic World, 1787–1838." PhD diss., Yale University, 2012.

Holcombe, William Henry. *Report on the Yellow Fever of 1867.* New Orleans: A. Eyrich, 1869.

———. *Yellow Fever and Its Homeopathic Treatment.* New York: W. Radde, 1856.

Holmes, Jack D. *Documentos ineditos para la historia de la Luisiana, 1792–1810.* Madrid: Ediciones Jose Porrua Turanzas, 1963.

Horn, Arthur E. "The Control of Disease in Tropical Africa: Part II." *Journal of the Royal African Society* 32, no. 127 (April 1933): 123–34.

Hornborg, Alf, J. R. McNeill, and Joan Martinez-Alier, eds. *Rethinking Environmental History: World-System History and Global Environmental Change.* Lanham, MD: Altamira Press, 2007.

Howard, Leland O. "The Yellow-Fever Mosquito." *USDA Farmers' Bulletin* 1354 (1923): 1–14.

Howard, Leland O., Harrison G. Dyar, and Frederick Knab. *The Mosquitoes of North and Central America and the West Indies.* Washington, DC: Carnegie Institute, 1912.

Huber, Leonard V. "New Orleans Cemeteries: A Brief History." In *The Cemeteries,* edited by Mary-Louise Christovich, 3–63. Gretna, LA: Pelican, 1974.

Huffard, R. Scott. "Infected Rails: Yellow Fever and Southern Railroads." *Journal of Southern History* 79, no. 1 (February 2013): 79–112.

Humphreys, Margaret. *Intensely Human: The Health of the Black Solider in the American Civil War.* Baltimore: Johns Hopkins University Press, 2008.

———. *Malaria: Poverty, Race, and Public Health in the United States.* Baltimore: Johns Hopkins University Press, 2001.

———. *Yellow Fever and the South.* Baltimore: Johns Hopkins University Press, 1992.

Hutson, Charles Woodward, ed. *Creole Sketches by Lafcadio Hearn* [1878–1881]. Boston: Houghton Mifflin, 1924.

Isenberg, Andrew C., ed. *The Nature of Cities.* Rochester, NY: University of Rochester Press, 2006.

Jackson, Thomas Wright. *Tropical Medicine: With Special Reference to the West Indies, Central America, Hawaii, and the Philippines, Including a General Consideration of Tropical Hygiene.* Philadelphia: P. Blakiston's, 1907.

Jentes, Emily S., Gilles Poumerol, Mark D. Gershman, David R. Hill, Johan Lemarchand, Rosamund F. Lewis, J. Erin Staples, Oyewale Tomori, Annelies Wilder-Smith, and Thomas P. Monath. "The Revised Global Yellow Fever Risk Map and Recommendations for Vaccination, 2010: Consensus of the Informal WHO Working Group on Geographic Risk for Yellow Fever. *Lancet Infectious Diseases* 11, no. 8 (August 2011): 622–32.

Johnson, James. *Influence of Tropical Climates on European Constitutions: Being a Treatise on the Principal Diseases Incidental to Europeans in the East and West Indies, Mediterranean, and Coast of Africa.* London: Thomas and George Underwood, 1827.

Johnson, Walter. *Soul by Soul: Life Inside the Antebellum Slave Market.* Cambridge, MA: Harvard University Press, 1999.

Jones, A. P. "Yellow Fever in a Rural District." *New Orleans Medical News and Hospital Gazette* 1 (1854): 180–89, 205–9.

Jones, James. "Outlines of Lectures on Yellow Fever." *New Orleans Medical and Surgical Journal* (1858): 500–517.

Jones, Joseph. "Yellow Fever Epidemic of 1878 in New Orleans." *New Orleans Medical and Surgical Journal* (March 1879): 683–715.

Justin, Placide. *Histoire politique et statistique de l'île d'Hayti, Saint-Domingue.* Paris: Briére, 1826.

Keating, John McLeod. *A History of Yellow Fever: The Yellow Fever Epidemic of 1878, in Memphis, Tennessee.* Memphis: Howard Association, 1879.

Kein, Sybil, ed. *Creole: The History and Legacy of Louisiana's Free People of Color.* Baton Rouge: Louisiana State University Press, 2000.

Keith, Jeanette. *Fever Season: The Story of a Terrifying Epidemic and the People Who Saved a City.* New York: Bloomsbury Press, 2012.

Kelly, Howard A. *Walter Reed and Yellow Fever.* Baltimore: Norman, Remington, 1906.

Kelman, Ari. "New Orleans's Phantom Slave Insurrection of 1853: Racial Anxiety, Urban Ecology, and Human Bodies as Public Spaces." In *The Nature of Cities*, edited by Andrew C. Isenberg, 3–23. New Brunswick, NJ: University of Rochester Press, 2006.

———. *A River and Its City: The Nature of Landscape in New Orleans*. Berkeley: University of California Press, 2003.

Kilbride, Daniel. "Southern Medical Students in Philadelphia, 1800–1861: Science and Sociability in the 'Republic of Medicine.'" *Journal of Southern History* 65, no. 4 (1999): 697–732.

Kiple, Kenneth F., ed. *The African Exchange: Toward a Biological History of Black People*. Durham, NC: Duke University Press, 1987.

———. *Blacks in Colonial Cuba, 1774–1899*. Gainesville: University Press of Florida, 1976.

———. *The Caribbean Slave: A Biological History*. Cambridge: Cambridge University Press, 1984.

———. "Future Studies of the Biological Past of the Black." *Social Science History* 10, no. 4 (1986): 501–6.

———. *A Moveable Feast: Ten Millennia of Food Globalization*. Cambridge: Cambridge University Press, 2007.

———. "Response to Sheldon Watts, 'Yellow Fever Immunities in West Africa and Beyond: A Reappraisal.'" *Journal of Social History* 34, no. 4 (2001): 969–74.

———. "A Survey of Recent Literature on the Biological Past of the Black." *Social Science History* 10, no. 4 (1986): 343–67.

Kiple, Kenneth F., and Kriemhild Coneè Ornelas. "Race, War, and Tropical Medicine in the Eighteenth Century Caribbean." In *Warm Climates and Western Medicine: The Emergence of Tropical Medicine, 1500–1900*, edited by David Arnold, 63–79. Amsterdam: Rodopi, 1996.

Kiple, Kenneth F., and Brian T. Higgins. "Yellow Fever and the Africanization of the Caribbean." In *Disease and Demography in the Americas*, edited by John W. Verano and Douglas H. Ubelaker. Washington, DC: Smithsonian Institution Press, 1992.

Kiple, Kenneth F., and Virginia H. King. *Another Dimension to the Black Diaspora: Diet, Disease, and Racism*. Cambridge: Cambridge University Press, 1981.

Kiple, Kenneth F., and Virginia H. Kiple. "The African Connection: Slavery, Disease, and Racism." *Phylon* 41, no. 3 (1980): 211–22.

———. "Black Tongue and Black Men: Pellagra and Slavery in the Antebellum South." *Journal of Southern History* 43, no. 3 (1977): 411–28.

———. "Black Yellow Fever Immunities, Innate and Acquired, as Revealed in the American South." *Social Science History* 1, no. 4 (1977): 419–36.

Kmen, Henry A., ed. *The Manhattaner in New Orleans: Or, Phases of 'Cresent City' Life by A. Oakey Hall.* Baton Rouge: Louisiana State University Press, 1976.

Knights of Honor. *Report of the Central Relief Committee.* Memphis: S. C. Toof, 1879.

Koch, Tom. *Cartographies of Disease: Maps, Mapping, and Medicine.* Redlands, CA: ESRI Press, 2005.

Kolb, C. R., and J. R. Van Lopik. *Geology of the Mississippi River Deltaic Plain Southeastern Louisiana: Technical Report No. 3-483.* Vicksburg, MS: US Army Engineer Waterways Experiment Station, 1958.

Kovalenko, L. G., O. V. Viktorov-Nabokov, E. M. Ruban, E. M. Skrynik, and L. A. Korneeva. "The Repellent Action of the Mannich Bases of Phenol Methoxy Derivatives for *Aedes Aegypti* Mosquitoes and *Xenopsylla Cheopis* Flea." *Meditsinskaia Parazitologiia* (1989): 68–71.

Kraemer, Moritz U. G., Marianne E. Sinka, Kirsten A. Duda, Adrian Q. N. Mylne, Freya M. Shearer, Christopher M. Barker, Chester G. Moore, et al. "The Global Distribution of the Arbovirus Vectors *Aedes Aegypti* and *Ae. Albopictus*." *eLife* 4 (2015): 1–18.

LaBarre, Delia, ed. *The New Orleans of Lafcadio Hearn: Illustrated Sketches from the Daily City Item.* Baton Rouge: University of Louisiana Press, 2007.

LaChance, Paul F. "The Foreign French." In *Creole New Orleans: Race and Americanization,* edited by Arnold R. Hirsch and Joseph Logsdon, 101–30. Baton Rouge: Louisiana State University Press, 1992.

Landau-Ossondo, M., N. Rabia, J. Jos-Pelage, L. M. Marquet, Y. Isidore, C. Saint-Aimé, M. Martin, P. Irigaray, and D. Belpomme. "Why Pesticides Could Be a Common Cause of Prostate and Breast Cancers in the French Caribbean Island, Martinique: An Overview on Key Mechanisms of Pesticide-Induced Cancer." *Biomedicine and Pharmacology* 63 (2009): 383–95.

La Roche, René. *Yellow Fever, Considered in the Historical, Pathological, Etiological, and Therapeutical Relations.* Philadelphia: Blanchard and Lea, 1855.

Lear, Linda. *Rachel Carson: Witness for Nature.* New York: Henry Holt, 1997.

Le Gardeur, René J., Jr. "The New Orleans Theater, 1792–1803." *Southern Quarterly* (2007): 85–115.

———. "The Origins of the Sugar Industry in Louisiana." In *Green Fields: Two Hundred Years of Louisiana Sugar,* 1–28. Lafayette: Center for Louisiana Studies, 1980.

Le Page du Pratz, Antoine Simon. *The History of Louisiana.* Edited by Joseph G.

Tregle Jr. Baton Rouge: Louisiana State University Press, 1975. First publication 1774.

Lewis, Charles Lee. *David Glasgow Farragut: Admiral in the Making.* Annapolis: U.S. Naval Institute, 1941.

Lewis, P. H. "Article V: Thoughts on Yellow Fever." *New Orleans Medical Journal* (May 1844): 31–44.

Lewis, Peirce F. *New Orleans: The Making of an Urban Landscape.* Santa Fe, NM: Center for American Places, 2003.

Li, Shang-jen. "British Imperial Medicine in Late Nineteenth-Century China and the Early Career of Patrick Manson." PhD diss., London University, 1999.

Ligon, Richard. *A True and Exact History of the Island of Barbados.* Edited by Karen Ordahl Kupperman. Indianapolis: Hackett, 2011.

Lima, José Benton Pereira, Marcella Pereira Da-Cunha, Ronaldo Carneiro da Silva Júnior, Allan Kardec Ribeiro Galarado, Sidinei Silva Soares, Ima Aparecida Braga, Ricardo Pimentel Ramos, and Denise Valle. "Resistance of *Aedes Aegypti* to Organophosphates in Several Municipalities in the State of Rio De Janeiro and Espírito Santo, Brazil." *American Journal of Tropical Medicine and Hygiene* 68, no. 3 (2003): 329–33.

Lind, James. *An Essay on Diseases Incidental to Europeans in Hot Climates.* London: T. Becket and P. A. Hondt, 1768.

——. *An Essay on Diseases Incidental to Europeans in Hot Climates.* Philadelphia: William Duane, 1811.

Lister, Joseph. "On a New Method of Treating Compound Fractures, Abscess Etc., with Observations in the Conditions of Suppuration." *Lancet* 89, no. 2274 (March 1867): 387–89.

Logsdon, Joseph, and Caryn Cossé Bell. "The Americanization of Black New Orleans, 1850–1900." In *Creole New Orleans: Race and Americanization,* edited by Arnold R. Hirsch and Joseph Logsdon, 201–61. Baton Rouge: Louisiana State University Press, 1992.

Louisiana State Medical Society, Annual Session of 1879. "Abstract of Proceedings." *New Orleans Medical and Surgical Journal* 7 (July 1879): 81–217.

Löwy, Ilana. "What/Who Should Be Controlled? Opposition to Yellow Fever Campaigns in Brazil, 1900–1939." In *Western Medicine as Contested Knowledge,* edited by Andrew Cunningham and Bridie Andrews. Manchester, UK: Manchester University Press, 1997.

Mackay, Alexander. *The Western World; or, Travels in the United States in 1846–47: Exhibiting Them in Their Latest Development Social, Political, and Industrial; Including a Chapter on California.* 3 vols. London: Richard Bentley, 1850.

Manning, Patrick. *Slavery and African Life: Occidental, Oriental, and African Slave Trades.* Cambridge: Cambridge University Press, 1990.

Manson, Patrick. *The Relation of the Panama Canal to the Introduction of Yellow Fever into Asia.* London: Bedford Press, 1903.

———. *Tropical Disease: A Manual of the Diseases of Warm Climates.* New York: William Wood, 1919.

Marks, Harry. "Epidemiologists Explain Pellagra: Gender, Race, and Political Economy in the Work on Edgar Sydenstricker." *Journal of the History of Medicine and Allied Sciences* 58, no. 1 (2003): 34–55.

Marshall, Mary Louise. "Samuel A. Cartwright and States' Rights Medicine." *New Orleans Medical and Surgical Journal* 93, no. 2 (1940): 1–12.

Massad, Eduardo, Francisco Antonio Bezerra Coutinho, Marcelo Nascimento Burattini, Luis Fernandez Lopez, and Cláudio José Struchiner. "Yellow Fever Vaccination: How Much Is Enough?" *Vaccine* 23 (2005): 3908–14.

Matas, Rudolph, Frederick William Parham, and Thomas Smith Dabney. *Special Articles on Yellow Fever.* New Orleans: L. Graham, 1897.

May, J. Thomas. "The Medical Care of Blacks in Louisiana during the Occupation and Reconstruction, 1862–1868: Its Social and Political Background." PhD diss., Tulane University, 1971.

———. "A 19th Century Medical Care Program for Blacks: The Case of the Freedman's Bureau." *Anthropological Quarterly* 46, no. 3 (1973): 160–71.

McCandless, Peter. *Slavery, Disease, and Suffering in the Southern Lowcountry.* Cambridge: Cambridge University Press, 2011.

McCarthy, Michael. "A Century of U.S. Army Yellow Fever Research." *Lancet* 357 (2001): 1772.

———. *Typhoid and the Politics of Public Health in Nineteenth-Century Philadelphia.* Philadelphia: American Philosophical Society, 1987.

McDowell, Peggy. "New Orleans Cemeteries: Architectural Styles and Influences." *Southern Quarterly* 27 (1986): 9–27.

McGrew, Roderick E. *Encyclopedia of Medical History.* McGraw Hill, 1985.

McNeill, J. R. *Mosquito Empires: Ecology and War in the Greater Caribbean, 1620–1914.* Cambridge: Cambridge University Press, 2010.

———. "Yellow Jack and Geopolitics: Environment, Epidemics, and the Struggles for Empire in the American Tropics, 1640–1830." In *Rethinking Environmental History: World-System History and Global Environmental Change,* edited by J. R. McNeill, Alf Hornborg, and Joan Martinez-Alier, 199–220. Lanham, MD: AltaMira Press, 2007.

McNeill, William. *Plagues and Peoples.* New York: Doubleday, 1977.

McPherson, James. *Battle Cry of Freedom: The Civil War Era.* Oxford: Oxford University Press, 1988.

Menard, Russell R. *Sweet Negotiations: Sugar, Slavery, and Plantation Agriculture in Early Barbados.* Charlottesville: University of Virginia Press, 2006.

Merleaux, April. "Sugar and Civilization: Race, Empire, and the Cultural Politics of Sweetness in the United States, 1898–1939." PhD diss., Yale University, 2010.

Milner, U. R. *Yellow Fever Not Imported, nor Contagious, but Indigenous; and Intrinsically Identical with Our Paludal Fevers: Preventable by Well Determined and Wisely Executed Local Sanitary Measures: Quarantine a Widespread Calamity and Should No Longer Be Tolerated: A Lecture before the Academy of Sciences of New Orleans, at Its Regular Meetings, Tuesday Evenings, November 16 and December 18, 1879.* New Orleans: M. Jones Scott, 1880.

Mintz, Sidney. *Sweetness and Power: The Place of Sugar in Modern History.* New York: Penguin Books, 1986.

"The Mississippi Jetties," *Scribner's Monthly* 19, no. 1 (November 1879): 46.

Moch, Leslie Page. "The European Perspective: Changing Conditions and Multiple Migrations, 1750–1914." In *European Migrants: Global and Local Perspectives*, edited by Dirk Hoerder and Leslie Page Moch. Boston: Northeastern University Press, 1996.

Monath, Thomas P. "Review of Treatment of Yellow Fever." *Antiviral Research* 78 (2008): 116–24.

———. "Yellow Fever." In *Tropical Infectious Diseases*, edited by P. F. Weller and D. H. Walker, 1253–64. Philadelphia: Churchill Livingstone, 1999.

———. "Yellow Fever: An Update." *Lancet Infectious Diseases* (2001): 11–20.

———. "Yellow Fever: Victor, Victoria? Conqueror, Conquest? Epidemics and Research in the Last Forty Years and Prospects for the Future." *American Journal of Tropical Medicine and Hygiene* 45, no. 1 (1991): 1–43.

Montejo, Esteban. *The Autobiography of a Runaway Slave.* Translated by Iocasta Innes. Edited by Miguel Barnet. New York: Pantheon Books, 1968.

Montella, Isabela Reis, Ademir Jesus Martins, Priscila Fernandes Viana-Medeiros, José Bento Pereira Lima, Ima Aparecida Braga, and Denise Valle. "Insecticide Resistance Mechanisms of Brazilian *Aedes Aegypti* Populations from 2001 to 2004." *American Journal of Tropical Medicine and Hygiene* 77, no. 3 (2007): 467–77.

Moore, Jason W. "Sugar and the Expansion of the Early Modern World-Economy: Commodity Frontiers, Ecological Transformation, and Industrialization," *Review* 23, no. 3 (2000): 409–33.

Moore, John Hebron. "The Cypress Lumber Industry of the Lower Mississippi

Valley during the Colonial Period." In *The Louisiana Purchase Bicentennial Series in Louisiana History*, vol. 1, *The French Experience in Louisiana*, edited by Glenn R. Conrad, 585–602. Lafayette: Center for Louisiana Studies, 1995.

Moreau de Saint-Méry, Médéric Louis Elie. *Description topographique, physique, civile, politique et historique de la partie française de l'isle Saint-Domingue*. Philadelphia: Printed by author, 1797.

Morris, Christopher. *The Big Muddy: An Environmental History of the Mississippi and Its Peoples from Hernando de Soto to Hurricane Katrina*. Oxford: Oxford University Press, 2012.

Mulrooney, Margaret M., ed. *Fleeing the Famine: North America and Irish Refugees, 1845–1851*. Westport, CT: Praeger, 2003.

Myrick, Herbert. *The American Sugar Industry: A Practical Manual on the Production of Sugar Beets and Sugar Cane, and on the Manufacture of Sugar Therefrom*. Springfield, MA: Orange Judd, 1899.

Navarro, José Cantón. *History of Cuba: The Challenge of the Yoke and the Star*. Havana, Cuba: SI-MAR S.A, 2001.

Nepstad, Daniel C., Claudia M. Stickler, and Oriana T. Almeida. "Globalization of the Amazon Soy and Beef Industries: Opportunities for Conservation." *Conservation Biology* 20, no. 6 (2006): 1595–1603.

New Orleans Board of Health. *Official Report of the Deaths from Yellow Fever, Alphabetically Arranged, Gives the Name, Age, Nativity, Residence, and Date of Death of Each and Every One Who Died during the Epidemic of 1878*. New Orleans: W. L. Murray's, 1878.

New Orleans Citizens. *Proceedings of a Mass Meeting Held in New Orleans, December 6, to Return Thanks for the Succor Extended to the City during the Epidemic of 1878*. New Orleans: A. W. Hyatt, 1878.

Ngalamulume, Kalala. *Colonial Pathologies, Environment, and Western Medicine in Saint-Louis-Du-Senegal, 1867–1920*. New York: Peter Lang, 2012.

———. "Keeping the City Totally Clean: Yellow Fever and the Politics of Prevention in Colonial Saint-Louis-du-Sénégal, 1850–1914." *Journal of African History* 45, no. 2 (2004): 183–202.

Nott, Josiah Clark. "The Cause of Yellow Fever." *New Orleans Medical and Surgical Journal* 4 (March 1848): 563–601.

———. *An Essay on the Natural History of Mankind: Viewed in Connection with Negro Slavery: Delivered before the Southern Rights Association*. Mobile: Dade and Thompson, 1851.

———. "An Examination into the Health and Longevity of the Southern Sea Ports of the United States, with Reference to the Subject of Life Insurance." *Southern Journal of Medicine and Pharmacy* 2 (1847).

———. "The Mulatto a Hybrid—Probable Extermination of the Two Races, If the Whites and Blacks Are Allowed to Intermarry." *American Journal of Medical Sciences* (July 1843).

———. *Two Lectures on the Natural History of the Caucasian and Negro Race.* Mobile: Dade and Thompson, 1844.

———. "Yellow Fever Contrasted with Bilious Fever: Reasons for Believing It a Disease Sui Generis; Its Mode of Propagation; Remote Cause; Probable Insect or Animacular Origin, &c." *New Orleans Medical and Surgical Journal* 4 (1848).

Nott, Josiah Clark, and George R. Gliddon. *Indigenous Races of the Earth; or, New Chapters of Ethnological Inquiry.* Philadelphia: J. B. Lippincott, 1857.

———. *Types of Mankind; or, Ethnological Researches, Based upon the Ancient Monuments, Paintings, Sculptures, and Crania of Races, and upon Their Natural, Geographical, Philological and Biblical History.* Philadelphia: J. B. Lippincott, 1868.

Obadale-Starks, Ernest. *Freebooters and Smugglers: The Foreign Slave Trade in the United States after 1808.* Fayetteville: University of Arkansas Press, 2007.

O'Hara, Leo James. *An Emerging Profession: Philadelphia Doctors, 1860–1900.* New York: Garland, 1989.

Oldmixon, John. *The British Empire in America, Containing the History of the Discovery, Settlement, Progress, and State of the British Colonies on the Continent and Islands of America,* 2 vols. London: J. Nicholson, 1708.

O'Leary, Cecilia Elizabeth. *To Die For: The Paradox of American Patriotism.* Princeton. NJ: Princeton University Press, 1999.

Olschner, Kay. "Medical Journals in Louisiana before the Civil War." *Bulletin of the Medical Library Association* 60, no. 1 (1972): 1–13.

O'Malley, Gregory. "Beyond the Middle Passage: Slave Migration from the Caribbean to North America, 1619–1807." *William and Mary Quarterly* 66, no. 1 (January 2009): 125–72.

———. *Final Passages: The Intercolonial Slave Trade of British America, 1619–1807.* Chapel Hill: University of North Carolina Press, 2014.

O'Neill, Karen. *Rivers by Design: State Power and the Origins of U.S. Flood Control.* Durham, NC: Duke University Press, 2006.

Otto, John Solomon. *The Southern Frontiers, 1607–1860: Agricultural Evolution of the Colonial and Antebellum South.* Westport, CT: Greenwood Press, 1989.

Packard, Randall. *The Making of a Tropical Disease: A Short History of Malaria.* Baltimore: Johns Hopkins University Press, 2007.

———. "Visions of Postwar Health and Development and Their Impact on Public Health Interventions in the Developing World." In *International Development and the Social Sciences: Essays on the History and Politics of Knowledge*, edited by Frederick Cooper and Randall M. Packard, 93–118. Berkeley: University of California Press, 1997.

Palmer, Steven. "A Cuban Scientist between Empires: Peripheral Vision on Race and Tropical Medicine." *Canadian Journal of Latin American and Caribbean Studies* 35, no. 9 (2010): 93–118.

Patterson, K. David. "Yellow Fever Epidemics and Mortality in the United States, 1693–1905." *Social Science and Medicine* 34, no. 8 (1992): 855–65.

Patton, G. Farrar. *The Louisiana State Board of Health, Its History and Work, with a Brief Review of Health Legislation and Maritime Quarantine in Louisiana*. New Orleans, 1904.

Peard, Julyan G. *Race, Place, and Medicine: The Idea of the Tropics in Nineteenth-Century Brazilian Medicine*. Durham, NC: Duke University Press, 1999.

———. "Tropical Medicine in Nineteenth-Century Brazil: The Case of the Esola Tropicalista Bahiana." In *Warm Climates and Western Medicine: The Emergence of Tropical Medicine, 1500–1900*, edited by David Arnold, 108–32. New York: Rodopi, 1996.

Pedersen, Jean Jay. "The Antiquity of Sylvan Yellow Fever in the Americas." PhD diss., University of California–Los Angeles, 1974.

Pierce, John R., and Jim Writer. *Yellow Jack: How Yellow Fever Ravaged America and Walter Reed Discovered Its Deadly Secret*. Hoboken, NJ: John Wiley, 2005.

Pierson, George Wilson. *Tocqueville and Beaumont in America*. Oxford: Oxford University Press, 1938.

Placide Justin. *Histoire politique et statistique de l'île d'Hayti, Saint-Domingue*. Paris: Briére, 1826.

Ponlawot, Alongot, Jeffrey G. Scott, and Laura C. Harrington. "Insecticide Susceptibility of Aedes aegypti and *Aedes albopictus* across Thailand." *Journal of Medical Entomology* 42, no. 5 (2005): 821–25.

Poor, Henry V. *Manual of the Railroads of the United States*. Vol. 5. New York: H. V. & H. W. Poor, 1872.

———. *Manual of the Railroads of the United States*. Vol. 22. New York: H. V. & H. W. Poor, 1889.

Porch, James W., and Fred Muller. *Panama via New Orleans: Report of the Board of Trade Committee, November–December*. New Orleans, 1904.

Powell, J. H. *Bring Out Your Dead: The Great Plague of Yellow Fever in Philadelphia in 1793*. Philadelphia: University of Pennsylvania Press, 1949.

Power, John Logan. *The Epidemic of 1878, in Mississippi: Report of the Yellow*

Fever Relief Work through J.L. Power, Grand Secretary of Masons and Grand Treasurer of Odd Fellows. Jackson, MS: Clarion, 1879.

Pritchett, Jonathan B., and Insan Tunali. "Strangers' Disease: Determinants of Yellow Fever Mortality during the New Orleans Epidemic of 1853." *Explorations in Economic History* 32 (October 1995): 517–39.

Public Health Reports and Papers v. V, Presented at the Meetings of the American Public Health Association. Boston: Houghton, Mifflin, 1880.

Putaporntip, Chaturong, Thongchai Hongsrimuang, Sunee Seethamchai, Teerayot Kobasa, Kriengsak Limkittikul, Liwang Cui, and Somchai Jongwutiwes. "Differential Prevalence of *Plasmodium* Infections and Cryptic *Plasmodium Knowlesi* Malaria in Humans in Thailand." *Journal of Infectious Diseases* 199 (2009): 1143–50.

Pym, William. *Observations upon the Bulam Fever Which Has of Late Years Prevailed in the West Indies, on the Coast of America, at Gibraltar, Cadiz, and Other Ports of Spain.* London: J. Callow, 1815.

Quinn, D. A. *Heroes and Heroines of Memphis; or, Reminiscences of the Yellow Fever Epidemics That Afflicted the City of Memphis during the Autumn Months of 1873, 1878, and 1879, to Which Is Added a Graphic Description of Missionary Life in Eastern Arkansas.* Providence, RI: E. L. Freeman, 1887.

Rajatileka, Shavanthi, William C. Black IV, Karla Saavedra-Rodriguez, Yuwadee Trongtokit, Chamnarn Apiwathnasorn, P. J. McCall, and Hilary Ranson. "Development and Application of a Simple Colorimetric Assay Reveals Widespread Distribution of Sodium Channel Mutations in Thai Populations of *Aedes Aegypti*." *Acta Tropica* 108 (2008): 54–57.

Reardon, Jenny. *Race to the Finish: Identity and Governance in an Age of Genomics.* Princeton, NJ: Princeton University Press, 2005.

Rediker, Marcus. *The Slave Ship: A Human History.* New York: Viking, 2007.

Reed, Merl E. "The New Orleans Short Lines." In *The Louisiana Purchase Bicentennial Series in Louisiana History*, vol. 14, *New Orleans and Urban Louisiana*, edited by Samuel C. Shepherd Jr. Lafayette: Center for Louisiana Studies, 1996.

Reiter, Paul. "Climate Change and Mosquito-Borne Disease." *Environmental Health Perspectives* 109 (2001): 141–61.

Report of the New Orleans Central Relief Committee to All Those Who Have So Generously Contributed to the Yellow Fever Sufferers of New Orleans, from the Great Epidemic of 1878. New Orleans: Clark & Hofeline, 1879.

Report of the Sanitary Commission of New Orleans on the Epidemic Yellow Fever of 1853, Published by Authority of the City Council of New Orleans. New Orleans: Picayune Office, 1854.

Reys, Natalie. *Saint-Louis du Sénégal a l'epoque précoloniale: L'emergence d'une Société Métisse Originale, 1650–1854.* Paris: Université de Paris, 1982.

Richey, Emma C., and Evelina P. Kean. *The New Orleans Book.* New Orleans: L. Graham, 1915.

Rightor, Henry, ed. *Standard History of New Orleans, Louisiana.* Chicago: Lewis, 1900.

Robertson, Robert. *A physical journal kept on board His Majesty's ship Rainbow: During three voyages to the coast of Africa and West Indies, in the year 1772, 1773, and 1774: To which is prefixed, a particular account of the remitting fever, which happened on board of His Majesty's sloop Weasel, on that coast, in 1769.* London: E. and C. Dilly, 1777.

Robertson, S. E., B. P. Hull, O. Tomori, O. Bele, J. W. LeDuc, and K. Esteves. "Yellow Fever: A Decade of Reemergence. *Journal of the American Medical Association* 276, no. 14 (1996): 1157–62.

Rocco, Fiammetta. *Quinine: Malaria and the Quest for a Cure That Changed the World.* New York: HarperCollins, 2003.

Rodrigue, John C. *Reconstruction in the Cane Fields: From Slavery to Free Labor in Louisiana's Sugar Parishes, 1862–1880.* Baton Rouge: Louisiana State University Press, 2001.

Rodríguez, Antonio Acosta. *La población de la Luisiana España, 1763–1803.* Madrid: Ministerio de Asuntos Exteriores, 1979.

Rogers, Molly. *Delia's Tears: Race, Science, and Photography in Nineteenth-Century America.* New Haven, CT: Yale University Press, 2012.

Rogers, Thomas D. *The Deepest Wounds: A Labor and Environmental History of Sugar in Northeast Brazil.* Chapel Hill: University of North Carolina Press, 2010.

Rosenberg, Charles E. *Explaining Epidemics and Other Studies in the History of Medicine.* Cambridge: Cambridge University Press, 1992.

Ross, Ronald. *First Progress Report of the Campaign against Mosquitoes in Sierra Leone (1901): Memoir V, Part I.* London: University Press of Liverpool, 1901.

Rothstein, William. *American Physicians in the Nineteenth Century: From Sects to Science.* Baltimore: Johns Hopkins University Press, 1972.

Rotz, Philip D. "Sweetness and Fever? Sugar Production, *Aedes aegypti*, and Dengue Fever in Natal, South Africa, 1926–1927." *South African Historical Journal* 68, no. 3 (2016): 286–303.

Roughley, Thomas. *The Jamaica Planter's Guide or a System for Planting and Managing a Sugar Estate or Other Plantations on That Island and throughout the British West Indies in General.* London: Longman, Hurst, Rees, Orme, and Brown, 1823.

Rush, Benjamin. *An Account of the Bilious Remitting Yellow Fever as It Appeared in the City of Philadelphia in the Year 1793.* Philadelphia: Thomas Dobson, 1794.

Ryan, James Gilbert. "The Memphis Riots of 1866: Terror in a Black Community during Reconstruction." *Journal of Negro History* 62, no. 3 (1977): 243–57.

Saikku, Mikko. *This Delta, This Land: An Environmental History of the Yazoo-Mississippi Floodplain.* Athens: University of Georgia Press, 2005.

Sall, Amadou A., Ousmane Faye, Mawlouth Diallo, Cadhla Firth, Andrew Kitchen, and Edward C. Holmes. "Yellow Fever Virus Exhibits Slower Evolutionary Dynamics Than Dengue Virus." *Journal of Virology* 84, no. 2 (January 2010): 765–72.

Sarbough, Timothy J. "The Spirit of Manifest Destiny: The American Government and Famine Ireland, 1845–1849." In *Fleeing the Famine: North America and Irish Refugees, 1845–1851,* edited by Margaret M. Mulrooney, 45–57. Westport, CT: Praeger, 2003.

Satchell, Veront. *Sugar, Slavery, and Technological Change: Jamaica, 1760–1830.* Saarbrücken, Germany: VDM Verlag Müller, 2010.

Savitt, Todd L. *Medicine and Slavery: The Diseases and Health Care of Blacks in Antebellum Virginia.* Urbana: University of Illinois Press, 1978.

———. *Race and Medicine in Nineteenth- and Early-Twentieth-Century America.* Kent, OH: Kent State University Press, 2007.

———. "Slave Health and Southern Distinctiveness." In *Disease and Distinctiveness in the American South,* edited by Todd L. Savitt and James Harvey Young. Knoxville: University of Tennessee Press, 1988.

———. "The Use of Blacks for Medical Experimentation and Demonstration in the Old South." *Journal of Southern History* 48, no. 3 (1982): 331–48.

Savitt, Todd L., and James Harvey Young, eds. *Disease and Distinctiveness in the American South.* Knoxville: University of Tennessee Press, 1988.

Scarano, Francisco A. *Sugar and Slavery in Puerto Rico: The Plantation Economy of Ponce, 1800–1850.* Madison: University of Wisconsin Press, 1984.

Scheube, B. *The Diseases of Warm Countries: A Handbook for Medical Men.* Edited by James Cantlie. London: John Bale, Sons & Danielsson, 1903.

Schmidt, H. D. *The Pathology and Treatment of Yellow Fever: With Some Remarks upon the Nature of Its Cause and Its Prevention.* Chicago: Chicago Medical Press Association, 1881.

Schotte, J. P. *A Treatise on the Synochus Atrabiliosa.* London: M. Scott, 1782.

Schwartz, Stuart B. *Sugar Plantations in the Formation of Brazilian Society: Bahia, 1550–1835.* Cambridge: Cambridge University Press, 1985.

Scott, Rebecca J. "Defining the Boundaries of Freedom in the World of Cane:

Cuba, Brazil, and Louisiana after Emancipation." *American Historical Review* 99, no. 1 (1994): 70–102.

———. *Degrees of Freedom: Louisiana and Cuba after Slavery.* Cambridge, MA: Belknap Press of Harvard University, 2005.

———. "Fault Lines, Color Lines, and Party Lines." In *Beyond Slavery: Explorations of Race, Labor, and Citizenship in Postemancipation Societies,* edited by Thomas C. Holt, Frederick Cooper, and Rebecca J. Scott, 61–106. Chapel Hill: University of North Carolina Press, 2000.

Searing, James F. *West African Slavery and Atlantic Commerce: The Senegal River Valley, 1700–1860.* Cambridge: Cambridge University Press, 1993.

Shannon, Richard. *Practical Observations on the Operation and Effects of Certain Medicines in the Prevention and Cure of Diseases to which Europeans are Subject in Hot Climates.* London: Vernor and Hood, 1794.

Silliman, Benjamin. *Manual on the Cultivation of the Sugar Cane and the Fabrication and Refinement of Sugar.* Washington, DC: Francis Preston Blair, 1833.

Singh, B., L. Kim Sung, A. Matusop, A. Radhakrishnan, S. S. Shamsul, J. Cox-Singh, A. Thomas, and D. J. Conway. "A Large Focus of Naturally Acquired *Plasmodium Knowlesi* Infections in Human Beings." *Lancet* 363 (2004): 1017–24.

Sitterson, Joseph Carlyle. "Expansion, Reversion, and Revolution in the Southern Sugar Industry, 1850–1910," *Bulletin of the Business Historical Society* 27, no. 3 (1953): 129–40.

———. *Sugar Country: The Cane Sugar Industry in the South 1753–1950.* Louisville: University of Kentucky Press, 1953.

Slosek, Jean. "*Aedes Aegypti* Mosquitoes in the Americas: A Review of Their Interactions with the Human Population." *Social Science Medicine* 23, no. 3 (1986): 249–57.

Smith, Billy G. *Ship of Death: A Voyage That Changed the Atlantic World.* New Haven, CT: Yale University Press, 2013.

Smith, Tom W. "Changing Racial Labels: From 'Colored' to 'Negro' to 'Black' to 'African American.'" *Public Opinion Quarterly* 56, no. 4 (1992): 496–514.

Soluri, John. *Banana Cultures: Agriculture, Consumption, and Environmental Change in Honduras and the United States.* Austin: University of Texas Press, 2005.

Soper, F. L., H. Penna, E. Cardoso, J. Serafim Jr., M. Frobisher Jr., and J. Pinheiro. "Yellow Fever without *Aëdes Aegypti:* Study of a Rural Epidemic in the Valle Do Chanaan, Espirito Santo, Brazil, 1932." *American Journal of Hygiene* 18, no. 3 (1933): 555–87.

Spielman, Andrew, and Michael D'Antonio. *Mosquito: A Natural History of Our Most Persistent and Deadly Foe.* New York: Hyperion, 2001.

Spinzig, Carl. *Epidemic Diseases as Dependant upon Meteorological Influences.* St. Louis: Ahner, Menning, 1874.

———. *Yellow Fever: Nature and Epidemic Character Caused by Meterorological Influences, Verified by the Epidemics of Shreveport and Memphis in 1872, by That of Savannah in 1876, by the Great Epidemic of the Mississippi Valley in 1878, and (in the Appendix) by the One of Memphis in 1879.* St. Louis: Geo. O. Rumbold, 1880.

Spletstoser, Fredrick Marcel. "Back Door to the Land of Plenty: New Orleans as an Immigrant Port, 1820–1860." PhD diss., Louisiana State University and Agricultural and Mechanical College, 1978.

Sprague, E. K. "Present Status of the Bacteriology of Yellow Fever." In *Yellow Fever: Its Nature, Diagnosis, Treatment, and Prophylaxis, and Quarantine Regulations Relating Thereto, by the Officers of the U.S. Marine Hospital Service,* 428–32. Washington, DC: Government Printing Office, 1898.

Staples, J. Erin, and Thomas P. Monath. "Yellow Fever: 100 Years of Discovery." *Journal of the American Medical Association* 300, no. 8 (2008): 960–62.

Starr, S. Frederick, ed. *Inventing New Orleans: Writings of Lafcadio Hearn.* Jackson: University Press of Mississippi, 2001.

Steiner, Paul E. *Disease in the Civil War: Natural Biological Warfare in 1861–1865.* Springfield, IL: Charles C. Thomas, 1968.

———. *Medical History of a Civil War Regiment: Disease in the Sixty-Fifth United States Colored Infantry.* Clayton, MO: Institute for Civil War Studies, 1977.

Stepan, Nancy. *Beginnings of Brazilian Science: Oswaldo Cruz, Medical Research and Policy, 1890–1920.* New York: Science History Publications, 1976.

———. *Eradication: Ridding the World of Diseases Forever?* Ithaca, NY: Cornell University Press, 2011.

———. *The Idea of Race in Science: Great Britain 1800–1960.* Hampden, CT: Archon Books, 1982.

———. "The Interplay between Socio-Economic Factors and Medical Science: Yellow Fever Research, Cuba and the United States." *Social Studies of Science* 8, no. 4 (1978): 397–423.

———. *Picturing Tropical Nature.* Ithaca, NY: Cornell University Press, 2001.

Sternberg, George M. "The Microscopical Investigations of the Havana Yellow Fever Commission." In *Proceedings of the American Association for the Advancement of Science* (1881): 381–86.

———. *Report on the Etiology and Prevention of Yellow Fever.* Washington, DC: U.S. Marine Hospital Service, 1887.

Sternberg, Martha. *George Miller Sternberg: A Biography*. Chicago: American Medical Association, 1920.

Stowe, Steven M. *Doctoring the South: Southern Physicians and Everyday Medicine in the Mid-Nineteenth Century*. Chapel Hill: University of North Carolina Press, 2004.

———. "Seeing Themselves at Work: Physicians and the Case Narrative in the Mid-Nineteenth Century South." *American Historical Review* 101, no. 1 (1996): 41–79.

Striffler, Steve, and Mark Moberg, eds. *Banana Wars: Power, Production, and History in the Americas*. Durham, NC: Duke University Press, 2003.

Strode, George K. *Yellow Fever*. New York: McGraw-Hill, 1951.

Stubbs, W. C. "Origin and Evolution of the Sugar Industry in Louisiana." In *Standard History of New Orleans, Louisiana*, edited by Henry Rightor, 646–729. Chicago: Lewis, 1900.

Sublette, Ned. *The World That Made New Orleans: From Spanish Silver to Congo Square*. Chicago: Lawrence Hill Books, 2008.

Sugar in Hawaii: The Story of Sugar Plantations, Their History, Their Methods of Operation and Their Place in the Economy of Hawaii. Honolulu: Hawaiian Sugar Planters Association, 1949.

Sutter, Paul. "Nature's Agents or Agents of Empire? Entomological Workers and Environmental Change during the Construction of the Panama Canal." *Isis* 98, no. 4 (December 2007): 724–54.

Sykes, W. H. "Contributions to the Statistics of Sugar Produced within the British Dominions in India." *Journal of the Statistical Society of London* 13, no. 1 (1850): 1–24.

Tapper, Melbourne. *In the Blood: Sickle Cell Anemia and the Politics of Race*. Philadelphia: University of Pennsylvania Press, 1999.

Tepper, Michael. *American Passenger Arrival Records: A Guide to the Records of Immigrants Arriving at American Ports by Sail and Steam*. Baltimore: Genealogical Publishing Company, 1988.

Thanispong, Kanutcharee, Sunaiyana Sathantriphop, and Theeraphap Chareonviriyaphap. "Insecticide Resistance of *Aedes Aegypti* and *Culex Quinquefasciatus* in Thailand." *Journal of Pesticide Science* 33, no. 4 (2008): 351–56.

Thernstrom, Stephan, ed. *Harvard Encyclopedia of American Ethnic Groups*. Cambridge, MA: Belknap Press of Harvard University, 1980.

Thévenot, J. P. F. *Traité des maladies des Européens dans les pays chauds, en spécialement au Sénégal*. Paris: J. P. F. Baillière, 1840.

Tikar, S. N., Arkaja Kumar, G. B. K. S. Prasad, and Shri Prakash. "Temephos-

Induced Resistance in *Aedes Aegypti* and Its Cross-Resistance Studies to Certain Insecticides from India." *Parasitology Research* 105 (2009): 57–63.

Toledo-Pereyra, Luis H. *A History of American Medicine from the Colonial Period to the Early Twentieth Century*. Lewiston, NY: Edwin Mellen Press, 2006.

Tomes, Nancy. *The Gospel of Germs: Men, Women, and the Microbe in American Life*. Cambridge, MA: Harvard University Press, 1998.

Tomich, Dale. "Small Islands, Huge Comparisons: Caribbean Plantations, Historical Unevenness, and Capitalist Modernity." *Social Science History* 18, no. 3 (1994): 339–58.

Tomori, Oyewale. "Yellow Fever: The Recurring Plague." *Critical Reviews in Clinical Laboratory Sciences* 41, no. 4 (2003): 391–427.

Touatre, Just. *Yellow Fever: Clinical Notes*. Translated by Charles Chassaignac. New Orleans: New Orleans Medical and Surgical Journal, 1898.

Trask, Benjamin H. *Fearful Ravages: Yellow Fever in New Orleans, 1796–1905*. Lafayette: Center for Louisiana Studies, 2005.

———. "The World of 'Septic Vapours': Yellow Fever and United States Shipping, 1798–1905." *Northern Mariner<th>/<th>Le marin de nord* 15, no. 2 (April 2005): 1–18.

Trudeau, Carlos. *Plan of the City of New Orleans and the Adjacent Plantations*. December 1798 ,24. Rare Book and Texana Collections, University of North Texas Libraries, Denton, TX.

Tucker, Richard. *Insatiable Appetite: The United States and the Degradation of the Tropical World*. Berkeley: University of California Press, 2000.

United Fruit Company Medical Department. *Annual Report, 1912*. Boston: Press of Geo. H. Ellis, 1913.

———. *Annual Report, 1913*. Boston: Press of Geo. H. Ellis, 1914.

———. *Annual Report, 1914*. Boston: Press of Geo. H. Ellis, 1915.

———. *Annual Report, 1915*. Boston: Press of Geo. H. Ellis, 1916.

United Nations, Department of Economic and Social Affairs, Population Division. *World Urbanization Prospects: The 2014 Revision*. New York: United Nations, 2015.

US Navy Department Bureau of Medicine and Surgery. *Report on Yellow Fever in the U.S.S. Plymouth in 1878–'9*. Edited by Philip S. Wales. Washington, DC: Government Printing Office, 1880.

Usner, Daniel H. "The Frontier Exchange Economy of the Lower Mississippi Valley in the Eighteenth Century." In *The Louisiana Purchase Bicentennial Series in Louisiana History*, vol. 1, *The French Experience in Louisiana*, 554–77. Lafayette: Center for Louisiana Studies, 1995.

Vainio, J., and F. Cutts, eds. *Yellow Fever*. Geneva: World Health Organization, 1998.

Valenčius, Conevery Bolton. *The Health of the Country: How Americans Understood Themselves and Their Land*. New York: Basic Books, 2002.

Viesca-Treviño, C. "Epidemics and Diseases during the Independence Period in Mexico." *Revista Médica del Instituto Mexicano del Seguro Social* 48, no. 1 (January–February 2010): 47–54.

Vogt, Paul L. *The Sugar Refining Industry in the United States*. Philadelphia: University of Pennsylvania, 1908.

Walker, William. *The War in Nicaragua*. Mobile, AL: S. H. Goetzel, 1860.

Wallis, Brian. "Black Bodies, White Science: Louis Agassiz's Slave Daguerreotypes." *American Art* 9, no. 2 (Summer 1995): 38–61.

Warner, John Harley. *The Therapeutic Perspective: Medical Practice, Knowledge, and Identity in America, 1820-1885*. Cambridge, MA: Harvard University Press, 1986.

Watts, David. *The West Indies: Patterns of Development, Culture, and Environmental Change since 1492*. Cambridge: Cambridge University Press, 1987.

Watts, Sheldon. "British Development Policies and Malaria in India, 1897–c. 1929." *Past and Present* 165 (1999): 141–82.

———. *Disease and Medicine in World History*. London: Routledge, 2003.

———. *Epidemics and History: Disease, Power and Imperialism*. New Haven, CT: Yale University Press, 1997.

———. "From Rapid Change to Stasis: Official Responses to Cholera in British-Ruled India and Egypt." *Journal of World History* 12, no. 2 (2001): 321–74.

———. "Response to Kenneth Kiple." *Journal of Social History* 34, no. 4 (2001): 975–76.

———. "Yellow Fever Immunities in West Africa and Beyond: A Reappraisal." *Journal of Social History* 34, no. 4 (2001): 955–67.

Webb, James L. A. *Humanity's Burden: A Global History of Malaria*. Cambridge: Cambridge University Press, 2009.

———. *The Long Struggle against Malaria in Tropical Africa*. Cambridge: Cambridge University Press, 2014.

White, C. B. *Disinfection in Yellow Fever as Practised at New Orleans in the Years 1870 to 1875 Inclusive*. Washington, DC: American Public Health Association, 1876.

White, Howard A. *The Freedman's Bureau in Louisiana*. Baton Rouge: Louisiana State University Press, 1970.

Willoughby, Christopher D. E. "Running Away from Drapetomania: Samuel Cartwright, Medicine, and Race in the Antebellum South." *Journal of Southern History* (forthcoming, 2018).

Wilson, Charles Morrow. *Ambassadors in White: The Story of American Tropical Medicine.* New York: Henry Holt, 1942.

Woloson, Wendy A. *Refined Tastes: Sugar, Confectionery, and Consumers in Nineteenth-Century America.* Baltimore: Johns Hopkins University Press, 2002.

Worboys, Michael. "Germs, Malaria and the Invention of Mansonian Tropical Medicine: From 'Diseases in the Tropics' to 'Tropical Diseases.'" In *Warm Climates and Western Medicine: The Emergence of Tropical Medicine, 1500–1900,* edited by David Arnold, 181–207. Amsterdam: Rodopi, 1996.

World Health Organization. *Dengue: Guidelines for Diagnosis, Treatment, Prevention, and Control.* Geneva: World Health Organization and the Special Programme for Research and Training in Tropical Diseases, 2009.

———. "Meeting of the Emergency Committee under the International Health Regulations (2005) concerning Yellow Fever." www.who.int/mediacentre/news/statements/2016/ec-yellow-fever/en/#.

———. "Yellow Fever." www.who.int/mediacentre/factsheets/fs100/en/.

———. "Yellow Fever Situation Report." www.who.int/emergencies/yellow-fever/situation-reports/2-june-2016/en/.

Yanochik, Mark A., Mark Thornton, and Bradley Ewing. "Railroad Construction and Slave Prices." *Social Science Quarterly* 84, no. 3 (September 2003): 723–37.

Ziegler, Vanessa M. "The Revolt of 'the Ever-Faithful Isle': The Ten Years' War in Cuba, 1878–1878." PhD diss., University of California–Santa Barbara, 2007.

Index

Note: page numbers in *italics* refer to illustrations; those followed by "n" indicate endnotes.